SEX AND THE SOUL

DONNA FREITAS

SEX AND THE SOUL
Juggling Sexuality, Spirituality,
Romance, and Religion on
America's College Campuses

Updated Edition

OXFORD
UNIVERSITY PRESS

OXFORD
UNIVERSITY PRESS

Oxford University Press is a department of the
University of Oxford. It furthers the University's objective
of excellence in research, scholarship, and education
by publishing worldwide.

Oxford   New York
Auckland   Cape Town   Dar es Salaam   Hong Kong   Karachi
Kuala Lumpur   Madrid   Melbourne   Mexico City   Nairobi
New Delhi   Shanghai   Taipei   Toronto

With offices in
Argentina   Austria   Brazil   Chile   Czech Republic   France   Greece
Guatemala   Hungary   Italy   Japan   Poland   Portugal   Singapore
South Korea   Switzerland   Thailand   Turkey   Ukraine   Vietnam

Oxford is a registered trade mark of Oxford University Press
in the UK and certain other countries.

Published in the United States of America by
Oxford University Press
198 Madison Avenue, New York, NY 10016

Library of Congress Cataloging-in-Publication Data
Freitas, Donna.
Sex and the soul : juggling sexuality, spirituality, romance, and religion
on America's college campuses / Donna Freitas. — Updated Edition.
pages   cm
Includes bibliographical references and index.
ISBN 978-0-19-022128-7 (pbk. : alk. paper)
1. College students—Religious life—United States.
2. Church college students—Religious life—United States.
3. College students—Sexual behavior—United States.
4. Church college students—Sexual behavior—United States.   I. Title.
BL625.9.C64F74   2015
205'.664088378198—dc23   2014035795

1 3 5 7 9 8 6 4 2
Printed in the United States of America
on acid-free paper

SEX AND THE SOUL IS AFFECTIONATELY DEDICATED
TO THE TWENTY-ONE STUDENTS WHO TOOK MY DATING CLASS
AT ST. MICHAEL'S COLLEGE AND, MOST ESPECIALLY,
TO THOSE SEVEN WHO WENT ON TO BECOME MY RESEARCH
ASSISTANTS THE FOLLOWING YEAR: AMANDA, BECKY,
JOSIE, ORLA, MAUREEN, ROBYN, AND RYAN. YOUR COURAGE,
ENERGY, DEDICATION, AND, MOST OF ALL, BRILLIANCE
WERE NOT ONLY ESSENTIAL TO THIS PROJECT, BUT INSPIRED
AND CHANGED ME AS A TEACHER AND SCHOLAR.
I WILL BE FOREVER GRATEFUL.

Foreword

Lauren Winner

On my many visits to college campuses—both religious and non-sectarian schools, both public and private—I have spoken with hundreds of students about their religious lives and their sexual habits. Their stories have lodged in my heart and my mind, and I have long wished for some way to convey them to friends and colleagues. Donna Freitas has done the work for me, and I am enormously grateful. In *Sex and the Soul*, we meet dozens of college students and listen to them describe their sexual experiences and their sometimes halting efforts to connect those experiences to their religious and spiritual commitments. We meet Emily Holland, a 21-year-old married evangelical with a self-described great sex life; Mandy Mara, a Catholic student who introduces us to the "yes girls" on her campus; and countless others.

In addition to the stories, I am also grateful for Freitas's statistics. When I was writing a book about Christian sexual ethics, I was constantly frustrated by the paucity of informative data about unmarried Christians' sexual behavior. Freitas has provided an eye-popping amount of statistical information about the sexual activities of American college students—statistics that are nuanced by inclusion of information about religious identification and religious practice—which is a huge gift to those of us who are interested in the intersection of religious identity and sexual practice.

The central question animating the book you now hold in your hands is: what is the relationship between sexual experimentation and spiritual formation on American college campuses today? After a year of intensive study on seven campuses—and in-depth interviews with 111 students—Freitas's findings defy easy summary. For my money, her most significant conclusion is that in the main, it is only evangelical students who ponder the connections between sexuality and spirituality. Students who identify as Catholic, mainline Protestant, "spiritual but not religious," or any other religious persuasion tend not to connect their spiritual or religious commitments to their sexual choices. (As someone who teaches at a mainline divinity school, I admit that I find this deeply disturbing.)

Freitas opens up the world of college students to us with her depictions of the sexual culture on different campuses. Her analysis of the culture of purity she found at evangelical colleges (a discourse into which women especially are plunged) is incisive, as is her discussion of the theme parties—maids and millionaires, jock pros and sport ho's—that she found at nonevangelical campuses. In a sense, these two trends reveal themselves to be two sides of one coin: though evangelical campuses prove to be consistently different from what Freitas calls "spiritual" campuses, both are places in which women bear the brunt of discourses about sexuality. Given that Freitas's topic is the intersection of sexuality and spirituality and that we live in a culture where women are presumed to be the bearers of spiritual, religious, and moral meaning has terrifically important implications.

Freitas goes beyond titillating thick description. By carefully listening to students talk about the culture of rampant sex on many of their campuses, she has found that most don't like the rules of the game. Some go along with the rules anyway, and some—in a complicated blend of acceptance and resistance—simply pretend to go along.

We Americans, of course, disagree among ourselves about sexual ethics. Same-sex unions, sex outside of marriage (and if so, under what circumstances), birth control, abortion, and cohabitation are all widely debated issues. Yet it seems safe to say that, regardless of one's political or religious persuasion, most of us don't like the idea of our sons or daughters passing their college weekends at millionaires and maids parties. (Even the implications for formation of class identity are staggering—imagine the female students at that party growing up and employing maids who did not have the benefit of a college education. How will their experiences of discursively classed sexual objectification at college shape the way they treat their employees?) Put it this way: few people think unbridled promiscuity and long strings of essentially anonymous sex are good for America's college students. In that way, this book is alarming (but not, I think, alarmist).

And yet I also closed this book encouraged. The encouragement came from the voices of the students themselves. Sometimes confused, but always thoughtful; sometimes contradictory, but always passionate, the students to whom Freitas introduces us are struggling to make meaning of their messy, embodied lives. They reject pat platitudes and seem to know that something about the sexual cultures on their campuses is not as it should be. This book, hopefully, will prompt not just academics, but other university employees, as well as pastors, friends, and parents, to think more deeply about how we can help those students in our lives make better sense of the questions about spirituality and sexuality they face during college.

The portrait Freitas has drawn and the conclusions she has reached are so subtle and provocative that I imagine most readers will find themselves reacting as I did: sometimes agreeing, sometimes disagreeing, at times sounding a wholehearted *amen*, and at times arguing vociferously with the page. That's because Freitas provides exactly what anyone picking up this book should be looking for. She invites readers into the world of America's best-educated young people; she asks some of the most important questions about formation on college campuses today; and, resisting sound bites, she hazards some very challenging answers.

Contents

Preface

Extra! Extra! Read all about it!

Dating 101

We, the students of RS 350: Dating and Friendship, believe that an honest conversation
about sex, love, intimacy, hooking up, dating, and other relationships found
on campus is both valid and necessary. Although these issues are widely discussed
post–weekend debauchery, they are rarely spoken of with depth and maturity.
We have benefited from addressing such issues in a spiritual context within
our classroom and want to extend the opportunity to the rest of our
college community. We invite not only the students but the faculty, staff,
and administration to participate as well. We hope you enjoy.

—*Student Mission Statement for* Dateline SMC, *April 28, 2005*

GRASSROOTS REVOLUTION

On a cold March day in a tiny room in the basement of a classroom
building, 21 college students began plotting a sexual revolution on
campus. The unrest had been growing for a while, but the tipping point
sticks in my memory.

It was just after spring break. A few of my students had done the low-
key, girlfriend road trip to somewhere local, or gone home for a quiet
week with family. One went to see a longtime boyfriend. But most of

them had returned tanned and tired from Florida and the Caribbean. They'd partied hard. They'd hooked up. They'd drunk until the wee hours of the morning and then dragged themselves onto the beach by noon, only to start the cycle over again. Many were seniors, so spring break—in its classic, alcohol-soaked, sun-drenched form—was the beginning of one final season of partying that would last until graduation.

I don't remember who said it first—that the campus hookup scene made her unhappy, even depressed, though she embraced it as if it were "the best ever," just a normal part of the college experience. She thought she was *supposed* to like it, but to be honest, she actually hated it. Her fellow classmates nodded their heads in silent agreement. Then the entire group set aside their willingness to remain complicit about peer attitudes regarding sex on campus and made confessions of their own.

We're not happy with the hookup culture, they said. We feel a constant pressure to do things that make us feel unsettled. We want meaningful relationships that integrate spirituality (whatever that turns out to be) into our dating lives (whatever that turns out to mean). We live in a community that says one thing and does another. We need to talk about this and not just within the walls of one classroom.

"Can we change things?" became the class refrain.

My students decided they wanted to challenge the campus hookup culture with, of all things, *theology*. They had read everything from the Song of Songs to novels about sex and romance. To my surprise, it was Joshua Harris's evangelical dating manual *I Kissed Dating Goodbye* that really blew them away. They were shocked that, somewhere in America, there existed entire communities of people their age—evangelical youth—who really did "save themselves" until marriage, who engaged in old-fashioned dating with flowers, dinner, and *maybe* a kiss goodnight. They reacted as if Harris described a fantasy land—offering them a glimpse into a world they secretly desired but didn't believe still existed. Somewhere in between the readings and discussions, their dismay about campus hookup culture and its lack of romance took root and grew like a weed until they could no longer ignore it. They wanted to stop hookup culture from dominating their lives. They wanted the right to demand more from their peers when it came to sex and relationships—more joy, more satisfaction, more commitment—and less sex. Maybe even *no* sex.

Make no mistake, these students didn't suddenly become pro-abstinence and antisex, nor did they deny that sex could be very pleasurable. Many of them knew this to be true from personal experience.

Nor did they believe that good sex was entirely absent from campus. Sure, some people were enjoying sex, especially in the moment. The problem was that hookup culture promoted reckless, unthinking attitudes and expectations about sex, divorcing it from their larger value commitments—religious, spiritual, or otherwise. After a few years of living in this environment they felt exhausted, spent, emptied by the pressure to participate in encounters that left them unfulfilled.

During class, we began to bat around ideas for confronting campus hookup culture: holding a student-led panel discussion, engaging in a public debate, writing an op-ed article for the school newspaper. In the end, we decided to produce our own newspaper, one devoted to sex, dating, religion, and spirituality. The purpose was to challenge the sexual ethic on campus with both personal experience and religious wisdom—in the hope of making romance and relationships more meaningful. The audience would be anyone and everyone who'd listen. The student body. The faculty. The administration. The college president. We would have to raise money to pay for printing—I had ideas for covering that. My students would have to find someone to give them a crash course in newspaper design. They would need to learn to write like journalists, too.

"Can we really do this?" they wanted to know.

Yes, I agreed, stunned that this unplanned brainstorming session was turning into a massive plot to change student life. I'd never seen students so motivated, so courageous. I was a little nervous about how the wider campus—their peers, faculty, and the administration— would receive a newspaper dedicated to sex and religion. But then, how often does a professor find students so impassioned about class that they decide to act on what they've learned?

With that yes began the most fulfilling and inspiring month in all my years of teaching. The twenty women and one man in my dating class took up the task of publishing a newspaper with gusto. Article ideas were proposed and assigned. Students divided themselves into groups: editorial, layout, production, advertising, and logistics. One day, I came into class to find the front pages of every major newspaper in the country taped to the walls, my students studying them intently. Article drafts were written, edited, rewritten, and edited again—seven, eight, nine times. The publication date neared and the students worked in shifts around the clock. I'd head to the computer lab at 9 at night to find almost everyone either proofreading or working on layout. My students would send me home around midnight, laughing because I was tired at that hour and they were just getting going.

We debated titles. *Holy Sex* was a favorite, but I shot it down quickly. *The Missionary Position* was another, but I rolled my eyes and said absolutely not. In a moment of inspiration, one student called out *Dateline*, and we all agreed it was perfect—appropriate and topical—so *Dateline SMC* it was.

The date we'd set for distribution approached and the students could barely contain their excitement. They were nervous, too. They'd put themselves out there. They'd bared their souls. What would everyone think?

CHANGING MINDS, ONE ARTICLE AT A TIME

The religion class I've been taking this semester has begun to challenge my view
of the very thing I used to see as exterior to my spiritual life. Suddenly,
sex has become an issue within my spiritual identity. But where exactly
does it fit in with my religion? Or does sexuality not fit in at all?

—*from "Drink, If You've Done* It *in the Road,"* Dateline SMC

"It's a *real* newspaper." The student who'd made the early morning trek to pick up *Dateline SMC* from the printers had awe in her voice.

"Yes it is," I agreed, amazed by the stacks of papers that looked as professional as the *New York Times*. I was proud of what my students had achieved. And the day was only beginning. My dating class had big plans.

There was a group ready to pick up papers to distribute door to door in the residence halls. There was another signed up for shifts to hand copies to people coming in and out of the student center and near the cafeteria. A third crew waited to hit the faculty offices, especially those professors whom students had persuaded to devote at least one class period, if not the entire day, to discussing the articles in *Dateline SMC*. There were even people stationed on the quad, handing out papers to everyone who walked by.

It wasn't long before the campus was buzzing about sex and religion. My students became campus celebrities, especially among first-year women. Throughout the day, into the evening, and over the weekend, people walked up to these neophyte journalists to talk about the articles. People told them how they'd spoken truth, said aloud some things that they'd thought to themselves but were afraid to admit, wrote of feelings they didn't know anyone else on campus shared, made them feel less alone. Most startling to my students were those who explained that, because of such-and-such an article, they had decided *not* to hook up that night—they deserved more and would wait until they found someone who wanted the same.

I'd never seen a group of students so empowered.

"We really made a difference," they said.

IT TAKES A CAMPUS

In our dating class, I learned there are many Christians who view dating
as a form of foreplay that will inevitably lead to sex. Young Christian
writers like Rebecca St. James and Elisabeth Elliot represent a movement
in Christianity that employs "sex" and "dating" interchangeably, as if they are
synonymous. This mind-set not only seemed absurd to me, but unproductive
for an honest conversation about dating and spirituality. People can date
and not have sex. I personally have dated without having sex. But that was
in high school; that was before I had sex. Since starting to have sex, that has
never been the case. Sex has been a part of my dating habits since sex has been
a part of my life. Some of my relationships have even started with sex. . . .
Until recently my faith has been completely absent from my dating life.
Somehow, something that I try to let dominate every other aspect of
my life has failed to permeate this one. So, I decided to give up sex and
dating because I don't know how to date without sex anymore. . . .
There *[are]* virgins, born-again virgins, and then there's me:
a "thinking-it-through virgin." I feel I have no right to apply the
word "virgin" to myself, but there is a kinship somewhere between my
recent decision and a kind of virginity.

—*from "Virgins, Born-Again Virgins, and Me: Reflections on Why
I'm Not Having Sex (for Now),"* Dateline SMC

When I decided to offer a "dating class" through the Department of Religious Studies at St. Michael's College, I didn't think about whether it would be popular. But the course filled within minutes on the first day of registration, and I spent the better part of that week a bit blindsided, fielding phone calls and visits from students trying to convince their way onto the roster. At the time I had no idea that this class would eventually affect the entire campus, not only the students enrolled. Nor did I have any inkling that it would transform my sense of self as a teacher, shape my concerns about college campus culture, and shift the direction of my future research.

If there is one thing I learned from this experience, it is that there's strength in numbers. Alone and silent, my students felt uneasy about hookup culture and about admitting their longing to find meaning through spirituality. Even though the majority had been raised within a faith tradition, students thought that religion had nothing to say to them about sex and dating and that expressing dissatisfaction with hookup culture was somehow verboten, even at a Catholic school. But when a handful among them found the courage to speak out, the others found their voices. And what voices! At first, I was taken aback by students' stories about the party scene and the degrading experiences that many of them, especially the women, endured regularly. We are ostensibly living in the era of feminism and post–sexual revolution. Weren't my students supposed to be beneficiaries of these movements, empowered and in control of their sexuality? I was even more surprised to learn exactly how powerless they felt to change this culture that made them so unhappy—at least before they realized that the person next to them (and the person next to *that* person) wished she or he could change things, too. And somehow they'd landed on spirituality as a potential way out of these circumstances.

The students' stories, discussions, and newspaper articles made painfully clear that hookup culture does not help young women and men discover the thrill of sexual desire or romantic passion, of falling madly in love and expressing this love sexually. Within hookup culture, many students perform sexual acts because that's "just what people do," because they are bored, because they've done it once before so why not again and again, because they're too trashed to summon any self-control, because it helps them climb the social ladder, and because how else is a person supposed to snag a significant other in a community where nobody ever dates? Living within hookup culture means putting up an "I don't care" front about behavior, occasionally if not frequently submitting to unwanted experiences, and, in many cases, slowly chipping away at personal standards, expectations, sense of self, and respect until these are sublimated so fully that a student almost can't remember what they were in the first place.

Although sex *could* be good on campus—and my students knew this—they found living within hookup culture far from healthy. It fostered a sense of unease in their daily lives, and it turned romance into a fantasy almost outside the realm of possibility. It forced many of them to alternately feel ambivalent or disappointed or highly stressed about sex, often without fully realizing why, and only occasionally happy and fulfilled. All of this combined led them to seriously consider the purity standards that Joshua Harris prescribes for young evangelicals. Not because they hoped to convert, but because it helped them to see how something as powerful as religion can hold an entire community accountable in ways that might, in the end, relieve them of all this sexual pressure.

As I looked through this new window into my campus community, I couldn't help but wonder if students at other schools felt the same way. I wondered if there were other Catholic colleges where religious affiliation didn't seem to influence the sex and party scene on campus, or if there were colleges whose religiosity contributed to a healthier social culture, or if social conditions were better at nonreligious schools. Were there students like mine across America—seeking spirituality but without much direction, trapped in a hookup culture that coaxed many of them into behavior that made them feel ashamed? Or was the experience about which my class spoke specific to our community? If other students felt comfortable enough to speak freely, would they express the same wish that mine did: *if only we could change things.* . . .

Anyone who has worked with college students long enough, and listened to them carefully enough, knows that, for lots of different reasons, they maintain dual personalities of sorts. They project one image to their peers for the purposes of navigating the social scene. But in private, even in the classroom, they can be very different people. When I embarked on the study chronicled in this book, I drew on my years of teaching in various sorts of classrooms—both high school and college, traditional and alternative—and many years of experience in student affairs, working and living in the residence halls, to help guide my conversations with students. My hope was to widen the conversation about sex and religion on campus beyond a single classroom to offer insight on a broader scale.

What follows are the stories and reflections of college students from around the United States who, like the courageous writers of *Dateline SMC*, shared their feelings about religion, faith, and spirituality and about relationships, romance, and sex. There are hard data, too, and I note trends because there are some, but the students' stories are this project's backbone and its reason for being. Each time I walked into a room to meet a student, I did so as a teacher, excited to hear what this person had to say, curious to know what she or he might teach me, grateful for their willingness to open up, and hopeful that the student's courage to talk might benefit other students who struggle with similar questions, hang-ups, triumphs, and regrets.

Remember that behind each story—which may seem sweet, shocking, sad, or even fascinating for its quirks—stands a real person who could be your daughter or son, your student, your friend. These are young people who sat down with me for hours to tell me the most intimate details of their lives.

This book is essentially a tribute to those students. I hope it does them justice.

Acknowledgments

First and foremost I thank the Louisville Foundation, which gener-ously funded the research, assistance, and travel necessary for this project, and in particular the foundation's president, Jim Lewis, for his excitement and guidance regarding my grant work. I'd also like to thank the Department of Religion at Boston University for providing me a vibrant home base while I took time away to write.

My gratitude to Dr. Molly Millwood and Dr. Jeffrey Adams from the Department of Psychology at St. Michael's College for their expertise and assistance in the development of the online survey, and for being such important conversation partners throughout this study. I could not have done this project without you both.

My thanks to the many colleagues who have taken an interest in this project and offered up their encouragement, support, guidance, and advice over the last several years, especially Lauren Winner, Stephen Prothero, Jason King, Sharon Lamb, and Elizabeth Dreyer. To my graduate assistants Abby Love Smith and Per Smith, for their detailed attention to the manuscript. To all my wonderful friends and family who listened to me speak passionately about this project during its many different stages, and who not only offered their ears but also their opinions and ideas.

For their assistance with hundreds of hours of transcription, as well as lending their personal opinions and experiences on campus during the development of this project from a "course on dating" to a national study, I thank the following undergraduate researchers: Ryan, Amanda, Becky, Robyn, Josie, Orla, and Maureen, as well as Mercedes and Alyisha for their additional assistance, and, of course, all those who participated in my spring 2005 Dating and Friendship course—a group of students I will never forget.

Many thanks to Elda Rotor for her enthusiasm about this project from the very beginning and for acquiring this book at Oxford University Press. To Theo Calderara for seeing this manuscript through to publication, for his amazing editing and willingness to endure so many phone calls and concerns from yours truly. To everyone at Oxford for taking this book so seriously and giving this project so much support.

Miriam Altshuler, my agent, is an author's dream. Enough said.

To the campus contacts who facilitated survey distribution and the interview process at the seven colleges and universities that participated in this study—thank you for your assistance and your belief in the importance of the questions and issues that ground this study.

And last, but certainly not least, to all those college students who participated in this study, I send my deepest gratitude. Due to privacy concerns I cannot name you, but please know *you* are this project's soul. Together you comprise the voices that will start meaningful conversations far beyond the pages that follow.

SEX AND THE SOUL

Welcome to College

Meet Amy Stone: Tour Guide, Fashion Model, Straight-A Student

I question my faith every day.

—*student at a Catholic college*

THE GIRL WHO (ALMOST) HAS EVERYTHING

If you were to visit a certain small Catholic liberal arts school in a bitterly cold but beautiful corridor of the Northeast, chances are you'd run into Amy Stone.[1]

Amy is the kind of girl you see on the cover of college brochures. A tall, raven-haired fashion model (for real) whom you might expect to meet on the streets of New York City, Amy is dressed as if she just walked off a magazine shoot. She'd be a shoo-in for the most popular sorority at any southern school—the lucky girl who always has a gorgeous date for the football game—unless she's dating the quarterback. She could be the face of an ad for snowboards or skiwear—maybe because that's her job: showing off clothes, accessories, and a dazzling smile for the cameras.

Articulate, thoughtful, athletic, and intelligent, Amy is that person whom most of her peers long to be. Everything about her is meticulous, from the perfect manicured nails to the hip jewelry dangling from her wrists, neck, and ears. Even her posture is just right, recalling the era when women spent many an hour balancing stacks of books atop their heads. Amy exudes so much confidence as she answers my questions that I find myself wondering whether she rehearsed her responses beforehand.

Everything about Amy seems out of place—too flashy and polished—for such a tiny, out-of-the-way Catholic school. What sparked her decision to enroll? I inquired. It wasn't the Catholic affiliation that attracted her; she's Methodist. She came here because she wanted to be a big fish, and she worried that at a large public university she might be just another pretty girl. Amy carefully selected a small college that reminded her of the high school where she had really shone. Smiling wide, as she does many times during our conversation, Amy informs me that her plan is working.

"I am involved in the student ambassador program, the founder's society. . . . I am a tour guide, and next year, I'll be a student coordinator for alumni functions," says Amy, who at 19 is a sophomore. "If I had chosen to go to [a public university], I really wouldn't have had these opportunities." Amy wanted the chance "to excel and be counted." She is effusive about her choice of college. "I think every experience so far that I have had at [this school] has been positive," she answers, flashing another smile.

> I love this school. I love the people. I love the professors. I love my friends that I've made here and the connections that I have made and the networking opportunities that I have had. It really has rung true what I thought [about the school as I] was coming in—a community where you walk across campus and all the students know your name and the professors call you by name.

On the surface, Amy is a star: the student everybody knows or at least knows about, the girl everyone either wishes to be or dreams of dating, the daughter that would make a parent proud, the student a professor would bend over backward to admit into an already crowded class, the ideal spokesperson for a college, the one promising prospective students: "this could be you!"

By day Amy adopts the uniform of the average college girl. She describes herself as "preppy" and wears "Ralph Lauren Polo shirts and Gap jeans or khakis" all the time and a "charm bracelet and usually [her] silver ball earrings to class."[2] When it's warm outside, she wears flip-flops and denim skirts.

Going out at night is another story. "When I go out, I like to get dressy," Amy writes in her journal. "Usually I will wear long jeans with heels or boots and a tank top with beads or other such accessories. . . . I have sophisticated shirts and skirts and more wild and provocative attire as well." Amy writes about one specific outfit she wore recently that made her feel especially sexy: "Last weekend I wore a black lace halter top with a 'Very Sexy' bra from Victoria's Secret underneath (one of the convertible ones so no straps are visible with halter tops). The bra made my boobs huge and the shirt was low cut and black and lace. The combination of those things created a lot of attention."

"I like to look hot when I go out," Amy explains. "I like to be looked at."

Amy senses that looking "hot" gives her sexual power over men on campus. Yet she also insists that dressing sexy has relatively little to do with sex. "This attention is not so people will desire me or want to hook up with me," she writes. "It is simply to give me a confidence boost and help me feel good about myself." As Amy understands things, dressing sexy is about *her* feeling empowered and not about pleasing guys or allowing them to dictate what she wears.

Amy studies hard and plays hard. The party usually begins in the residence hall with "pre-gaming"—drinking before heading out to the real party. As the night goes on, girls drink as much as guys because, Amy tells me, "alcohol is the catalyst of finally making [something into] an intimate relationship." When I ask why, she explains, "Alcohol just makes it easier. You would never just walk up to someone and just start making out with them if you weren't intoxicated. It makes your inhibitions go."

Sometimes, Amy goes to theme parties, events where students dress up according to a particular set of stereotypes—"pimps and ho's," "CEOs and office ho's," and "golf pros and tennis ho's," to name the most popular. Girls wear as little as possible, sometimes nothing more than lingerie. Like many students I interviewed at Amy's Catholic college, Amy says theme parties are a campus tradition. Current seniors went to theme parties when they were first-years, and now it is their right and privilege to carry on the practice by holding their own. Amy often "stumbles" upon these events. Though, as she put it, she doesn't intentionally dress the part. Amy worries about getting a reputation, since the "girls who are going to go all out and have everything hanging out and showing [at a theme party]—those are the girls who are going to be labeled as easy or a slut." It doesn't occur to Amy that the premise of a "ho's" party is that *all* the girls who attend adopt the role of "whore." By their very design, most theme parties are about sex and power, with guys in the dominant positions—the CEOs and the sports pros—and girls acting the part of the sexually submissive, sexually suggestive, sexually available, and sexually willing ho's at their beck and call.

During our conversation, Amy's concern about being labeled negatively comes up repeatedly. Girls have to work harder academically, she explains, since they are expected to have good grades. Girls have to look perfect. Girls have to "be the responsible ones." Girls have to be willing to hook up because that's the only way to get a guy, but every time they do, they risk social ruin by imperiling their reputations. Girls also have to live with an apparent contradiction: they want committed relationships, but boys do not. "Guys have it easy," Amy says on three separate occasions. All boys worry about, she adds, are sports and partying.

"When I am out I just want to be fun," Amy writes. "I don't want to be one of those jealous girls or one of those girls who gets super-emotional when she drinks. I just want to be fun," she emphasizes. "That is the image I portray and try to live by. I don't take myself too seriously and simply want to have a good time ... singing and dancing required."

Amy may be campus royalty, but, as she explains in depressing detail, being a "fun" princess comes with a price. Amy has dark stories to share—stories that one wouldn't expect to hear from the girl who seems to have everything. They are stories permeated by struggles with sex, struggles with her soul, and struggles trying to relate the two. "Being fun" has led Amy down a painful path.

THE BIG MAN ON CAMPUS WANTED HER "V-CARD"

As it turns out, Amy doesn't dress sexy just for herself but is trading sexiness for male attention. She has known only disappointment when it comes to sex and romance. There is one major thing that the girl who seems to have everything is missing: a boyfriend. Amy thought college would be all about falling in love with the guy she'd be with forever. But she in fact has never even had a boyfriend.

"You hear about my parents' generation, who met the loves of their life in college, who had this great whirlwind relationship and decide[d] to get married and have kids," Amy says wistfully. "Then I got here, and I said, 'Oh my God, it's totally not like that at all.' People don't generally want to have relationships." Almost everybody is single, Amy explains, especially the first-year students and sophomores.[3] "I remember as a freshman...I was out at a party with this guy, and I thought he was really into me," she says with some sadness:

> We were at a dance party and we were kissing, and someone came up to me and told me he had a girlfriend at a different school. I was blindsided. It took a little bit of figuring out my freshman year that this is how a lot of people are. They'll either have a girlfriend at another place and all they're interested in is hooking up, or they will not have a girlfriend at all and just want one-night stands.

During most of our interview, Amy maintains the same poised manner she had when she first walked into the room. Yet once our conversation turns to Amy's personal sexual history, her composure falters. Amy really wants to find a boyfriend, someone who will love her. She's tried everything she knows: hooking up, being friends with benefits, playing hard to get. Nothing has worked. Most of her efforts have produced only heartache. Amy is still a virgin, she explains, though she has performed oral sex on a number of boys. But what worries Amy and makes her ashamed is not her experience, but her *in*experience.

Being a virgin—even a popular, beautiful one—is difficult. "It puts a mark on your head," Amy says. Amy's virgin status made her the subject of a bet among members of the most popular male sports team on campus: Who would be the first to persuade Amy to have sex?

Not long before our interview, Amy was "sort of with someone," she begins, but they "weren't calling each other boyfriend and girlfriend." This "someone" was the star of the varsity soccer team—as big a man on campus as a small liberal arts college can boast. Amy admits she was drawn to him because he was an athlete. "We were hooking up," Amy says, eyes darting to the ground. "We didn't have sex, although that was just because I told him that I didn't want to." They were "together" every weekend for a month and a half before it ended. "I found out from guys on his soccer team that his intention was to have sex with me, and that was basically why he was with me." The notorious virgin-fashion model on campus was to be a notch on this soccer star's belt, and his teammates were cheering him on, betting on the day he would finally persuade Amy to give in.

"I was devastated," Amy confesses. She felt both betrayed and humiliated to learn that her sexual innocence had become a topic of locker room conversation:

> Our third time hooking up, we came very close to having sex. I told him that we weren't going to have sex... and he said OK. So afterwards we were just cuddling and whatnot, and he asked me if I was a virgin. I remember we were lying in the spooning position, and I didn't feel like we should be having this conversation in the spooning position. We needed to be face to face. So I turned around, and I looked at him right in the eye, and I said, "This is between you and me, promise me this won't be locker room talk." Those were my exact words. He said, "Of course." I told him that, yes, I was a virgin. Then for half an hour we talked about the reasons I was a virgin, how I wanted my first time to be, the reason I was saving it for something special. And he was so respectful and told me that, yes, of course your first time should be special, I really respect you for waiting this long.... So I didn't think anything of it. I believed that he wouldn't talk about it.

Luckily, Amy explains, one of the other soccer players felt bad for her. He told Amy how his teammate was boasting that he was going to "take her v-card." By then, the soccer star and Amy had already hooked up many times–he was the first person on whom she performed oral sex.

Amy's bad experiences did not stop there. In her journal, Amy recounts a regretful encounter with a different guy on campus. "[One] night that I was very drunk," she writes:

> I threw up at a party. The room was spinning and I needed to go to bed. Friends at the party had the guy I was with at the time take me back.... When we went to bed we began to hook up and I obviously was not in the state to be doing so. The next thing I know I was giving him oral sex. He was basically masturbating into my mouth because I was too drunk to do anything more than hold my mouth there.

Many would consider this a sexual assault, but Amy doesn't go that far. Several other women I interviewed spoke of instances where they did not consent to sexual acts, yet the guys they were with went ahead anyway. Amy simply reports that it was "disrespectful of him to still want oral sex even though I was that drunk."

"In that instance we were not connecting and I was simply the means for him to get off," she writes. "I never confronted him about it," she adds, "but after that I knew he was not who I thought he was."

Amy expresses a consuming frustration when it comes to sex and romance, and begins to seem less like a princess and more like the average college woman I met—vulnerable, burned by at least one guy and who, behind closed doors, admits to regret, shame, and dismay about some of her past experiences. Amy also shares an inability to find her heart's desire: a real boyfriend, one who loved and respected her, and who would admit to their relationship in public by doing something as simple as asking her on a date or holding her hand while walking across campus. Amy can win the admiration of the entire campus in all sorts of ways, but she can't win at love. Despite her pull on the social scene, Amy is powerless to change her peers' expectations about dating and sex, so she goes with the crowd while at the same time clinging to the hope that she'll find one good guy somewhere.

Amy is unsure whether she will save herself for marriage. She used to think she would be a virgin on her wedding day, but now she just hopes that her first time won't be something she regrets—that it will happen with someone who at least respects her, even if he doesn't love her. Her experience with the soccer player has made her leery about trusting guys. Sometimes she even lies about the fact that she is still a virgin. "I mean," she says, "if [the soccer player] was talking about wanting to take my v-card, you never know who else is thinking that. If that is for some bizarre reason a priority for guys to take someone's virginity, [then] knowing that I'm a virgin is not necessarily going to be a good thing."

Amy has learned several lessons so far from her on-campus sexual experiences: that being a virgin makes her a target and that she has to be careful who knows about her virginity. Amy feels she "escaped" sexual ruin, but she feels humiliated that word is out on campus: the fashion model is a virgin. She is dismayed that, even at a small school where people seem so friendly and she's experienced so much success, her body is a "hot commodity" and her virginity a coveted "prize." Who knew that a Catholic campus would prove to be a place where sexual inexperience was something either to hide or to get rid of as quickly as possible? Where you could see members of that same soccer team at church on Sunday mornings, as if religion and sex, mass and morality, had nothing to do with each other?

NEWS FLASH: STUDENT INTEREST
IN SPIRITUALITY SOARS

That today's college students are fascinated by religion and spirituality may come as a surprise to some, but word is spreading fast at America's institutions of higher education.[4] Harvard professor Peter J. Gomes pronounced in the *New York Times*: "There is probably more active religious life now [on campus] than there has been in 100 years."[5] Affiliation as religious and/or spiritual (to varying levels of intensity and practice) is at an all-time high among young adults—at approximately 82%.[6] But teens and college students diverge significantly when it comes to the "spiritual but not religious" demographic—a group that believes it possible and often desirable to separate spirituality or "being spiritual" from organized religion. Sociologist Christian Smith claims that the number of "spiritually seeking" high school students—his version of the "spiritual but not religious"—is "exceedingly few" (between 2% and 3%) and that America's 13- to 17-year-olds are very "traditional" in religious activity and churchgoing: they are remarkably similar to their parents.[7] A UCLA study, by contrast, reports that there are many more college students in the "spiritual but not religious" group (35%) and that almost half of college students report that "it is 'essential' or 'very important' that college[s] encourage their personal expression of spirituality."[8] Taken together, these studies suggest that something important is happening in the religious and spiritual lives of America's youth when they go away to college. It would seem that only about 47% of high school students are retaining the traditional religious affiliations of their families after leaving home, and even more are questing once they walk through the campus gates.

Evidence also demonstrates that America's teens and college students are exceedingly sexually active—anywhere from 73% to 85% (depending on college institution type).[9] Since most religions forbid sexual activity outside of marriage, it is difficult not to wonder whether there is a correlation between the drift of college students away from traditional religion—especially in practice—and their immersion in a sexually active college culture.[10]

Could the pressure to have sex and to conform to gendered sexual stereotypes on campus account for what seems like a drop in traditional religious practice among college students and an explosion of interest in personal spirituality? Or might a strong religious and/or spiritual identity that is both personal and communal (and not simply private) help students to navigate and even resist sexual expectations set for them by their peers? Could students' experience with regard to "sex and the soul" vary depending on whether students attended religiously affiliated or religiously *un*affiliated schools?

What underlying factors account for the apparent ambivalence, lack of fulfillment—and, in the case of Amy Stone, anxiety—about sex and romance among college students? How should colleges and universities respond to the kind of degrading behavior to which Amy was subjected—and to which she subjected herself—when it becomes the norm? What changes in campus culture might transform the unhealthy, inadequate dimensions of college students' experience, empowering them to follow their impulses to search for higher forms of meaning and dignity? Might religion and spirituality hold some of this wisdom?[11]

SEVEN SCHOOLS AND A MULTITUDE OF QUESTIONS

To investigate these questions, I crisscrossed the country interviewing students at seven different colleges and universities—some that sit atop national rankings, some that wish they could land any ranking at all, and some that fall in between.[12] As the weather became warmer and winter turned to spring, I made my way through campuses that were almost hidden among bustling city blocks and high-rises and others that were the center of life in tiny rural towns. The institutions I chose to visit divide into four types: Catholic, evangelical,[13] nonreligious private, and public. In every case, student participation was voluntary, and all participating schools and students were promised anonymity. I assigned pseudonyms to all the people I interviewed and, in rare instances, changed details to protect a student's identity.[14]

- Visit 1 was to a Catholic liberal arts school with a student population of about 1,500 located just outside of a large city that borders the Midwest.
- Visit 2 was to an urban nonaffiliated private school with a student population of about 50,000 (both undergraduate and graduate) located in the mid-Atlantic region.
- Visit 3 was to an evangelical school with a little more than 1,000 undergraduates located in a small town in the Deep South, where all faculty must sign a statement of faith.
- Visit 4 was to an urban nonaffiliated private school with a student population of over 30,000 (both undergraduate and graduate) located in New England.

- Visit 5 was to a public school with a student population of approximately 30,000 (both undergraduate and graduate) in a small southern city.
- Visit 6 was to a midsize evangelical school with an undergraduate population of approximately 4,000 students in the Midwest, where all faculty must sign a statement of faith.
- Visit 7 was to a Catholic liberal arts school of a little more than 2,000 students in a rather isolated region of the Northeast.

More than 2,500 undergraduates at these seven colleges and universities volunteered to take an extensive online survey concerning their sexual experiences and religious and spiritual commitments; the survey was open to a sizable portion of the student population at the large universities and was distributed to the entire student body by e-mail at the smaller schools.[15] From 534 volunteers collected via the online survey, 111 of these students (between 13 and 19 students per school, a total of 63 women and 48 men) were randomly selected for exhaustive, one-on-one, face-to-face interviews with me, and they also chronicled their thoughts in online journals solicited for this study.[16] The stories told by students in the interviews coupled with their journal responses shape the bulk of the narratives shared in each chapter.

I had hoped for about 150 participants per school and was unprepared for the overwhelming response to the online survey (especially from women, who accounted for 67% of respondents) and the sheer number of students who wanted to be interviewed. This high level of interest immediately suggested something important about my study: there are college students all across America, the majority of them women, who are eager not only to talk about sex, relationships, religion, and spirituality as individual subjects, but who are deeply curious about what these same topics—which often seem to them disparate and irreconcilable—might have to say to one another. Significant numbers of students across varying institutions in higher education want to have conversations about sex *in relation to* the soul.

CONFRONTING THE SEXUAL ETHOS OF COLLEGE LIFE

What I discovered about sexual mores among students during my travels was, at first glance, not surprising at all. Students from evangelical colleges follow conservative Christian teachings about sexual restraint. Catholic schools seem more adept at creating lapsed Catholics than anything else.[17] Many of the young Catholics I interviewed were apathetic about their faith tradition, and some literally laughed out loud at Catholic teachings on sex. I also learned that hookup culture doesn't discriminate based on an institution's reputation, wealth, rank, or religious affiliation (at least if that affiliation is Catholic). But then, students at all four school types are far more alike in their desires, struggles, and disappointments regarding sex than I had ever imagined. Although a few seem happy with the status quo in their communities, all live in a sexual culture that they have neither invented nor ratified; whether it is one of excessive restraint or excessive freedom depends on the school. All face unrealistic expectations with regard to sex—though different ones.[18] And most want to find a better way forward.

Positive student stories—stories of pleasurable sex, self-approval, and happiness with past experiences—were rare. I would have loved to hear more—and those positive stories that *were* disclosed I pass along here. But most of what students talked about was negative, and so the majority of stories I tell about sexual identity and experiences follow suit.

When I first heard tales of college girls dressing like whores for parties and offhand remarks about boys taking advantage of girls nearly passed out from drinking, it did more than give me pause. It made me wonder if the media hype about today's young girls linking feminism and empowerment to their "right" to perform fellatio on any guy who asks is more than simply hype.[19] Some students' stories, like Amy's, read like an excerpt from Ariel Levy's *Female Chauvinist Pigs: Women and the Rise of Raunch Culture*. What Levy calls "raunch" and what I refer to as "hookup culture" is definitely *not* about the joys of free love, but about the ways in which young women have been persuaded to participate in activities that were once only fantasies in the minds of men. "Raunch culture isn't about opening our minds to the possibilities and mysteries of sexuality," writes Levy. "It's about endlessly re-iterating one particular—and particularly commercial—shorthand for sexiness."[20] This "shorthand for sexiness" is written by and for men. One of Levy's principal examples of this is the *Girls Gone Wild* media empire, but one of the ways I encountered this shorthand woven into the campus social scene was through events like the "CEOs and office ho's" theme parties.[21] College women are learning to attach a male-defined and male-controlled sense of sexiness to self-worth (or have this pervasive societal message reinforced while at school), as Amy Stone does, not only through this dimension of party culture, but also in light of the ways that hookup culture sets different expectations and values about sex for women and men. "Sexiness is no longer about being arousing or alluring, it's about being worthwhile," Levy explains. "Hotness has become our cultural currency, and a lot of people spend a lot of time and a lot of regular, green currency trying to acquire it."[22]

The majority of students on campus go along with hookup culture more in the form of campus gossip and cafeteria conversation than by living out its most lurid extremes on a regular basis. Hooking up is a behavior that generally refers to having a physically intimate encounter with someone with whom you are not in a long-term relationship— often someone you just met. Students define hooking up as anything from making out one night to having oral sex with someone random to having sexual intercourse with someone with whom you have hooked up many times before.[23] Students have parallel phrases for hooking up, such as "friends with benefits." Occasionally, the term "one-night stand" pops up. But most students talk about hooking up freely, using "hookup" as the common noun.

Students typically perceive hooking up as a social norm at college, even if their personal "numbers" are rather low. Many who do take part regularly in the hookup scene eventually realize that it doesn't feel so "normal" or even "fun" for them to behave this way after all. Unfortunately, most are left to suffer in silence, while continuing to support this culture by default in public.[24]

TWO BASIC CATEGORIES: THE EVANGELICAL AND THE SPIRITUAL

The only exception I found to hookup culture was at America's evangelical colleges.[25] Life at an evangelical school is, in a sense, enclosed by the Christian faith in a manner suggestive of what sociologist of religion Peter Berger calls the "sacred canopy."[26] At evangelical schools, a student can expect certain things: their peers are Christian unless they say otherwise, and students pray regularly, share certain Christian beliefs, do Bible study, go to church on Sundays, went to youth group in high school, and hope to someday marry a good Christian with whom they can start a family. If students identify as "spiritual" (as most do), their spirituality is always particular to the Christian faith. Evangelical campus culture is religiously infused on every level, and students assume that their peers are saving themselves for marriage unless told otherwise. A quest for purity and chastity reigns supreme on these campuses—sometimes with an iron fist.

On the other hand, more than 78% of the students at religiously unaffiliated private and public colleges self-identify as "spiritual," which suggests that they live under their own version of a sacred canopy.[27] And the two Catholic schools in my survey had more in common with the unaffiliated colleges than with evangelical schools in this regard; though many students at Catholic colleges profess attachment to an amorphous spirituality, traditional religious attitudes and practices among them are negligible. I also found that the divide between sex and the soul is not between religiously affiliated and secular campuses but, rather, is between evangelical campuses and everyone else. In their sexual behaviors and in their attitudes about sex and religion, students at Catholic schools are virtually indistinguishable from those who attend religiously unaffiliated colleges.

So although the most straightforward way of classifying the seven schools I visited might seem to be by institutional affiliation—four grouped together as religiously affiliated, and three as religiously unaffiliated or secular—this division doesn't capture the reality of *student* culture on campus. A more accurate and useful way to classify these schools would be to weight student attitudes toward sex and the soul above "official" affiliation. This leads to a division in which there are only two major categories of colleges and universities: what I will call "spiritual colleges," which I base on the priority that even students at secular schools reportedly place on spirituality; and evangelical colleges, where students are both highly religious *and* highly spiritual in affiliation and practice, and where most students at least practice and value chastity.

This alternative grouping of schools, once allowed, reveals even more complex differences between the student experience at the spiritual and the evangelical colleges. While life at an evangelical school is predictable—due to its deep-rooted, unified commitment to living out the Christian faith—it is far harder to pin down the basic things a student can expect from life at a spiritual college, given that "the spiritual" famously eludes definition. Students enrolled at a spiritual college can assume that value will be placed on diversity, an almost unlimited sense of freedom, a work hard/play hard party ethic, and, of course, the hookup culture. Yet, the freedoms of a spiritual college— many of which would be outlawed on an evangelical campus—do not necessarily make life easier or more liberating for the students, especially when it comes to sexual freedom. While student curiosity about religion and, most of all, spirituality is piqued, high levels of interest in religion and spirituality seem to have no effect on reining in or shifting the pressures of hookup culture at spiritual colleges—again distinguishing them from evangelical colleges, where religious commitment *does* translate into a culture of sexual restraint. Though many students at nonevangelical colleges profess an interest in "spirituality," most have no idea what to do about either spirituality or religion, or where to find the resources for living a more spiritual life. They tend to hide their religious and spiritual longings deep inside themselves.[28]

SEEKING TO RECONCILE SEX AND MEANING

When I set out to test the relationship between sex and the soul among America's college students, I had no idea how marginal an influence religion has become in sexual matters among students. Evangelicals aside, most students live their sexual lives as if they are religiously unaffiliated—as if their religious and spiritual commitments simply do not matter. This separation of religion and sex among such a wide swath of American youth has important consequences, not least of which is the inability of most religious affiliations to effectively empower youth to resist the sexual excesses of both college hookup culture and mainstream American popular culture.

The "spiritual but not religious" cohort may be characterized above all by its ambiguity. I suspect that what is appealing about "spirituality" as opposed to "religion" is precisely that it is undefined—spirituality appears to be a symbolic label adopted to free oneself from the moral obligations and rituals of tradition. Students know even before college that their sexual yearnings and, for some, practices do not fit into the do's and don'ts of their faith. But once they arrive on campus and encounter unfettered sexual freedom, many want something outside themselves—something divine—to help them make sense of what can be a disorienting experience. The key question is not so much why and how spirituality and religion are apportioned among the college population, but how religious and spiritual beliefs, practices, and affiliations are affected (if at all) when sex is added to the mix—and vice versa.

Some students respond to sexual distress by developing a private world of personal spirituality, which they hope will guide them through the indignities and assaults of hookup culture. Here again, Amy Stone turned out to be an interesting example. During her time at college she shifted away from the faith tradition of her youth and toward the more private realm of spirituality, which she saw as a safe space in which to try to understand her sexual experiences. But personal spirituality—entirely unmoored from a particular faith tradition—was too ill defined and private to help her dig out of the hookup scene.

Amy Stone also serves as a classic example of why, even at a Catholic institution, religion doesn't matter much when it comes to sex and romance. Students at Catholic schools know little about what Catholicism teaches about sex, and what they do know seems to them irrelevant at best and ridiculous at worst.

In the end, when students at the spiritual colleges like Amy try to fix their lives, they find that they are navigating the waters of sexuality and spirituality pretty much alone.

AMY'S FAITH: "GOD IS THE MAN WITH THE PLAN"

During our interview, I press Amy to talk more about being a Methodist at a Catholic institution. Her religious affiliation doesn't make her feel uncomfortable or out of place, she says, because she can barely tell that the school is Catholic anyway. "I don't feel like I am at a Catholic college so much as I feel that I am at a place where you can explore your spirituality," she says. "I think there are a lot of opportunities on campus to explore your spirituality, but not necessarily Catholicism." Amy attends mass about twice a month with her Catholic and non-Catholic friends. "Obviously, when you are walking across campus and you see [a priest] you are reminded you are at a Catholic institution. But I don't think every day, 'Oh I am at a Catholic school.'" This laissez-faire attitude about Catholicism might make her college's administrators blanch, but Amy's views are common. Whatever Catholic culture there is at the Catholic schools I visited is subtle or bordering on nonexistent—at least according to the students.

Though Amy says she is Methodist, she adds that she is "more spiritual than religious." She thinks of religion in terms of doctrine and constraints. "To me, spirituality is who you are as a person and what guides who you want to be," Amy explains. "Religion is more [about] following a certain set of beliefs. I think that is why I veer away from it a little bit, because I don't agree with everything that a certain church might say is right or wrong."

Growing up in her local Methodist community was tough for Amy. Though mainline Protestant, like so many of the Catholic students I interviewed, Amy used words like "forced" and "dreaded" in relation to her devout mother's efforts to get her to go to church services and

Sunday school. Today, though, Amy says that she is more grateful than resentful of her mother's efforts. "I still identify as Methodist, but that is because I love my church family and love attending the services and love applying the sermon to my life," Amy writes in her journal. "Other than that, I have my own understanding of God and spirituality. I have a strong sense of God and an even stronger sense of my own spirit. Although I don't like following the beliefs of one organized religion, [growing up Methodist] allowed me to explore what I believe."

What exactly does Amy believe? To start: she believes that faith, your belief in God, your sense of spirituality are personal things that you don't really share with friends. Just because you go to mass only sporadically and don't stick to "one organized religion" doesn't mean that you can't cultivate a vibrant spiritual life. Spirituality begins with a turn inward, and it speaks to whatever you are confronting at a particular moment. "I look within myself for my spirituality and to answer the meaning of life," Amy writes in her journal. She also relies on such resources as popular Christian books and the Bible—unlike most students at her Catholic college. In fact, Amy is the only student I interviewed at that school who mentions having a Bible on her bookshelf. "When I am having a really tough time I will turn to the Bible," she writes. "Each time I have found comfort in passages." She is a fan of Rick Warren's bestseller, *The Purpose Driven Life*, too, "because it helped me see God in all areas of my day-to-day existence."

Faith in God is a major part of Amy's spiritual identity, though like many believers she struggles with doubts. "Sometimes I long for God to touch me and point me to a religion and say, 'This is the way,'" she writes. "Sometimes I feel that maybe I am missing the boat by not being Catholic or Jewish. But then I remind myself that this life is [a] life given to me by God to do good. As long as I am doing good and growing into the best person I can be I am good in his eyes. I am not sure what is in store for me when this life ends, but I have faith that it will be good."

"God is the *man* with the *plan*," Amy tells me at several points during our interview, and always with a smile on her face. Each time, she emphasizes "man" and "plan," as if this is a fun rhyme she repeats to herself often. This same phrase recurs in her journal. Believing that God has a plan not only for the world but also for her particular life comforts Amy. Her relationship with this "man with the plan" is intense, intimate, and constant—everything that her relationships with boys are not. Amy turns to God for just about everything, good and bad, large and small. "I pray to God and give him my problems. I turn to him in turmoil and tell him that I know I must go through suffering because it is part of a grander plan," Amy writes.

> I pray and try to engage in what I consider an open-ended conversation with God. I pray in times of joy and sorrow. I ask for guidance.... Sometimes I feel that I am very close to God and sometimes I feel like I am aimlessly wandering. When I feel aimless I make myself pray more and keep an open dialogue throughout the day.... That is how I try to keep God in my mind and our relationship real and strong.

Amy's personal relationship with God matters tremendously to her, and she maintains that relationship through prayer. But now that she is at college, this onetime Sunday school teacher keeps her faith hidden. Sex is a popular topic of conversation among just about everybody at her school, Amy says, but religion and spirituality are not. Save for the rare crisis—when Amy and her friends might offer up prayers for one another—Amy's spiritual life lacks a communal dimension. When she prays, she prays in private. Unlike the evangelical students I met, prayer among friends or between Amy and a faculty member or another adult mentor in her community is almost nonexistent. Whereas God might indeed "be everywhere" for Amy, he is clearly not very social.

God doesn't have much to say about Amy's sexual and romantic life, either. When Amy talks so explicitly to me about her sexual past and present, her spiritual leanings aren't even a whisper, and this "man with a plan" disappears from our conversation. For Amy, and for many of her peers, keeping prayer private and spirituality personal amounts to the separation of religion from their social lives. When it comes to her stories about sex, Amy's intense spiritual identity and devotion to God simply go missing.

Amy confesses that she doesn't have any idea what the official Methodist stance is on sex outside of marriage. "We didn't talk about it in Sunday school," Amy says when I ask what, if anything, she learned about dating and sex in her church community while she was growing up. "It wasn't preached in sermons. We didn't talk about practical issues at all."

But she describes her church community as "open and affirming" when it comes to sexual minorities, so she suspects that kids who had premarital sex would be OK, too. Amy says that she wouldn't be embarrassed telling members of her home church if she had sex. But even if she were embarrassed, and even though the Methodist Church probably prohibits such behavior, none of that would stop her from having sex if she decided she wanted to. This is because her "spirituality" is what she draws on when it comes to sex, not religious teachings or guidance from her Methodist community.

As Amy tries to articulate why she allows spirituality rather than religion to influence her sex life, her usual poise falters, and she stumbles over her words for the first time in the interview:

> My spirituality and my sense of self, where I am at spiritually, where my, how do I want to say it, it's like where, I think that my spirit and who I am at that time comes into play more than, more than religion [with regard to sex]. Like if, if my church said you can't have premarital sex, that wouldn't stop me from having premarital sex. It would be how I feel about myself and my decisions.

To Amy, the girl with the strong relationship with God who prays all the time and sees God everywhere, sex is a personal choice that each individual must face without reference to religion, a decision she imagines she must face without the help of the man with the plan. This choice is not entirely divorced from God, however, since Amy believes that sex and dating can affect a person's relationship with God. "I really think that all experiences will affect your spirituality in some way," she explains. "Whenever my self is affected, my relationship with God is affected too, because I am leaning on him for different things and asking new things of him." Amy also thinks that sex can be a "sacred" or "spiritual" experience in certain circumstances, and she has experienced sexual intimacy (though not intercourse) as a "spiritual connection" with certain boys. "When you are hooking up with someone and you are staring into their eyes," she says. "You can almost see the connection drawing from eye to eye. I think that that can be very spiritual."

In her journal, Amy writes of a time when she felt that a hookup was a spiritual experience for her. It happened the second time she got together with someone. "We had gotten to know each other and had a lot of fun around each other," she writes.

> When we went back to his room all the sexual attraction that had been building throughout the night was released. We shut the door and immediately started kissing and taking each other's clothes off. It was intense. The hook up was emotional. We looked deep into each others [sic] eyes. We could not stop kissing and showing affection. The best part was when it was over, we lay in bed and cuddled for hours. We talked about family and life. This encounter was special because we

connected as emotionally as we connected physically. It was spiritual. I grew as a person and I will always consider it special.

Though Amy can speak of two moments in her sexual history that she considers not only positive, but significant enough to call spiritual—because they include an "emotional" aspect—neither of these occurred in the context of a committed relationship. Amy still has never had a boyfriend, something she deeply desires. Fearing that the kind of romance she once expected isn't in the cards, she is trying to put the best possible spin on her hookups. Although Amy may privately identify a sexual encounter as "spiritual" in retrospect, neither she nor her hookup partner openly labeled their experience together as spiritually significant. This part of the story—the spiritual part—Amy kept from her friends, too.

Navigating sexuality in relation to spirituality, as Amy Stone is struggling mightily to do, is for most American college students a private affair. But unlike most of the students I interviewed, Amy has found in her personal spirituality at least the beginnings of a resolution to her search. It may not be perfect, but at least she can see a way forward, however dimly lit and lonely it appears to be.

I believe that the student stories I share in these pages express better than any charts the conundrum in which America's college students find themselves with respect to sex and the soul. In what follows, you will meet more students. Some you will encounter because of the fascinating ways that religion shapes (or fails to shape) their lives. Others you'll meet because they have fought so hard to meet religious or cultural standards about sex or have failed at romance and have no idea how to recover. The overwhelming majority do not know how to reconcile their religious identities with their sexual selves. Students such as Amy, who have crept toward resolution and compromise in these areas creatively and as best as their personal resources allow, are few and far between.

THE VARIETIES OF COLLEGE RELIGIOUS EXPERIENCE

*I wouldn't, like, walk up to somebody on the corner
and be like, you know, "Jesus, Jesus, Jesus!"*

—*student at a Catholic college*

ONE

The Spiritual Colleges
Souls Adrift

Religion? It's one of those no-no topics of conversation.

—*student at a nonreligious private university*

SEARCHING ALONE? MAX BRADLEE

Before Max Bradlee walks into the room, I expect to see yet another seemingly well-mannered frat boy from the public university I'm visiting. When I look up from my desk, I am startled. I find myself staring into the eyes of a boy who looks like Marilyn Manson.

Tall and lanky, Max waits patiently in the doorway, his head tilted slightly, his long, dyed-black hair hanging like a curtain along one side of his face. I invite him in and he removes his dark jean jacket, folding it neatly over a chair. He extends his hand to shake mine and I notice the thick charcoal lines that outline his eyes, the deep blue, chipped polish on his fingernails, and the almost black lipstick that turns his mouth into a gloomy, indigo smudge. Against all the makeup, his face is ghostly white.

"I'm Max," he says politely. He sits down, and we begin.

When I ask for his religious affiliation, Max says that he is an agnostic but that he grew up in a religious household. Soon it is clear that

Max's religious upbringing more closely resembles that of the students I have met at evangelical colleges than it does that of his peers at this university.

"My Mom brought me up as a Lutheran," he says in a soft voice. She enrolled him in Bible study and youth groups when he was in middle school and high school. "My father was a Catholic, but he didn't go to church a lot. But I guess he considered himself Christian because he'd go to my Mom's church. When I was younger, I guess I identified with [the Lutheran church], but I don't really see myself as a Christian anymore." During high school, Max "just kind of stopped going" to church, and he hasn't been back since. His mother was very disappointed, he says, "but she was respectful of my opinion."

I ask Max what made him leave church. "I don't know," he answers, his dark eyes glancing out the window, at the floor, anywhere but directly into mine. "I guess at the time I didn't value religion much at all. I just thought religion was kind of like, I don't know, kind of a social control or something that people need to add to their lives when they don't really have much that they can make meaning of. But I've changed since then."

"How so?" I ask.

At this point, our conversation takes a more personal turn and Max says that although he is an agnostic, he considers himself "spiritual but not religious." Max is not the first student I've interviewed to apply this label to himself. But I soon realize he is more advanced than most in his efforts to understand what this means for his life. When I ask him to explain the difference between religion and spirituality, he says that religions are organized under "a specific set of principles" and have particular modes of worship and a distinct institutional structure. Spirituality is less defined. It allows someone to step outside of institutional structure and even away from belief in God. Spirituality, for Max, has to do with having "a connection to all life and to people and the world."

Though Max labels himself "spiritual but not religious," he has not given up on religion. He is on a quest of sorts and hopes to find a religion he can "identify with." Lately, Max has spent time exploring Judaism by attending a series of public lectures on the tradition. He takes religious studies classes, reads books by religious leaders, and debates the pros and cons of various religious and philosophical traditions with friends "all the time." Together, Max and his friends are trying to understand which religion might best help them to chart a fulfilling life path. "They discuss their [quest], and I discuss mine," he explains. They are seeking answers to questions about life's meaning and how to rank their commitments, relationships, and professional pursuits. But he admits that everyone seems a bit up in the air about where this search will take them.

"How did this religious quest start?" I ask Max.

"I guess it happened in college," he answers:

Taking philosophy classes, I've learned that religion is important to so many lives. And religious teachings can be a good thing. I've been reading the Dalai Lama's book on global ethics, and I've been identifying with Buddhism a lot. But all religions, even Christianity, have things—like liberation theology—that are not necessarily religious dogma but [are] rather positive social attitudes.

The fact that Max mentions "liberation theology"—a theology originally inspired by Marxism and a socially progressive rereading of the Christian Gospels among Latin American theologians—shows an uncommon level of sophistication in his religious vocabulary and intellectual pursuits.[1] I interviewed 39 students[2] who categorized themselves as either "spiritual" or "spiritual but not religious," and an additional 5 who said they were "more spiritual than religious."[3] Of these, only Max and a few others proved to be spiritually adventurous. The rest had a difficult time not only describing their beliefs and practices, if any, but also articulating what spirituality might mean. For most, "spiritual but not religious" indicates little more than a distaste for organized religion and a vague interest in something more—what, they are not sure. It was rare for a student to associate openly and confidently with a worldview, humanistic or otherwise, on which they relied to guide them.

Max also stands out because although he does not belong to a faith community or attend religious services, he is pursuing religious and spiritual questions in practice. And unlike Amy Stone, he is doing this with friends rather than "searching alone."[4] As a rule, students at spiritual colleges—especially the men—divorce religious and spiritual questioning from their social lives. Max and his friends, on the other hand, are seeking answers in community.

ENTICEMENTS TO EXPLORE: WHAT SPARKS
SPIRITUAL SEEKING?

Another student exploring different religious paths in earnest—trying them on for the purposes of figuring out if one might fit—is Todd

Walden. Todd is a very funny, bright-eyed 21-year-old junior at the public university, who identifies both as a Christian unencumbered by allegiance to any particular denomination *and* as "spiritual but not religious." Like a number of other young men to whom I talked, he began thinking about faith for reasons that were, well, somewhat less than spiritual.

"I met a girl," he says, and we both laugh.

He was 17 then. "She was a big church girl, and she went to a Baptist church, and I went with her a few times," Todd says, continuing to chuckle at the absurdity of pursuing a girl all the way into a pew. He wasn't focused exclusively on getting the girl, however. "I listened to what the preacher had to say, and I took a lot from it," he says. "It was a pretty strong experience for me. So after that I became more aware of a higher existence and a sense of moral obligation and repentance." But since going to college, Todd's awareness of these things "has weakened," as he puts it. Most of his buddies just want to party and could not care less about religion, morals, or going to church or synagogue. As for Todd, he has continued his churchgoing in fits and starts, and once again a woman is involved.

"I actually went to the nondenominational church down the street for a few months with a friend of mine—she's a girl, and it was a nice experience," Todd says. "I got a lot from it, but I couldn't identify with people there. I just didn't feel like I fit in." This disappointed Todd, but it hasn't stopped him from continuing to explore Christianity:

> I've always kept up with a lot of books about Christianity and religion. I read daily devotionals. I read *The Purpose Driven Life* by Rick Warren. I pray. But I don't adopt the accepted method of praying for a Christian, operating as a Christian in a set religion, so I've kind of had my own relationship with Christianity since I was 17. It has set a foundation for my spiritual being, I guess.

Todd's parents and sister have no particular faith affiliation. Maybe Episcopalian or just "general Christian," he supposes, if he has to pick. "Growing up, there were never any strict guidelines we were supposed to follow as far as worship, God, or a higher power." Todd's family rarely went to church, and when they did it was because his grandfather wanted them to. But now his mother and sister are doing some seeking themselves: they are dabbling with Buddhism, which "just goes to show how open-minded they are about faith and religion," he says with pride.

Though Todd self-identifies as Christian, he insists that he does not consider himself religious. "I think spirituality is something that is beyond the human eye, beyond the human experience," he says. "I think to find spirituality, you have to really look deeper into things and not just take what you've been told in religious sermons or a book. I think spirituality is deeper than man-made religion." Todd feels happy about where he is spiritually, despite the fact that he hasn't found a church he likes and that he isn't comfortable sharing his spiritual side with friends—unless one of those friends happens to be a woman in whom Todd has a special interest. Todd isn't going to let his buddies affect his search, he explains with confidence. "I'm on my path," he says. End of story.

Jake Stein, a boisterous 21-year-old senior at a nonreligious private university, grew up in a Jewish household with a mother who was "really into it"—Judaism, that is. Jake, however, describes himself as "kinda Buddhist." As a child, Jake's family celebrated the Sabbath faithfully and belonged to the local synagogue. He learned Hebrew, attended Hebrew school, and had his bar mitzvah. Yet when it was time to choose a college, Jake steered clear of religious institutions because he has "very strong issues with Western religions." Going to a secular university was his way of escaping the "weirdness" of his religious past. "I've gone through every kind of weird Judaism thing you can imagine, and my best friend was one of those, like, crazy 'I think I'm Jesus' people, so I've seen every aspect of the weird Christian thing, too," he says, rolling his eyes and laughing.

Like Max and Todd, Jake hasn't given up on religion. He's exploring Japanese Buddhism, and describes himself as "definitely spiritual and *attempting* to be religious." "I've always loved Japanese culture," Jake explains.

> And Zen was always one of those things I really liked because there's no religious doctrine when you get down to it. It's just kind of about being in the moment, focus[ing] on what you're doing, which seemed to be really cool. I've been to maybe five or six Zen centers. I do meditation by myself, too, because while it's fun going sometimes, I don't like getting up early on Saturday.

Jake doesn't believe in God—"I never trusted or believed in the Judaic teachings I was raised with—the idea of an all-powerful god is ludicrous," he writes in his journal. But he has not given up on divinity altogether. "I believe in an ethereal essence or energy, un-personified, and un-relatable, but flowing through most things." When I ask what sparked his interest in Asian religions, Jake says somewhat sheepishly that "it was experimenting with drugs." In his journal, he elaborates on his journey from drugs to the divine:

> While I am aware that this sounds cliché, it remains true nonetheless that experiences [with drugs] opened my eyes to the possibility of a spiritually active world.... Drugs allowed me to pursue the ascetic and disorienting [spiritual] states that religious founders usually assumed to find and make for themselves. While it didn't give me the same spiritual/religious experiences that lead others to start religions, it did give me an understanding of how people could believe in some spiritual or religious teaching or that there could even be some spiritual force in the universe.

Jake says he no longer pursues this chemical path to "enlightenment" and instead has turned to practicing meditation on a regular basis and taking lots of religious studies classes, which allow him to further explore Asian traditions.

It has become fashionable to refer to people like Max (who seeks an intellectual, spiritual home with friends), Todd (who pursues girls down a spiritual path), and Jake (who laced his spiritual pursuit with drugs) as typical of the "spiritual but not religious" crowd. But most of the so-called seekers I met weren't at all like these young men. Sure, there are basic similarities between them: an allergic reaction to all things dogmatic and a rejection of institutional religion. Yet, most students who identified themselves to me primarily as spiritual often do little more than disassociate themselves from a religious upbringing that they now find oppressive—a way to wash away the dogma and doctrine or what they regard as the fictional Santa Claus–like God of their parents, while at the same time retaining some affinity, however vague, with Meaning (whatever that is). For most, claiming the label "spiritual" seems enough to satisfy. The added step of finding new forms of worship, of seeking personal enlightenment through religious study, or even expressing the hope to one day find a tradition they like is not even on the radar. Few do anything actively or practically to pursue a spiritual path.

At all three types of spiritual colleges, a large number of students answered "none" when I asked about their religious affiliation (22 out of the 75 interviewed at these three school types, or 29%),[5] though many of them later applied the label "spiritual" or "spiritual but not religious" to themselves when given the opportunity.[6] Students in this category often spoke of parents who had grown up in strict religious households, who felt a lot of resentment toward religion, and who believed they must shield their kids from the experience of forced church or synagogue attendance that they had endured as children. Many of these students chalked up their lack of religiosity and undeveloped spiritual life to their parents' desire to avoid influencing them about faith and belief, which translated into having no religious background to draw on or even reject in their young adult lives.

Then there were students like Jess Levy, who fall somewhere between the Jake Steins, whose families were "really into" a faith tradition, and those students whose parents remained mute on the subject.

Jess attends a nonreligious private university, and although he identified as Jewish in the initial demographic questions, he later described himself as "not really religious and not really spiritual either." Jess doesn't belong to a synagogue and has not once attended services since entering college—and he's a junior now. His friends don't attend religious services either, and religion *never* comes up in conversations, Jess tells me. His exposure to the Jewish tradition at home consisted of going to services only on high holidays like Rosh Hashanah and Yom Kippur, but he can't remember when the high holidays were this year, and he thinks he may have had classes on those days so he didn't go home. "I guess I put class before religion," he says.

Though Jess's family belonged to the same Orthodox synagogue as his grandparents when he was young, it wasn't long before they switched to a Reform synagogue. Eventually, they stopped going to Friday night services. "It was important to go to synagogue on the high holidays. . . . In a way I think it was important, but like, looking back, I don't know." Jess pauses a long time before finishing, "[My parents] tried to make it important, but really saying it and doing it are two different things."

Saying it and doing it are two different things. This is a perfect summary of what I heard from a number of students. Their parents made some effort to have them attend services or religious education classes, but the broader familial message was that religion wasn't that big a deal, expendable even. Although Jess was content with this experience, I met plenty of students who were not only spiritually unmoored, but angry that their parents hadn't effectively raised them in a faith tradition. All around they saw friends thinking about faith and God and struggling over whether to stay or leave a particular church or denomination, and they wished they had something to fret about in the religion department. In some cases, their inexperience with and inability to process religious feeling was the very thing that sparked them to label themselves "spiritual"—a way to sound more like their friends, make them feel less conspicuous. These students wished their parents had given them *something*.[7]

RELIGIOUS DIVERSITY AND THE SEPARATION
OF CHURCH AND COLLEGE

"Coming from the Hindu religion, it is very easy to pray at home and go to the temple to pray," says Padma Dasari, a dark-skinned young woman with beautiful eyes, long black hair, and a gravelly voice. "Growing up, I was affiliated with a very religious family, and once a week we would have what are called *satsangs* at our house for the neighborhood," Padma says. "A religious priest would come over for a service and read from a holy book. And every Sunday morning, I would go to temple, and I would learn how to sing, and I would dance in the shows."

When Padma was growing up, she knew that, as a Hindu, she was "pretty different" religiously from her New England friends. But in college, being a Hindu became even more difficult. At home with her family, Padma tells me, she was required to fast one day a week. Lately, this practice has all but disappeared from her life. "It's hard to keep up the fasting tradition when you have to go to school and eat at dining halls." Padma hasn't taken advantage of the weekly Tuesday services at her nonreligious private university, and though she's part of the Hindu Council on campus, she rarely goes to meetings. Her parents understand that it is difficult to practice her Hinduism at college, and Padma isn't too hard on herself, either. "I know that when I'm out of college, I will probably be as religious as I was before," she says. "But for the time being, I'll go to the temple once every month." Although Padma considers herself both spiritual and religious, she is, at least "for the time being, more spiritual than religious." It's just too hard for a college student to follow all the rituals of the Hindu tradition, she stresses. Without family around to hold her accountable, Padma can't seem to muster the energy or enthusiasm to maintain her faith in practice.

Once again, her friends aren't helping matters, either. Padma doesn't discuss her Hindu background, despite the fact that she has an altar in the apartment she shares with roommates. (In Hinduism, she explains, you can practice at home, though she adds, wistfully, even there she doesn't pray as much as she used to.) Religion just isn't a popular topic of conversation. She and her friends practice something of a "don't ask, don't tell" policy. "If they wanted to know about [my religion], I would definitely talk to them about it," Padma says. "I wouldn't volunteer any information unless I was asked, though."

Though Padma's Hinduism seemed unique in the sea of evangelicals and Catholics (lapsed or otherwise) whom I interviewed, she was by no means the only student who affiliated with a non-Christian tradition. I could relate other fascinating faith histories of students who grew up as secular Jews or atheists or Sikhs or even as Hindu, like Padma. One student at a public university told me she was a longtime pagan! She "knew" she was pagan by the age of 12, she said, and she described her understanding of the divine as "a higher power that permeates all things, animate and inanimate," and that lives "in her" as she "is in nature." But recounting these varied histories might give the false impression that religious diversity at a university or college somehow magically creates a lively, open forum for discussing religion. After interviewing students at the public and nonreligious private universities, it became clear that although these institutions are much more religiously diverse than are the Catholic and evangelical schools I visited (a statistic about which these colleges boast), religion remains resolutely private—something students typically don't speak about personally or even debate philosophically with friends. Students claimed they speak about sex "all the time" with friends—that it is one of the most popular topics of conversation on campus—but faith talk is another story. You would never know how religiously diverse the student body really is unless you sat down in private as a researcher and encouraged students to reveal what they obviously regard as quite personal.[8] In theory, religious diversity should enhance student dialogue and exchange about faith. But if a college does not intentionally cultivate and invite personal, religious expression, students end up navigating a campus atmosphere that makes faith talk awkward, and even unwelcome, the so-called benefit of this diversity lost in students' real experiences.

As I pursued students' stories, I discovered that, for many of them, the only truly safe space for discussing matters of religion seemed to be in a journal; students who were shy or even uncomfortable discussing their faith histories in person suddenly flourished on the page. Of the 111 interviewees, 107 chose to answer in journal format a series of optional questions ranging from what books they were reading to descriptions of a recent night out with friends to their sense of the divine (if any) and the course of their own "spiritual autobiography." This exercise offered some of the most interesting and surprising insights about students' spiritual pursuits, especially regarding the difference between what they find acceptable to admit in a conversation about faith, versus what they are comfortable expressing in private. With many students, I only understood the nature and fullness of their religious pursuits and spiritual reflections when I turned to this written commentary.

One student at a nonreligious private university who labeled himself "just spiritual" and claimed he was not engaged in pursuing religious or spiritual activities at college during our in-person interview offered this anecdote in his journal:

> Now that I am in college, my spirituality is provided for with dance. In my dance classes, I can truly say that I experience something that is out of this world. Only when I dance do I lose sight of every problem and every ache in my body. Even when I go home over breaks, I always try to take a dance class. I know how much my body and mind needs [*sic*] this release and reconnection with itself. Dance has become a big part of me and a valve through which I can always re-center and connect with the inner me.

A young Chinese American woman who had been raised Buddhist told me during our interview that she is "undecided" about her religious affiliation. But in her journal, she writes:

> Belief and faith were irrelevant to me, for they were not pertinent to truth.... Above all, my adolescence was characterized by a search for objectivity, under which religion and spirituality do not fall. I wanted to state only what I knew for certain. Since I believed that there is no way to be certain about spiritual issues given our circumstances, there was no use in speculating about them.

Further along in this entry, which goes on for almost 3,000 words, she describes a turning point in her spiritual life, a change of heart, that came after what she said was a particularly lonely, depressing day:

> That night, I took a bath and prayed for the second time in my life. My prayer was more like a conversation in which I was trying to figure out the reasoning behind my experiences. Afterwards, I felt more clear-headed and optimistic. It seemed like I had gained a greater sense of faith in a purpose and reason for my life. This past year, it has been as if

religion has slowly penetrated my life without much conscious effort on my part. . . . I have gained a better understanding and appreciation of my family's religious roots. When I went back home for spring break, I paid closer attention to the shrine that my mother erected for worship and even tried bowing and praying in front of it. . . . By exploring different religions on personal and interpersonal, ideological and practical levels, I believe that I am slowly expanding the boundaries of my spiritual awareness. Although I am in no rush for answers, at least I'm willing and open to receive them if they arrive.

The only students exempt from this unspoken rule about nondisclosure at the spiritual colleges (including the Catholic institutions) were those who actively participated in campus ministry programs at a Catholic college or who identified strongly with parachurch groups, such as InterVarsity—a Christian fellowship which has chapters on most U.S. college and university campuses including the nonreligious private and public institutions.

One 19-year-old sophomore active in one of these groups likens attending the nonreligious private university that he now calls home to "living on the moon," because it is so different from what he was used to growing up. As a nondenominational Christian, he is able to express his faith commitments through the InterVarsity chapter on campus, but he divides his friends into two separate groups: "I have friends who I would not be comfortable at all talking to about spirituality," he explains with some resignation. "And I have friends who I could call at any hour of the night and ask them a question about a passage in the Bible. I haven't found a middle ground between the two groups yet." The more I noted these stories of faith and doubt carefully hidden away—stories of students searching mostly alone—the more I came to believe that many students who enter higher education nowadays are agreeing implicitly to compartmentalize whatever beliefs or doubts they have during their college experience. Whether this message comes from their peers or is (perhaps unwittingly) encouraged more broadly by faculty, staff, and administration is unclear. Regardless of its origin, students at nonreligious institutions experience a separation of church and college, an expulsion of religion from the public square that is so extreme that many of them are rendered mute on the subject. This is an odd reality even for a so-called secular school, given that institutions of higher education typically advertise themselves as places where students can openly pursue *any* kind of question or topic. It is also an unfortunate, missed opportunity at a point in history where dialogue about religion is of paramount importance on the global stage and one might imagine colleges and universities as places that would rather rise to the occasion, preparing the next generation for a world fraught with religious conflict, teaching their students how to encounter and engage religious diversity on both a personal and a critical level.

IN SEARCH OF AN UNSUPERVISED SPIRITUALITY

Another commonality among students interviewed at the spiritual colleges had to do with their attitude about organized religion. Whether students identified as "just spiritual," "spiritual and religious," or "spiritual but not religious" didn't seem to matter on this one issue. The dominant feelings toward organized religion were anger and apathy.

On the angry end were those students with personal gripes about religious institutions in general and often about the tradition they were reared in. As many put it, religion had been "shoved down their throats" as children, so they didn't want religion to impinge on their college experience—though they still identified as spiritual to some degree. (Parents can't seem to win when it comes to raising kids and religion: students who were not given a tradition were often angry, and students who were given a tradition were often angry.) This group of students believed that all public traces of anything smacking of religion should be erased from campus life. This attitude was especially common among students at the nonreligious private schools and the public university. The idea that college might be a place for exploring religion in new, less offensive ways, or even that religion was an important subject to explore for the sake of gaining this kind of literacy did not occur to them.[9]

At the other end of the spectrum were students who did not oppose a religious identity for their schools of choice, and who may have even considered going to a religiously affiliated institution, but who also felt strongly that religion should remain a private affair. Occasionally, these students showed a curiosity—often piqued by Eastern traditions—and enrolled in a religious studies course or two, but they restricted this behavior to theory and not practice, to the classroom and not the wider campus. The attitude was that a person should be laid-back about matters of religion.[10] Expressing or, at worst, *imposing* religious beliefs on another person was an offense they were not going to commit.

Most students have an altogether different attitude about religiously unaffiliated spirituality, however. Extraordinarily high numbers of students at the spiritual colleges—anywhere from 85% to 93%—registered at least some degree of spirituality in the online survey. This seems to indicate that most students long to find meaning and direction and, in many cases, seek a relationship of some sort with God or the divine, even if they don't tell anyone else, and even if they don't know how to develop, or have any intention of developing, this interest.

All students who participated in the online survey were asked to choose one of four possible associations with the terms "religious" and "spiritual." They could indicate that they were (a) both spiritual and religious, (b) spiritual but not religious, (c) religious only, or (d) neither. The percentage of students who identified as both or as (at least) spiritual are remarkably high across all institution types but, not surprisingly, are highest at the evangelical schools.

TABLE 1.1   Religious/Spiritual Label Breakdown among Students Surveyed

	Evangelical Schools	Catholic Schools	Private-Secular Schools	Public School	Total
	*609 students**	*472 students**	*355 students**	*188 students**	*2,455 students***
Spiritual and religious	558 (91.6%)	300 (63.6%)	166 (46.8%)	97 (51.6%)	1,609 (65.5%)
Spiritual but not religious	30 (4.9%)	92 (19.5%)	112 (31.5%)	72 (38.3%)	529 (21.5%)
Religious but not spiritual	19 (3.1%)	28 (5.9%)	23 (6.5%)	6 (3.2%)	118 (4.8%)
Neither	6 (1%)	53 (11.2%)	54 (15.2%)	13 (6.9%)	207 (8.4%)

*This number reflects students who marked a preference from one of the four options in the left-hand column and also indicated their university/college affiliation.
**This column reflects the total number of students who marked a preference from one of the four options in the left-hand column, including those who indicated their university/college affiliation and those who did not.

Perhaps even more interesting are the spiritual and religious tendencies of the students I interviewed in person. Each was asked how he or she would self-identify in terms of the labels "religious" and "spiritual." Only 6 (5%) registered that they were "neither spiritual nor religious," and 2 more (2%) said that they simply didn't know. That left 104 students (93%) across all four institution types who identified as at least somewhat religious and/or spiritual (though, as a result of their answers, I added an additional category—"more spiritual than religious"—because a number of students identified specifically in this way).

This is also remarkably high, and I see two possible explanations: (1) when students were given the chance to elaborate or explain their affiliations in a face-to-face interview rather than simply mark a multiple-choice survey, they were more likely to consider a topic which to them is

TABLE 1.2   Religious/Spiritual Label Breakdown among Students Interviewed

	Evangelical Schools	Catholic Schools	Private-Secular and Public Schools	Total
	36 students	*31 students*	*44 students*	*111 students*
Spiritual and religious	19	7	7	33 (30%)
Spiritual, and spiritual but not religious	7	13	26	46 (41%)
More spiritual than religious	9	4	1	14 (13%)
Religious	1	4	5	10 (9%)
Neither spiritual nor religious	0	3	3	6 (5%)
Don't know	0	0	2	2 (2%)

rather complicated; or (2) those who were interviewed were selected from among students who volunteered to have in-depth, in-person interviews related to the online survey topics—meaning that they already registered a high interest in religion and/or spirituality. (The latter is the more likely explanation, I believe.)

According to both the students interviewed and those who took the online survey, the major difference between what is spiritual and what is religious has to do with the personal versus the institutional. Evangelicals and everyone else tended to say that the spiritual is private and has to do with a personal relationship with God—how this relationship is cultivated with prayer, reflection, and so on. Religion, on the other hand, tends to be "organized," "institutional," having to do with following rules, doing "religious things" such as going to church, and practicing faith in a community.[11]

I believe that being "more spiritual than religious" or even just "spiritual" means something different for evangelical students than it does for students from Catholic, nonreligious private, and public institutions. Evangelicals tend to have a very active, practical religious life, even if they don't label themselves "religious," and although many students I interviewed at the spiritual colleges felt comfortable identifying as spiritual without having any corresponding communal practice, it was rare to find an evangelical student who did *not* express the spiritual in ritualistic, social, ethical, and legal ways. At the very least, these students prayed regularly, read the Bible on their own, and were serious about letting the do's and don'ts of their faith guide their actions. On the other hand, students who did not identify as evangelical typically did not do much if anything to express their spirituality— except for occasional prayer.

Of course, a number of students I interviewed defined "spiritual" in a way that did not fit with this general understanding of a personal relationship with God, and they offered a more humanistic take on the spiritual:

- "Spirituality is more like a common human experience. You'll stand at a concert looking around and you'll, like, get eyes looking back at you, and you'll both feel something and you can tell that the other person is feeling it. That is spiritual, the connectedness between people, and we all feel that it's right with the world at that moment."
- The spiritual is "how I feel if I'm in the woods by myself, or if I'm by myself in silence or doing art or listening to music."

- "When I picture spiritual, sometimes I picture like the hippie earth-loving kind of people."
- I am spiritual because, "like, I drink green tea and do tai chi."
- The spiritual is "your own story of how you came to be," and religion is a "set of rules for people who don't have their own story of how they came to be. Religion is like a pre-made spirituality that doesn't always work."

The same was true of students in the online survey. All students who marked "spiritual but not religious" were given the option of explaining what spirituality means to them, and how it differs from religion. Although many of these 404 respondents located the spiritual in the "experiential and the emotional" and the religious in the "ritual," "social and institutional," and "ethical and legal," some students spoke in humanistic terms of spirituality as self-awareness, or they distinguished spirituality from religion in terms of subject matter: spirituality is about humanity, whereas religion is about God. There were also those who provided far more complex differentiations than the average respondent:

- "Spirituality [is] a reverence/respect/belief/idea for/about a power(s)/energy(s)/entity(s) beyond oneself. Religion [is] participat[ion] in some form of established religion/ritual/form of worship on a regular basis, regardless of denomination/sect/ etc., also regardless of whether the establishing was done by oneself or another party, and regardless of how long the tradition has existed. The difference: one could be both spiritual and religious. Spiritual is in the mental realm however. Spirituality is characterized by thought and belief. Religious [*sic*] is characterized by action—doing something to participate in/ honor something. The two do not have to exist together, but neither are they mutually exclusive."
- "Spirituality is to me an understanding of the universe and where you fit into it. It is a way of understanding the way things work without having all of the answers and still being able to feel like you can have faith in some things. Religion on the other hand is something where you are told a specific doctrine that you either adhere to or believe in." "The main difference is that it is possible to be individually spiritual regardless of a belief system or structure that is set up and that other people belong to. To be religious you are practicing a

religion which entails structure, rules, doctrines and dogma while spirituality is not necessarily (but can still be) composed of these types of regulations. It is much more open and more of a feeling than a structured belief system."

- "Spirituality encompasses one's individual feelings in connection with whatever power(s) that they happen to believe in/identify with. When one states that they are religious, that, to me, means that they practice a specific religion and are fairly dedicated to it. The difference between spirituality and religion is huge! Anyone can have a spiritual connection with a higher power, multiple higher powers, the Earth, Nature, all living things, etc. Religion is something entirely different. Religion is a practice that some people feel the need for, possibly to aid in their connectedness, their spirituality. However, religion can be extremely limiting and I feel that there are many people who do not use religion for spiritual purposes, but only because it is the way they were raised and they feel obligated, or they have societal reasons for religion."

- "Religion is the routines and rules associated with a faith, a dogma that far too many people follow blindly without questioning it. Religion is politics; it gets used constantly in inappropriate ways to intimidate, coerce, and otherwise influence people in ways [that] should be criminal. I've seen a bumper sticker that says, 'Jesus saves, NOT Christianity,' and I couldn't have put it better myself. Spirituality, on the other hand, is the deeply personal component that SHOULD (though it often doesn't) accompany someone involved with a religion. Spirituality is about integrity and your position in life and everything around you. It's the driving force behind ethics, it's what makes us human, and regardless of religious affiliation, spirituality is an essential part of the human experience. The difference, then, is that religion is used to control populations, but spirituality is what sets you free."

Evangelical students aside, overall the idea of the spiritual typically has to do with a *lack of supervision*. Many students resist the rules, definitions, organization, and simple requirements that being "religious" entails—even those who identify as religious themselves. Students often express that they don't want to be told what to do or believe; they want (or, at least, they think they want) control of just about everything in their lives, and the spiritual seems to be a largely unsupervised way of maintaining a relationship with the divine and/or cultivating a sense of higher purpose or meaning in their lives.

Given that most of the students interviewed experience campus culture as marginalizing faith to the private realm, making conversations about beliefs and values difficult and, at times, embarrassing, if not impossible, an unsupervised spirituality is exactly what they are getting.[12] Although students who report feeling subjugated by religion can feel liberated by this kind of environment, this spiritual aloneness does little to help them create the meaning and find the direction they crave. Unsupervised spirituality pushes them to hide their faith interests from others, whereas a longing for meaning and a framework in which they can more skillfully make ethical decisions depends to a great extent on their ability to find a sympathetic community that subscribes to that same framework in practice.[13] The absence of any real consensus and the lack of basic openness about questions of faith—even within small-scale groups—at the spiritual colleges make it difficult for students to freely explore questions of faith and value, something the students I interviewed overwhelmingly want to do.

TWO

Why Catholic Schools (and Their Students) Are "Spiritual but Not Religious"

Without the monks running around,
you wouldn't know it's a Catholic campus.

—*student at a Catholic college*

RECOVERING CATHOLICS AND THEN SOME:
JUANITA ALVAREZ AND MADANJIT SINGH

Juanita Alvarez's hair falls in dramatic ringlets, framing her face and dark, playful eyes like a thick halo. She describes herself as a "recovering Catholic" who grew up in a *very* traditional Catholic family with a strict Catholic mother. They went to church every Sunday, and they lived and breathed Catholicism at home. Juanita ticks off all the different things that made her a "good Catholic girl" before college: she participated in youth groups, prayer meetings, Bible study, and was lead singer in the worship band at her parish—all rare activities for most Catholic youth I interviewed. In her journal, Juanita even recalls "carrying the Bible everywhere."

"My whole life before [college] was, you know, church, church, church," Juanita says with a sigh, then a shudder. "You know, I *had* to go to church. This is what I *had* to do." As Juanita reflects on her Catholic upbringing, she uses the word "forced" over and over. Whenever her mother worried that Juanita's faith was somehow "faltering" or "diminishing," she sent Juanita on weekend retreats to try to revive her daughter's commitment to Catholicism. "Growing up I had the sense that nothing else mattered in the world," Juanita writes. "My only point and goal in life was to be a server of God and to serve him always, never questioning his beliefs or the ideas that my parents wanted me to follow."

Juanita's father ruled the women in the family; women were to obey men always, no questions asked. All people were to obey the masculine God of Catholicism in much the same way. "Because my father was the male in the household, I had to do everything he asked of me without questioning his strict authority," Juanita writes. "I could never think for myself . . . since I was the female."

Going to college was a breath of fresh air for Juanita. She rarely goes to church any longer, and if she occasionally stops by her old youth group on visits home, she does so only for social reasons. Juanita still believes in God and prays regularly, but since leaving home her faith has become more personal, more her own—more "spiritual," she says. Being spiritual frees Juanita to think and do all sorts of things she was never allowed to even consider growing up: question her faith, express doubts, think about religion in an academic context, sleep in on Sunday mornings, and pursue a relationship with God in her own way. But she no longer considers herself religious, which worries her mother, who tells her she "needs to get back on track." Juanita responds that no one can "force her anymore." Not now that she's left home.

Catholic students like Juanita are not alone in their complaints about being force-fed religion at home. Madanjit Singh, 20 years old and a junior at a nonreligious private university, identifies himself as "formally Sikh." But his complaints about religion have almost as much to do with Catholicism as they do with Sikhism; prior to college, he attended Catholic school for 12 years. When I ask whether he enrolled in a nonreligious university on purpose, he says yes, adding that when people ask him about his religious background, he tells them that he "doesn't like religion."

Madanjit's falling away from Sikhism in part had to do with the language used in the temple he attended each week as a child. Temple services were only in Punjabi, he explains, a language he neither speaks nor understands, and so it was hard for him to feel connected to his family's tradition. Still, he wishes he knew more about Sikhism, and this lack of knowledge felt embarrassing to him at the Catholic school he attended growing up. In grade school and high school Madanjit was also embarrassed by being the only non-Catholic in a sea of Catholics. He was "forced" to go to mass every week, while at the same time he could not fully participate because he wasn't Catholic. But forced weekly mass is not what makes him so angry at the Catholic tradition. He traces his hostility back to second grade. He'd gone with his classmates to mass, all of whom were receiving the Catholic sacrament of first Communion. No one bothered to explain to Mandanjit what was happening, so when his classmates rose to approach the priest for Communion, he followed them. In response, the priest yelled at him, humiliating Mandanjit in front of his friends and their families. No one explained to Madanjit after the service why what he had done was unacceptable, either.

In his journal, Madanjit recounts another upsetting experience in which he was a participant—but not fully—in an activity sponsored by his Catholic school and was made to feel uncomfortable and isolated. "Senior year of high school, I took part in a religious retreat," Madanjit writes:

> A particular prayer service took place where many people claimed to have felt the Holy Spirit enter into their bodies, causing them to cry excessively and causing a release of their emotions. Almost no one questioned this practice or this idea, and I essentially snapped and left the retreat early. I felt deceived, and isolated, because I did not have the experience that the other people claimed to have had.

The experience turned Mandanjit against all religions, not just Catholicism. "I resolved to not give in to something I did not believe in," Madanjit goes on to say. "And for the first time in my life, I made a choice regarding religion. Ever since that time, I have regarded myself as not subscribing to any one formal religion."

Ever since that time, Madanjit has believed that children should not be made to participate in a religious tradition against their will.

Clearly, Catholicism has the power to alienate not only young Catholics but young people of other faiths as well. Evangelicals, by contrast, do much better at keeping their youth in the fold. What accounts for this difference? One answer may lie in the stories of two sisters attending the same Catholic college. Raised Catholic, they now consider themselves "just Christian" and are affiliated with a nearby evangelical community that has captivated them in ways that Catholicism never did.

JOYOUS CONVERTS: NEWLY EVANGELICAL AT A CATHOLIC SCHOOL

Sisters Jennifer and Jacie Stoltz are anything but jaded when it comes to religion. By the time I met these two young women, I'd grown accustomed to Catholic college students' eyes glazing over when I asked about faith. Catholicism, for most, had little relevance to daily life, and students would rather talk about something else, *anything* else.

Not Jennifer and Jacie.

Both juniors, both resident assistants, and both excellent students, Jennifer and Jacie are enjoying a religious renaissance of sorts at college. Their eyes light up and smiles shine on their faces when they talk about their relationship with God. Their energy is infectious, and their faith animates the way they talk and carry their bodies. Their presence brightens the dreary interview room where we are sitting and talking. As if they've just fallen in love for the first time, Jennifer and Jacie speak of Jesus as the object of their affections and of Christianity as the factor that has changed *everything* for them.

Neither Jacie nor Jennifer say unprompted that they enrolled at their college because it is Catholic, but as our discussion continues, Jennifer explains that since she had gone to Catholic school all her life, it feels right to continue. And Jacie says that now that she is at a Catholic school, she likes the fact that if she is having a bad day, someone might well say, "I'll pray for you." Both sisters say that professors and staff at their college talk a lot about "Catholic values" and how to "hold up" these values as a community—something the other students at their school do not say. Are Jennifer and Jacie simply listening and observing more carefully? Are they seeking out faith-based resources more actively than others? What makes these sisters' feelings about faith so positive?

Jennifer's and Jacie's attitudes are different from those of their Catholic peers for the simple reason that the two sisters have discovered evangelical Christianity. For Jennifer and Jacie, being evangelical *and* Catholic isn't an either/or proposition. Most important is taking whatever fires them up about their faith wherever and whenever they can get it.

"I grew up Catholic," Jacie says, explaining that her family went to church regularly. At college, however, she and her sister went church shopping—they weren't too concerned about denomination—just about having a good experience. "We looked up churches online and just bounced from church to church until we found one we felt was right for us," Jacie explains. "We loved it, *loved it!*" These explorations that carried them beyond Catholicism were motivated by factors other than just Sunday services. At their new church, which is nondenominational, they also found a widespread passion for faith and an environment in which they can explore Christianity in a more intense way. Jacie says that they "met more people who were, like, on fire and wanted to read the Bible and do more Bible studies and read spiritual books. . . . We weren't finding that at our [Catholic] church at home among people our age. So . . . that's kind of how it started."

Since then, Jennifer and Jacie have found other young people who were reared as Catholics but are now forgoing Catholic mass for nondenominational Protestant worship services geared toward college students. "You know, sometimes they have guest speakers," Jacie explains. "Sometimes they have worship, sometimes they have different bands. . . . It's really, like, modern [and] appealing to our age group." But what really seems to excite Jacie and her sister is a community of young people who are talking, really talking, about how to walk the Christian walk. These conversations energize Jacie in particular, and when I ask her about the discussions she enjoys the most, she turns to baptism. "Well, like, people baptizing people as babies," Jacie says.

> Some churches baptize people who are saved and find Christ. And that raises all types of questions: like a Catholic who doesn't make that decision on their own—what type of life will they lead? At these churches people were living [faith] out more. That's what we were finding: people felt it was *their* decision. . . . I don't know. I don't think the Catholic Church is wrong at all. . . . I think it's great. But I don't think I would have grown as much, [and] I don't think I would have read as much if I didn't look elsewhere. So I'm glad I did it and am still doing it.

This desire to meet people who are deciding for themselves how to live out their faith especially attracts Jennifer to evangelical churches. Jennifer explains her preference in the familiar language of religion versus spirituality:

You can do something religiously like get up and eat Cheerios religiously. And when I think of religious I think more of Catholicism just because there are so many rituals and things tied into it. And I think that is why I have strayed away from [Catholicism], because I felt like I was getting lost in it. I was losing my spirituality, which is my relationship with God and Jesus.

In her journal, Jennifer expands on why Catholicism alone fell short of satisfying her spiritual desires. "I didn't really question my faith in God as much as I did question my religion," Jennifer writes. "I found that I wasn't learning much in the Catholic Church. I would leave [mass] and realize that I had just recited the words and listened to a sermon and gotten absolutely nothing out of it." Like Jacie, Jennifer's decision to opt for evangelicalism was rooted especially in its different mode of worship. "Around my junior year in high school I began looking at Christian, Baptist churches," Jennifer writes. "I felt that they were run with less structure and repetition of phrases that seemed meaningless to me. I have found greater fulfillment in this type of service."

In my travels to Catholic colleges, I found it ironic that the two most committed Christians I interviewed were, for all intents and purposes, practicing evangelicals, even though both young women retained some ties to the Catholic faith. Finding a devout *Catholic* at a Catholic school was no easy task.

A GOOD CATHOLIC IS HARD TO FIND:
ADAM SPECTER AND MANDY MARA

Adam Specter is one of a few students I met with a Catholic background who became more interested and more invested in his faith since enrolling at a Catholic college. Adam is a heavy-set, confident young man. At 22 and a senior, Adam is a partier who regales me with stories about smuggling forbidden cases of beer into allegedly dry residence halls and about the "sluts" everybody knows on campus.

When I ask Adam to tell me about his religious background, he leans back in his chair and clasps his hands across his body. He almost becomes smug, as if he had prepared himself for just this series of questions. Adam says that he grew up Catholic but that his parents couldn't care less about passing on the faith to him or seeing him attend a Catholic college. Going to church was usually restricted to holidays.

And when Adam went to Sunday school, his parents would just drop him off and pick him up without darkening the church doors themselves.

Adam now studies hard, parties hard, and spends time with his girlfriend. He also makes time to attend church "two to three times weekly"—more than any other Catholic student I interviewed. When asked what accounted for this newfound interest in Catholicism, he leans forward this time, the black leather chair creaking under him, and answers with one simple word. "Availability," Adam states in a tone that suggests he has just given me the inside scoop on some stocks. Then he sits back in his seat, satisfied that he has just delivered a big secret.

In high school, neither Adam's parents nor his friends wanted to go to church with him. At a Catholic college, however, the possibility of finding someone willing to attend mass is "always there." But Adam also attributes the availability of religious and spiritual resources beyond church services to his deepening Catholic faith. Since coming to this college, Adam has engaged in a "search for personal meaning" and "spiritual guidance." Catholicism was there for the taking. Taking, it should be emphasized, is the operative word, because like so many other students I interviewed, Adam detests coercion in things religious. What he likes most about exploring his faith at a Catholic college is how laid-back the atmosphere is. "I mean it's there," Adam says, "but it's not being forced on me."

Although Adam shares an appreciation for this relaxed atmosphere with his lapsed Catholic friends, he feels that people at his school, from students and faculty to administrators and staff, go to extremes to ensure that Catholicism does not interfere with anyone's life. To illustrate what he means by this, Adam shares a rumor that a professor had recently resigned after being told that he was not allowed to pray in class. "It's almost like it's an anti-Catholic Catholic school," Adam says.

Adam describes himself as both spiritual and religious, and he sees spirituality and religion working hand in hand. "I look at religion as my set beliefs and . . . being closely associated with the Catholic church, and I see my spirituality as more my personal relationship with God," Adam explains. "For instance, I go to church, and participate in religious activities to heighten my personal spirituality. You know, I feel close to God in church."

Although Adam is the most devout Catholic I will meet during my travels, his Catholicism is still oddly detached from the rest of his life. It is something he does a few times a week at church, but not something he talks about with friends or faculty or seeks to integrate into his coursework, his relationship with his girlfriend, or his professional aspirations.

Like students at the nonreligious private and public universities, for Adam, it is as if faith is secreted away in a separate compartment in his life, like a cabinet he can open and shut at certain times of the week, a screened-off area of himself that is accessible to God alone.

Mandy Mara, on the other hand, is far more public about her Catholic faith. A first-year student at the same Catholic college as Adam, she wears her Catholicism like a pretty summer dress; it's not only something she flaunts, it's the calling card for membership in a tiny and exclusive social clique at her school: the campus ministry elite. I use the words "exclusive" and "elite" because when I asked other students at Mandy's college whether they ever participated in campus ministry activities, they told me over and over that campus ministry functioned more like a social club—if you weren't solicited for membership, then you need not apply. One student even described the campus ministry clique as "kind of mean." Mandy, however, gushes about the great social life that campus ministry offers her. Mandy's enthusiasm for Catholicism was nurtured long before college, while growing up in a devout family.

"I was brought up in a *very* Catholic family," Mandy says, her hands cupping her chin and elbows resting on the table between us. "My mom and dad are both Catholic, and they feel very strongly about the faith. They grounded me in [Catholicism] since I was very young, so my faith is very important to me." Growing up, Mandy went to church weekly and sometimes even to daily mass. Her family was very involved in their local parish and prayed together over meals. Mandy and her siblings went to catechism classes and maintained private prayer lives. When it came time to choose a college, there wasn't much question about whether Mandy would go to a Catholic school.

"I chose [my college] because of the values and beliefs I felt would be nurtured at a Catholic school," Mandy tells me.

Unlike so many of her peers, Mandy's commitment to Catholicism has not waned at college. Most of her friends also do campus ministry, and being active there makes her feel "very connected to the school." It also shelters her from hard-partying peers: Mandy has never been to a wild party, and she doesn't plan to go to any. She seems unaware that most of her fellow students regard campus ministry as an exclusive clique; from Mandy's perspective, it is the center of campus life. Mandy and her campus ministry buddies feed the homeless on Friday evenings and go to mass together on Sundays. They also do Eucharistic adoration once a week—a ritual that involves worshiping the real presence of Jesus in the consecrated host, a practice that many young Catholics have never even heard of. (Mandy was the only student I interviewed who mentioned this ritual.) Mandy goes to confession once a month, prays daily, and has regular "conversations with God." Doing these sorts of things is, according to Mandy, what it means to be religious. When I ask her whether she distinguishes spirituality from religion, she gets confused. She doesn't understand how anyone can possibly differentiate between the two, so she asks if we can skip that question.

Mandy is not confused, however, about her theological beliefs, which she describes in her journal with the enthusiasm of a true believer and language that could be straight out of the Baltimore Catechism:

> I believe that there is one true God. He has created me, all people and all of creation. He is all people's Father and is a merciful and loving God. People have to choose Him and live according to His will if we want to live in eternal life with Him. I feel close with God, because I know that He is the reason I am alive and He deserves all praise because He is my creator and I want to be with Him in heaven for all eternity, and I can gain this by living a life in accordance to His will. I go to weekly Mass, pray formal and informal prayers throughout the day and sometimes at certain times of the day. God is a spirit, but also came down from heaven as a man. I am Catholic, so I believe in the trinity. God is God and man. It is a mystery.

Like Adam, Mandy is an unusual young Catholic; one might call her an "evangelical Catholic"—to use a term coined by scholar William Portier in his article "Here Come the Evangelical Catholics."[1] She worries about her non-campus-ministry friends, their lack of faith, and their Catholic fatigue, and she feels obliged to explain her beliefs to others and how she practices her faith and why. Mandy hopes that she might help others to discover (or rediscover) the true faith. Witnessing in this way was nearly as common and natural as breathing among the evangelical Christians I interviewed. But it is foreign to the point of forbidden among most Catholics. Mandy was the only Catholic student I interviewed who was not only trying to bring others to a stronger faith, but felt it was her God-given duty to do so.

"Catholic?" The young man's voice rises suddenly as if he is asking *me* a question, or maybe because he's just really confused. I had just asked Jim Mahoney, a 19-year-old sophomore at one of the Catholic colleges, for his religious affiliation, if any. As our conversation continues, it is clear why his association with Catholicism comes with a question mark. His parents are Catholic, and he went to Catholic schools his entire life, but since getting to his Catholic college, he has ceased attending services. When it is up him, he has zero desire to have any association with the Catholic faith.

"I am just, I am not really religious," Jim says, struggling to explain. "I would say I am somewhat spiritual. I think about things more, like, intellectually or inwardly, but I don't really feel the need to go to church." Jim doesn't have much to say about his spiritual past or present—at least not during our interview. Take this brevity at face value and it would appear that Jim, like many students at the Catholic, nonreligious secular, and public colleges and universities, doesn't struggle with or think about faith much at all.

But when I turn to Jim's journal, I gain a whole new perspective on his religious and spiritual journey. In this space Jim—whose answers to my interview questions were curt and concise—goes on for more than 4,000 words. He writes with eloquence about growing up in the Catholic tradition, having blind faith as a young boy, beginning to question the existence of God and miracles, and then interrogating Catholic Church teachings about euthanasia, premarital sex, abortion, and the death penalty. In one particularly moving passage, Jim reflects with nostalgia on the faith he had when he was younger:

> One experience that I distinctly remember was my great-grandmother's death when I was in third grade. I sat down in my chair, closed my eyes, clasping my hands together and praying. At the time I felt like I was really praying to God and that my silent prayers would help to ensure that my great-grandmother went to Heaven and that God would help my family members overcome the loss. I just accepted the beliefs that had been taught to me in school and by my parents, just as a child accepts the existence of Santa Claus or the Easter Bunny.

Later in this narrative, Jim talks about the "new dimensions in his spiritual journey" that emerged during high school and college—dimensions that led him to question the relevance and even the existence of God:

I decided that it is perfectly plausible that people developed the idea of a Higher Being because of the fear of the unknown. People wish there to be a God, so that when we die there is a place that we actually go. To me, this is not extremely important; I do not find a problem with life being the termination of each individual being. I think that people say there must be a God to ensure that people act appropriately, but I think that people should be good based solely on the merit of their actions. I think that a man like Gandhi or Jesus did not act virtuously because of a belief in a higher being, rather they were virtuous because that is the just thing to be. This [was] the period in my life when I began to develop the idea that people should be just, kind, loving, etc. to their fellow human beings based on the merit of that action, not because one feels that "God wishes it to be done." . . . I currently have no distinct ideas of whether or not God exists, so I have tried to develop myself into someone whose actions are based on reason and virtue.

Part of the complex spiritual and religious portrait that Jim presents on paper is his decision to turn to meditation as a way of satisfying spiritual longings left unfulfilled by his loss of faith. "Prayer during this time for me developed into meditation, which for me means clearing my mind and relaxing," Jim writes. "Sometimes this leads to an internal conversation about my beliefs and other times I simply use it to relax."

What Jim's story and those of students across all the spiritual colleges tell us is that students who say very little about their religious or spiritual lives in person may open up when offered an opportunity to do so on the page. Student claims to be "spiritual but not religious" may seem empty when asked to describe their spirituality in conversation or even in a class. But give them a more private and personal space for expression, such as a journal, and the religious and spiritual impulses of these young people surface and, in many cases, turn out to be quite elaborate.

Christian Smith, author of *Soul Searching: The Religious and Spiritual Lives of American Teenagers,* found the high schoolers he surveyed about religion and spirituality to be remarkably boring—almost identical to their parents when it came to their religious beliefs. Yet he collected teens' stories only through phone calls and face-to-face personal interviews.[2] Smith and his research team are not alone in using conversation as the primary method for gathering narrative data about young adult religiosity and spirituality—it is a common approach. What I am suggesting here is that Smith and other researchers might have gotten a different, more nuanced portrait of teen religion and spirituality had their studies also asked participants to write about their beliefs in private. If young adults do not, as a rule, live in communities where they believe it is *normal, safe,* and *comfortable* to talk about a given topic—as was the case with religion among many of my participants at the spiritual colleges—then it makes sense that these students would hold back when questioned about a subject their peers and even their professors largely view as private and personal. But this is a generation accustomed to pouring out its most intimate thoughts and experiences online on MySpace and Facebook and in blogs. It should not really be so surprising then that these same young people would flourish on the page in ways that they don't in personal conversation, and that Catholic youth that seem apathetic on the surface, deep down aren't that apathetic after all.[3]

THE MARKS OF A CATHOLIC SCHOOL: CLASSROOM CRUCIFIXES AND HOSTILITY

A good deal of ink (and grant money) has been spilled on the "Catholic apathy" problem and on analyses of why so many young Catholics have abandoned the religious tradition of their parents. Sociologist Dean R. Hoge and his fellow researchers explored this apathy in a study of 848 Catholic youth, which resulted in *Young Adult Catholics: Religion in the Culture of Choice*.[4] Christian Smith devoted a chapter of *Soul Searching* to the epidemic of teen Catholic apathy.[5]

The Catholic students I talked to seemed to bear out this trend. As with students at nonreligious schools, private and public, the conversations about faith that I had with students at the two Catholic schools were short, with most students indicating meager interest in talking about their religious tradition.

Still, as with the journals which paint a more nuanced, invested portrait of students who would otherwise seem disinterested or unreflective about faith, I think *apathy* is the wrong word here. Many of the Catholic students I interviewed, at both Catholic and non-Catholic institutions, were eager to explore religion and, in particular, spirituality. When it came to talking about *growing up* Catholic, they even became quite passionate, resorting frequently to words like "forced" and "shoved" and "pushed" to describe their experiences. They portrayed themselves as having had no choice but to submit to activities in which they did not want to participate and to beliefs they found in some cases to be ridiculous. This sounds more like hostility than apathy.

The following quotations are representative of this disquiet among young Catholics:

- "I just feel like, I mean, my church, I feel like it's just dead."
- "By second grade I was enrolled in CCD (Confraternity of Christian Doctrine) [and] I really felt as if all the teachings were boring and stupid."
- "The Catholic church just felt like a monolithic beast to me when confirmation came around. I kept telling my parents that I didn't want to go any more, but they pushed."
- "I felt like I was being crushed, like someone was force feeding me my beliefs, *my* beliefs. I don't agree with the Catholic Church on many subjects. In fact, I disagree with its very hierarchy; it is truly un-Christian. Jesus taught equality: a hierarchy is unequal by definition. I currently hold no religious affiliation and will continue to do so. I don't want to tie my beliefs to any institution, and I want to make my own beliefs in my own terms."
- "When I was a lot younger, we were forced to go every Sunday to church. But my sister and I started talking to my Dad, [saying that] we really hate going to church and we just fall asleep and the priest doesn't even like us, so we just all talked as a family and said it's hypocrisy to be forced to go to church if you are not really in[to] it. . . . I never felt anything inside of me like, 'Oh, I really believe this,' or 'I am moved by what this person said,' so I don't miss it. It was just a chore that we had to do."
- "I remember wanting to be every other religion besides Catholic. . . . [Going to church] always seemed like an obligation we had to do."
- "It wasn't until probably high school when I really questioned why I do these things and the hypocrisy of so much of religion. . . . I just lost so much faith in the Catholic religion. It felt like so much of it was about money and politics and power."

Many Catholic students come to college eager to be free of force-fed faith, so they find the nonintrusive, "religion is a private matter between me and my God" atmosphere at Catholic colleges to be a huge plus. Catholic students seem relieved that the atmosphere at their colleges allows them to keep their tradition at arm's length. Most students wouldn't be caught dead reading the Bible unless it was for a class or admitting to praying unless it was behind closed doors or with a trusted friend or priest. Students who attend church tend not to advertise it, and they do everything in their power to restrict their faith to a small corner of their lives.

Of course, this is only one slice of the Catholic college experience. Journalist Colleen Carroll, in *The New Faithful*, attests to young Catholics newly enamored of Old World, conservative Catholicism, as does Naomi Schaefer Riley in *God on the Quad*, which found similar students at Notre Dame and Thomas Aquinas College. But Schaefer Riley focused on schools well known for their Catholic conservatism, and Carroll met young people at the Catholic University of America, Franciscan University of Steubenville, and again, Notre Dame University, all of which fall on the conservative end of Catholic higher education (some, like Steubenville, on the most extreme end).[6]

The colleges I visited are average Catholic liberal arts colleges. How to maintain and enhance a Catholic identity is a common concern among many faculty members and administrators at these more moderate Catholic colleges and universities, which sponsor frequent discussions, lectures, and even retreats in their efforts to pursue this question—a pursuit thoroughly examined in Melanie M. Morey and John J. Piderit, S.J.'s *Catholic Higher Education: A Culture in Crisis.*[7]

Perhaps most indicative of why Catholic colleges have reason to be worried about their identity is the fact that the number one reason that students I interviewed "knew" they were at a Catholic school had nothing to do with the piety of classmates or the practice of religious rituals. Instead, it was the crucifixes in the classrooms, a church on campus, the priests and/or monks walking through the quad, and the fact that religious/theological studies courses are a curriculum requirement. Aside from those trappings, the so-called Catholic college experience, according to the students actually experiencing it, was indistinguishable from that of nonreligious schools.[8] They may be angry at Catholicism, but their high levels of interest in spirituality and journal reflections about faith and God point beyond apathy to something potentially fruitful, if not altogether orthodox, that faculty, clergy, and administration at colleges concerned about the Catholic identity question might do well to investigate.

THREE

Evangelical Extroverts

Faithful and Diverse

*I cannot point to an exact day, week, month, or even year when
I began to know that a loving God became incarnate, died
for my sins, and communes with me. It just seemed
that at some time I eventually knew that the truth
of Christianity was for me.*

—*student at an evangelical college*

A STEP AHEAD: WENDY CAMPBELL

At 19, Wendy Campbell already knows her future: to become a biologist. Though only in her first year of college, she exudes confidence, speaking with a conviction unusual among the young women I interviewed. Wendy hesitates when telling me her undergraduate year, but only because she enrolled with enough advanced placement credits to be reckoned a sophomore by the registrar. From the moment she walks in the room, the vibe is ultra-serious and intellectual. She is friendly and talkative, but she rarely laughs or smiles. Her answers are no-nonsense. Our conversation returns regularly to science because her mind is so focused on her biology major.

Wendy is a deeply committed evangelical Christian. She doesn't see any contradiction between her faith and her future vocation. In fact, she believes that Genesis and evolution are perfectly compatible. Unlike most evangelical students I interviewed, Wendy did not choose to attend an evangelical college because of its religious affiliation. "They actually have a pretty good biology program, so that's why I'm here," she says.

Wendy's perspective on the relationship between science and religion has already been transformed by her coursework. One class hit Wendy particularly hard—it was about reconciling evolutionary science with Genesis. She can't stop thinking about it. "I've always been taught...creation science," Wendy says. "You know: six-day creation, 24 hours a day.... But this class really helped me see that, hey, evolution is actually possible, and it's OK." Wendy's recent and firm shift to evolutionary theory and her refusal to reconsider creationism (or its close cousin, intelligent design) complicate her faith—just as, she thinks, her faith complicates her chosen profession. "Because I'm a Christian, scientists will think of me as a second-class scientist," she explains. "And Christians...think that if you believe in evolution, you're a second-class Christian because you don't think God created the world. So it puts me in a really hard position. But that's what I've chosen, and I feel that it's correct." According to Wendy, it's possible to be *both* a committed Christian and a successful biologist.

Wendy considers herself both spiritual and religious. If you are just religious, she says, it "sounds like you just go through the motions." Spirituality is what creates the personal dimension of faith, which is something Wendy believes is paramount, essential to maintaining a relationship with God. Her background mirrors those of the highly committed evangelicals I interviewed. At home, she went to church every Sunday—twice—with her family. When she was little, she participated in a program called GEMS: Girls Everywhere Meeting the Savior. When she got older, she went to youth group. Her family prayed before meals and studied the Bible regularly both together and on their own.

Since she has come to college, Wendy's religious life has changed somewhat. She still goes to church every Sunday. But her spiritual habits have gotten "worse," she says. When I ask her to explain, she laughs awkwardly and offers up the first and only cringe of our conversation. "Well, I haven't been doing daily devotionals," she says. "I feel like I don't have time to...read the Bible...which is kind of sad.... It's not to say I'm not a Christian because I don't read the Bible daily, but, it's something that I should get back into and make time for. . . . I mean, I *try* my best to have a personal relationship with my God and my Savior."

CHRISTIAN REBEL: MOLLY BAINBRIDGE

Cocking her head to the side, Molly Bainbridge sighs deeply and appears pensive as she gears up to answer my questions. All of this young woman's responses are long, animated, and utterly riveting. A 22-year-old senior at a midwestern evangelical college, Molly oozes drama, and she has a long history of involvement in theater to match. Her speaking voice pitches up and down in an impressive range, from low-toned seriousness partnered by a stare from her bright hazel eyes, to high-pitched squeals of laughter, her head thrown back with glee and her long, wavy brown hair trailing down behind her chair. Molly's every move conveys the impression that she is posing for an admissions photo captioned, "See how much fun our students have?"

"Oh goodness," she says with a sigh and a deep breath when asked to describe her college experience: "I think [my college] is magnificent. I really love my professors here, and I think some of them are so amazing, and they're just so smart, and they care so much about their students, and they are as a whole just so open and honest." Molly speaks in long strings of modifiers, jumping passionately from one idea to another, taking quick, compulsive breaths that occasionally interrupt her rapid-fire pace. "Again, they're very, just, open and genuine with the students, and there *is* the role of the professor, but it's not, it's not like they have this *package* of education they have to sell you and they give it to you and watch you unwrap it."

All this enthusiasm comes from a born-again Christian who is also a liberal, a feminist, and a bisexual.

"I was kind of a feminist for my whole life, but [college] is where I became liberal politically [and] really concerned about social justice movements," Molly explains:

> I've had a lot of doubt in my faith and in my struggles, and this is where I felt accepted in having those struggles and where I have felt like I didn't necessarily have to fix everything tomorrow. You know what I mean: I don't have to come to any solid conclusions tomorrow because there are so many people who, well, we call each other the "Heretics Anonymous."

And who are the "Heretics Anonymous"?

"We believe heretical things, but we're still Christians and very strong Christians in some ways, but without ascribing to *all* of the doctrines."

It's comforting, Molly informs me, that she and her professors "are on the same page" as far as their religious background, which offers everyone a common platform from which to discuss—and debate—both faith and doubt:

> If in creative writing classes I want to sit down and talk to my professor about grace or the spiritual presence of God in my life, I know she already knows exactly what I'm talking about even though I know she might not hold the same opinions as I do. That's the great thing about [my college]: you don't have to sign anything saying, "I believe in Jesus Christ as my Savior." I think schools that make you do that are ridiculous.

Though Molly still identifies as a Christian, she is no stranger to doubt. Molly approaches Christianity as a kind of puzzle she is constantly trying to figure out. She doesn't feel alone in thinking this way, since many of her classmates are in the same boat: "I've found people who are just very committed to, um, figuring out how to live as a Christian in the world . . . how to live and serve God, how we feel we're called to . . . figuring out how we're going to live this way . . . and how to use ourselves, kind of, to our fullest, I guess." She believes "all of life is sacred and can glorify God." "There isn't a division between things I worship and things I don't," she elaborates. "You can be spiritual through everything because everything is inside of that circle [of life]."

Early in her teen years, Molly underwent a religious conversion—she was saved. But shortly after watching a series of horror movies, her faith hit a frightening roadblock. "That was when my paranoid fears of Satan set in," she says. "I spent the next, I'd say, two or three years afraid that Satan was going to steal inside of my mind and make me do the only unforgivable sin, which is blaspheming the Holy Spirit. I thought that Satan could somehow steal my thoughts and make me blaspheme and sever me from the Lord forever," she says, pausing to laugh and roll her eyes about her youthful angst. "I'm perfectly healthy now, but for a good three years I was a very legalistic Christian. God was all a bunch of rules, and I was breaking rules all the time, and I had promised God I would do something, but I couldn't follow through on it."

After years of stressing about Satan and not "living up to what God wanted," Molly finally experienced an important change of heart. "I had this revelation where I was just like, 'I'm not happy.' . . . it was like grace." She begins another long soliloquy:

> You hear sermons all the time as a Christian about how you can't be legalistic because there's grace and God doesn't love us for the rules that we can follow because we can't follow *all* of them. It was about that time that I had a very, very emotional experience because I found out my Dad was an agnostic and that he didn't believe, that he wasn't a Christian. This really, I mean, completely knocked me [out]. I remember going down into my room and just bawling, because, just because it was such a foundation, and if my Dad didn't believe it . . .

Molly trails off uncharacteristically, pausing to think before she continues into one of the most intense exchanges of our interview. "At that moment I was just in my room bawling and I felt it didn't come from inside of me," she says, her voice becoming a hush:

> There was something in my mind that said, "You need to let this go." And so I did. I needed to let [my faith] go, and I felt this physical wrenching in my chest, and I let it go. . . . From that day until this I've never been able to 100% say I am a Christian. All through junior high and high school I [was on] this roller-coaster of doubting in faith. . . . But through the whole thing I want to say that as much as I've doubted, I've very much always felt a very strong spiritual connection to God. I mean, what *I* call God. I've always prayed. . . . I've doubted Jesus. . . . I didn't want my faith to be a security blanket, so I let go of God, too, for a while, and that was really hard.

Since her Dad came out to her as an agnostic, Molly's once-perfect church attendance has dropped significantly. But she still goes to services occasionally, and enjoys the experience when she does. "I really love going to church and singing and taking Communion and participating in those rituals where you are actively worshiping," Molly says passionately, at which point our conversation turns back to what qualifies her as a card-carrying member of "Heretics Anonymous":

> I don't necessarily believe that all scripture was inspired by God, though I might believe that one day. . . . I mean, here's the thing: I've never been a rebellious doubter . . . [but] I'm a lot more of a universalist than traditional Christianity would allow for. I don't think that going to church every Sunday is going to save my soul, I don't think that's where my faith lies, and a lot of people in Heretics Anonymous would say the same thing. I mean we're kind of this merry band of doubters who

aren't necessarily in a hurry to [resolve our] active struggles. . . . I know that there is a presence in my life, a good and affirming presence and as long as that's there, I don't have to worry about the letter of the law. I need to worry about practicing and loving, and that's where a lot of us find ourselves. We're like, "OK. Let's love God and love each other."

She finishes by taking a deep breath and laughing.

COMMITTED, CONVERTED, AND CREATIVE

Biases about evangelicals abound in American culture. But few of the approximately 45% of Americans who identify as evangelicals fit the stereotypes.[1] Walking onto the campus of an evangelical college for the first time was like entering a world almost entirely apart from the other schools I had visited. At these institutions, faith is neither ignored nor suppressed. In fact, at these schools, faith is everything. It is the bedrock on which both the curriculum and the social life are built, and where religion is not only powerful, it is public.

As a professor accustomed to the religious anger and spiritual waywardness of Catholic college students, I was astounded by my conversations with undergraduates from these evangelical institutions.[2] Students talked easily and richly about their religious upbringing and their attempts to live and grow in their faith—a sharp contrast to the reticence of students at the spiritual colleges. The longest and most in-depth conversations I had about religion were at the evangelical colleges.

When I tell friends and colleagues about the different groups of students who participated in this study, antievangelical prejudices surface over and over. Many people believe that evangelical Christians are not intellectual, that there is little nuance to their beliefs, and that they are not capable of sustaining a well-reasoned argument. But there is nearly as much diversity inside evangelical culture as there is outside of it. And time after time during my interviews, these stereotypes were shattered. Wendy and Molly epitomize the complexity of personal and religious identities common among the evangelical students I interviewed—perfect examples of the committed Christian who grows intellectually and learns to push boundaries and think hard about her place in the world *because* of her own and her college's intense faith commitments, not in spite of them. Although, to be sure, I met stereotypical Religious Right types, I also encountered a wide range of political persuasions, including moderate Christian students who were on the fence about all sorts of issues, the occasional uncompromising Christian feminist, and the flamboyant and very out Christian lesbian. While both Wendy and Molly have particularly interesting stories to tell, the extent to which their studies, their social lives, and their future hopes revolve around their faith is typical of virtually all the students I interviewed at both evangelical colleges.[3]

A RICH MIX WITH ONE THING IN COMMON

"It's amazing here at [my college]," Kristen Parson tells me, "how learning can be worship."

After attending Catholic school her entire life, Kristen speaks ardently about why she converted from the tradition that her family still practices (much like sisters Jacie and Jennifer), joining a nondenominational church and later deciding to attend an evangelical college. In ninth grade, a friend invited Kristen to go to her church service one Sunday. The experience changed her life. "I finally understood what Christ is, what he did, and what he means to me," Kristen tells me. "With Catholicism, it was more like, 'here's some facts' and not like, 'what does it have to do with me?' Before, Jesus didn't really mean anything at all. [But then] it finally made sense, and I became Christian."

Hunter Ross, a 20-year-old sophomore who exudes energy, explains enthusiastically that, like so many of his classmates, he is challenged at his college not only academically "but also spiritually, socially, and emotionally." "You're challenged to look at everything from a Christian worldview," says Hunter. His family belonged to a Catholic church when he was very young, but they soon switched to a nondenominational church. Hunter spends a lot of our interview talking about the process of discernment—a spiritual evaluation process that helps one to make decisions about what to do in a given situation—and how he and his friends are learning to move beyond being "legalistic" in living out their faith and are trying instead to attain a kind of Christian wisdom that will help them sort through the many gray areas that everyone faces.

The "all faith, all the time" atmosphere of the average evangelical college is not for everyone, of course. Some students roll their eyes about certain dimensions of their campus culture. Others confess that they sometimes feel that the dose of Christianity they are getting at college is a bit dizzying. Some long for more religious diversity among the student body and greater freedom to participate in "secular" activities such as drinking, partying, and dancing (at one school I visited, there was a campuswide ban on dancing), and they express a desire to flee the "faith-filled" atmosphere now and then. But such critiques were sporadic and halfhearted.

For the most part, students at evangelical colleges listed Christian affiliation as a major reason that they chose to attend. For parents and students looking for a place where a person can grow in the Christian faith, build relationships in the context of religious community, and receive an education that integrates faith and learning, advocates and students both say there is no better place to go than an evangelical college.[4]

Students at evangelical schools often told me of their pride in certain core characteristics that define their campus communities:

- Students are encouraged in their faith by peers and supported in their "Christian walk" by friends as they struggle with family difficulties, academics, personal problems, or doubts about their faith.
- Faculty not only are open about their personal faith commitments but also integrate Christian teachings and values into their courses, encouraging and empowering students to integrate the material they are studying into their own understandings of their faith.
- Because students and faculty have, for the most part, the same religious commitments and values, faith is an integral part of the relationships they form at college.
- Though most students can identify a small group of hard partiers on campus, they typically enjoy non-alcohol-related socializing, and they express relief that their Christian culture largely shelters them from the hookup culture they see among friends attending public, nonreligious private, and Catholic colleges and universities.
- Open discussions of faith, both one on one and in a variety of faith-based campus activities, allow students to explore their religious commitments in community.
- Contrary to popular stereotypes, the fact that evangelical colleges are faith-based does not necessarily restrict student learning and growth by forbidding certain topics of discussion. On the contrary, this core commitment provides

students with a strong framework within which they can test their beliefs and values, discerning in the process where they fall in relation to what is presented to them as the Christian ideal.

This last characteristic is also the most important. Far from turning students into automatons, faith seems to make them more self-conscious and thoughtful; as a rule, I found that the more committed Christian students were also the more articulate and worldly. The students at evangelical colleges were more engaged, reflective, and nuanced during interviews than were students at spiritual colleges when it came both to their self-understanding as people of faith and to their understanding of their place and responsibilities in the wider world.

Many of the negative stereotypes about evangelicals stem from the idea that faith and reason are somehow incompatible—that religious traditions prevent believers from thinking for themselves. But it is precisely the intensity of immersion into an unequivocally Christian community that provides these students with a solid place from which to stand and observe, as well as a lens through which they can filter experiences and education. They are encouraged to cultivate a strong personal relationship with God and also to express their Christian commitments through various group activities and ritual practices. Not only are their communities centered on a very specific life compass—a shared commitment to the principles and practices of the Christian faith—but their colleges open doors to explore faith in light of a chosen major. These schools offer courses designed to look at various world events and political issues through the lens of faith, and most important of all, they help students raise challenges to and express doubts about the limits of Christianity and its tradition while in the company of faculty and peers asking similar questions.

EVANGELICAL VS. CATHOLIC: THE STATISTICAL DIFFERENCES

Virtually all the students to whom I talked at the evangelical colleges spoke of their experiences on campus as explicitly Christian at just about every level. They had every expectation that they would grow in their Christian walk in all sorts of ways—academically, socially, personally. All of the 36 students I interviewed at these two schools self-identified as Christians. Thirty-three (92%) identified themselves generically as "Christian," occasionally adding a modifier such as "nondenominational," "Protestant," or "evangelical." The 3 remaining students—one Pentecostal, one Baptist, and one Catholic—all identified explicitly with a particular denomination. On these campuses, 23 students (64%) offered, unprompted, that the Christian identity of their institution was a major reason—if not *the* reason—that they chose their particular college. Six more students answered yes when asked explicitly, raising the total claiming that the Christian identity of the college was a major factor influencing their attendance to 81%. Students saw attending a Christian college as a way to "strengthen faith," to be in an atmosphere "conducive to spiritual growth," and to "be in a place where [their] beliefs are accepted." Others felt that "God was leading them" to their particular Christian campus.

The contrast here with Catholic schools could not be more stark. Of the 31 students I interviewed at Catholic institutions, only 7 (23%) expressed, unprompted, that the religious affiliation of their college was a reason they decided to enroll. For this minority of students, the Catholic affiliation was one of many reasons listed, and a minor one at that. When asked explicitly whether the Catholic identity of their school was a factor in their choice of colleges, the number went up only to 17 out of 31, or 55%. Many Catholic school students actually said that the Catholic identity of the institution made them "unsure" about going to their school, and several were concerned that it would be "too religiously oriented." Moreover, those who described their school's Catholic affiliation as important in their choice of college generally explained their decision by describing Catholic schools as "small" or "nice communities." One simply said, "I went to Catholic schools all my life." End of story. Almost no one said they wanted to be in a Catholic environment among lots of practicing Catholics, or in a place where they could grow in their faith among fellow Catholics.

When asked to discuss their institution's religious identity and their interest in participating in Catholicism on campus, students at Catholic schools discussed their school's Catholicism largely in terms of the visuals discussed earlier: there was a large church in the center of campus, priests and/or monks walking around, and crucifixes in the classrooms. Rarely did anyone mention that a faculty member integrated faith into coursework, encouraged students to reflect on the role of faith in their college classroom experience, or shared her personal faith with students. When these factors *were* mentioned by interviewees, it was usually in the context of a required theology or religious studies course. Students considered faith and religion to be private, intimate topics that might be appropriate for discussions between close friends but were not appropriate to social life or the classroom (except for religious studies/theology courses). Those students who saw faith as part of their lives generally compartmentalized it. Rarely did they see religion or spirituality as the foundation for their lives or the compass guiding them during their college experience, never mind into the future.

As far as their own religious affiliations, only 17 out of 31 (55%) self-identified as "Catholic." And at one of the two Catholic schools I visited, "none" was a more popular religious affiliation than "Catholic." Even among the Catholics, however, students had little to say about how their faith affected their lives—it simply didn't. Catholicism seems to play almost no role in their studies or their relationships.[5]

THE DIFFERENCE BETWEEN EVANGELICAL SCHOOLS AND EVERYONE ELSE

Catholic, nonreligious private, and public colleges and universities—what I call the spiritual colleges—stand to learn something from their evangelical counterparts; evangelical colleges are interesting models for the kind of mentoring communities that Sharon Daloz Parks advocates in *Big Questions, Worthy Dreams: Mentoring Young Adults in Their Search for Meaning, Purpose, and Faith*.[6] To create a community where faith matters not just in theory but in reality, faith has to be a public value, not just a private one. Professors need to embrace the idea of themselves as "spiritual guides" of a sort and their syllabi as "confessions of faith." The campus should be a culture forged by a shared identity, mission, and values of its own, each forming a sense of itself as something special and set apart from the broader culture (and that does not trade solely on its sports teams for these dimensions).[7]

The only institutions at which I encountered a shared identity and common values—which I now believe are keys to a healthy college experience, especially when it comes to reining in hookup culture—were the two evangelical schools. One could argue that evangelical colleges have it easy here: almost the entire student body identifies as Christian, even if their communities are very diverse in other ways as with race, ethnicity, and class. But then, following this logic, one might imagine that Catholic schools would have the same advantage in this area. They do not, which is one of a number of reasons I grouped Catholic colleges with the nonreligious private and public schools. The near-universality of a Christian affiliation among students at evangelical colleges should not discount these schools as successes, not only in the domain of creating supportive, mentoring communities for their students to ask "big questions," but also in attracting a student population who enrolls precisely because they desire this kind of faith-integrated learning atmosphere. Most students at evangelical schools go to college in part to learn how to live a good Christian life in the presence not only of peers but also of mentors who can serve as role models for integrating the life of faith, the life of the mind, and the real world. Evangelicals are rightly renowned for integrating religion and culture; they were among the earliest adopters of radio, television, and the Internet (plus the organ and virtually every form of popular music). And this is likely one reason that their youth are not as alienated from faith as many Catholic youth are. But evangelicals are also adept at integrating religion and learning, values and education.

Overall, at the spiritual colleges I visited, no one seemed to have any idea how to integrate ultimate concerns with the proximate concerns of education. The closest any school seemed to get to an operative mission statement was "The sky's the limit." This may seem attractive because it offers students freedom. But the "sky's the limit" approach leaves most students with, at best, a vague sort of moral code either to adopt or to resist (and even then one they find difficult to articulate when asked)—unless they arrived with a formidable one to begin with. Many students in these environments find themselves acting without reflecting much on their behavior. They may be brilliant in the classroom, but they leave this learning behind when they step onto the larger campus. Their college community most likely boasts an idealistic mission statement on its Web site and in its student handbook and course catalog, designed to foster particular values and standards on campus, but these ideals seem trapped on the screen and the page. Moreover, if and when these students begin to feel unsettled about their social, relational, and sexual choices, most are uncertain about where to turn for possible answers or possible models for being in the world, and they are reluctant to commit to any one way of thinking, even for a short period of time. Many students seem afraid of realizing they have chosen poorly or acted wrongly. So they remain in limbo, committing to no one and nothing—a difficult place to be.

The sky's-the-limit model in which everything is possible and nothing either right or wrong is not an invention of the students I interviewed. It is championed in the admissions materials and on the Web sites of many Catholic, nonreligious private, and public schools, which repeatedly tell prospective students and their parents that "anything is possible" at their institutions. If you enroll, you will have "the whole world at your fingertips."[8] Students will stay up all night talking about "all sorts of things," and nobody will be breathing down their necks telling them what to think or do. Admissions materials at many Catholic schools actually play down their Catholic affiliation, relegating it to a fact of their heritage and implying that a student might not even notice it. In other words, attending a Catholic school is pretty much like attending a non-Catholic one. You too will be met with a diverse student body and "open-minded" faculty and administrators—open, that is, to a mind-boggling array of ideals and beliefs and apparently committed to none in particular.[9]

Things could not be more different at the evangelical colleges, where Web sites and admissions materials offer something very specific to potential applicants: Jesus. Their message is commitment to Christianity and an exploration of diversity and doubt within this religious framework, rather than openness to anything and everything under the sun. The message they send, through such slogans as "Burning with Jesus," or "Learning to Live for Christ," is that your college experience will be Christian through and through.[10] Your social life, your courses, your sports, and your major will revolve around your Christian faith. Your college will help you to integrate into your experiences what it means to be a Christian in today's world and what it means to be a Christian in your personal and professional life. You can expect faculty, staff, and students to be almost exclusively Christian. As a student, you will get the total Christian package.

Even within this very particular evangelical framework, these colleges boast that a student's faith will be challenged, that doubt is part of the deal, and that inquiry and hard questions are part and parcel of the Christian college experience. If you come here, these institutions say, you will find yourself among people who, like you, have questions, doubts, and struggles—you will not be alone. As you explore the world in the context of your faith, you will have all the institution's resources at your fingertips. You will not be searching alone as you find your own way into the world. True, all this will be happening in a community that has very stringent rules. You may even have to sign a "covenant" agreement restricting and even legislating your behavior and its potential judicial repercussions before you set foot on campus. If you stay up all night talking, it will probably be in single-sex housing.

This vast divide between the campus cultures of evangelical and spiritual colleges can be seen not only in admissions materials and on Web sites but also in the day-to-day experiences of students. For students at evangelical colleges and universities, the answer is always to turn to faith, Jesus, and God when a situation is confusing or difficult. A student might do this on a personal level only, in private prayer or reflection. Or she might do so in a communal way, in small groups of friends in her hall, in a conversation with a trusted faculty member, or through the activities of the campus chapel.

For students at spiritual colleges, by contrast, there is no one obvious place for a student to go when she is seeking answers. That is because she is supposed to go anywhere and everywhere! She has a myriad of thinkers, models, traditions, and cultural possibilities at her fingertips and can choose any one that feels right at the moment—even if no one else chooses it. All these options, all this freedom, simply add to the confusion for many students. Under these circumstances, many end up as perpetual wanderers, finding it extraordinarily difficult to locate themselves in any one place, to commit themselves to any one intellectual or moral framework. As a result, they have difficulty truly understanding their experiences. They act—especially in their social lives—with little if any reflection. The task of carving out a path for their lives, or developing a guiding compass with which to orient themselves in the world and assess their behaviors is barely on their radar. Many of the adults around them—the potential mentors who serve as staff, faculty, and administrators—are often reluctant to share personal views which might be interpreted as asserting influence over student beliefs or as somehow not rigorous academically, and therefore they are often perceived as equally noncommittal.[11] I am not suggesting the evangelical college as *the* model for identity, mission, and ethics at all institutions of higher education; there are many appropriate value systems, both humanistic and religious, that could serve this purpose well for a diversity of communities. But what if most colleges and universities do not advocate any particular value system, even a humanistic one, in practice? What if most colleges and universities, like their students, are afraid to "impose" any values at all on their community members? Some may see this is a plus. As a longtime professor and teacher, and researcher of this study, I have watched too many students floundering and faltering without any sense of direction, or any idea where to go to get any, to regard this hands-off approach as advantageous any longer.

When at least three-quarters of students across institution types, religiously affiliated or otherwise, register an interest in spirituality, faith, and religion, it seems a glaring problem that the majority of these students never find productive ways to explore or express these interests personally and academically during the college experience. Even where there is a vast diversity of belief and religious background, one would imagine the college campus as a place that would actively welcome its public expression in the service of learning, of character development, and of students discovering likeminded individuals and pursuing understanding among those who hold different views. Most colleges and universities provide mission statements meant to forge the kind of shared identity of which Daloz Parks speaks—or at least the appearance of one. Following through on these statements in practice is another story. When it comes to religion and spirituality, most campuses seem to be failing miserably, barely attempting (if at all) to create atmospheres where students feel welcome to pursue their "big questions" in this area and in whatever form their desires (and their professor-mentors) take them. This oversight has even bigger repercussions when it comes to sex, as student narratives will demonstrate.

THE ROMANTIC IDEAL

*For me, I'm looking for a deeper connection than
most people are looking for I guess.*

—*student at a nonreligious private university*

FOUR

Evangelical Purity Culture

Its Princesses and Warriors

> *I was taught very firmly that, that beyond kissing*
> *everything's pretty much sinful. A person should*
> *never go beyond kissing.*
>
> —*student at an evangelical college*

A PRINCESS OF PURITY

"Ooooh, sex is *wonderful!*" gushes Emily Holland, an unusual confession for someone at an evangelical college. Emily wears a smart, pale green suit, dressed as if our meeting is really a job interview. Her cheeks turn pink, her long eyelashes flutter, and her blue eyes dance as she draws out each syllable.

My eyes open wide as I try to hide my surprise.

It's not that I haven't met other evangelical students who have had sex. But they are typically regretful, mortified, angry, or fearful. Emily is decidedly different.

Like most of her peers, Emily grew up in a "very religious" household, went to church every Sunday (sometimes more than once), prayed and studied the Bible at home with her family, and was part of a youth group. She describes herself as "very involved and very religious and very spiritual." In her journal, she writes that she has "religious experiences all the time" because she "walk[s] every day with God." Emily decided to attend an evangelical college because she wanted to "surround herself" with fellow students and faculty who would "hold her accountable" in her faith.

Nonetheless, Emily is effusive about sex.

"I have a *very* healthy sex life," she continues happily. She then does something that makes me understand why she is not conflicted about sex: she takes her left hand from her lap and displays it on the table between us, revealing a big diamond ring. At 21, Emily is already married.

In Emily, I met what most evangelicals would call a true princess of purity: an unblemished, unspoiled young woman who—at least, according to the purity culture in which she lives—had every right to wear a white dress and to hold her head high as she walked down the aisle on her wedding day. Emily had done everything right: she not only remained a virgin until her wedding night, she also made it to the special day uncorrupted by any sexual intimacy aside from the occasional kiss.

In other words, Emily lived the fairy tale and was now embarked on a happily ever after with Prince Charming. And she isn't just proud of this accomplishment; she is smug. She knows that the overwhelming majority of her peers "fail" as princesses; most girls don't get the fairy tale. And while female classmates are deep into what is popularly known on campus as "the senior scramble"—the mad dash to find a husband by graduation—Emily can sit back, relax, and just watch. And she does.

When I ask Emily about sex at her school, her face lights up again. Even though they aren't supposed to, students at her college participate in casual sex, Emily reports, adding that this is a sad circumstance for everyone, especially women. When our conversation returns to her own sex life, she bursts with pride, eager to regale me with tales of promise rings, first kisses, and the dream-come-true wedding night.

Growing up, Emily had for eight years worn what she called a "covenant ring," given to her by her parents at her thirteenth birthday. "I made that vow to my parents and to God and to myself that I was going to save sex for marriage," Emily says:

> God not only commands [us to wait to have sex], but he commands us
> to do it for a reason. It's not just a stupid rule to follow. There are a lot

of emotions and a lot of hurt if it's not kept, so I knew the value of that. . . . And then, aside from that, I decided that the only person that I ever wanted to kiss was the man that I would spend the rest of my life with.

A series of studies have shown that young Christians find it difficult to keep the covenant these rings symbolize. In many cases, abstinence pledges do little more than postpone sexual intercourse for a few months, or turn those who try to keep them in the direction of other sexual activity.[1] But Emily was able to keep her promise. When I ask if her husband was in fact the first person, the *only* person, she has ever kissed, she sits up straight, and smiles. "First person!" she confirms with delight. And, according to her journal, the only intimate contact she ever had with a man other than her husband was holding hands a couple of times with a longtime boyfriend in high school.

The first kiss between Emily and her betrothed took place in a carefully choreographed courtship, one that reflected the values found in evangelical dating manuals and was designed above all else to preserve Emily's purity. Although some evangelical students insist on following the "first kiss at the altar" rule, Emily and her fiancé did not kiss until they were engaged, and then agreed "not to touch each other any place that a modest bathing suit would cover." "We weren't going to cross that line until we were married," she explains. "So definitely kissing was all we really had to do." As Emily recounts this experience, her voice sounds nostalgic, and her eyes turn dreamy as she remembers the exciting game of maintaining very particular boundaries up until their wedding night. When I inquire whether waiting had been a struggle during their engagement, Emily replies: "I don't regret it for a minute. It was very difficult, but I don't regret making that choice."

Emily's promise ring helped to bring her to the altar as a virgin, but it also played an important role on her wedding night. Emily chose to give the ring to her husband once they arrived at their hotel—just before they had sex. "We prayed together, and we committed everything that was going [to] happen that night to God," Emily says. "We wanted it to be completely special, and I presented [the ring] to him, saying, 'You know, I've saved myself for you, and here is a token of that.'"

According to Emily, staying pure before marriage has made her sex life as a married woman all the better. "I think we both understand the value of having saved [sex] for each other, and it's not at all a selfish act," Emily explains. The people who don't guard their purity, Emily says, are "setting themselves up for a lot of disappointment later on in life especially when they do find that one person." She continues:

> If I hadn't saved myself, and I met my husband who *did* save himself, I would be a big disappointment to him, and that would be very hard.... And it would be very disappointing to me had he not saved himself. So I think that you have to be careful in dating situations to realize that the person you're dating might not be who you end up with. It might not work out, so be careful what you give them.

Emily is an anomaly, even at an evangelical college. Most of the evangelical women I interviewed had, according to the extreme "battle" terms of the prevailing purity culture, already given away too much.

PURITY TALK AND THE EVANGELICAL ROMANTIC IDEAL

Dictionary definitions of "purity" are: "freedom from matter that contaminates, defiles, corrupts, or debases"; "freedom from moral corruption, from ceremonial or sexual uncleanness, or pollution"; a "stainless condition or character; innocence, chastity, [and] ceremonial cleanness."[2]

When something is impure, we imagine it is contaminated and corrupted, blemished. It is somehow dirty, profaned in a way that may make it necessary to discard or avoid. In *Purity and Danger*, anthropologist of religion Mary Douglas discusses in detail how we divide the pure from the impure and in the process discriminate between the sacred and the profane, the holy and the corrupt. She explains that our attempts at "purifying" are acts against being "polluted and toward 'dirt-avoidance.'"[3] This "dirt avoidance" can entail anything from tidying the house to avoiding sex. "For us," Douglas writes, "sacred things and places are to be protected from defilement. Holiness and impurity are at opposite poles."[4] Dirt is "a relative idea":

> Shoes are dirty not in themselves, but it is dirty to place them on the dining table; food is not dirty in itself, but it is dirty to leave cooking utensils in the bedroom, or food bespattered on clothing; similarly, bathroom equipment in the drawing room; clothing lying on chairs; out-door things in-doors; upstairs things downstairs; under-clothing appearing where over-clothing should be, and so on. In short, our pollution behavior is the reaction which condemns any object or idea likely to confuse or contradict cherished classifications.[5]

Following Douglas's reasoning, we could say the same about sex: sex is not dirty in and of itself, but it is dirty to engage in sexual activity or perhaps even to indulge sexual thoughts in ways that, in Douglas's words, "contradict cherished classifications." Within contemporary evangelical Christianity, the operative classification is marriage, understood as a kind of "purifying container" for the messiness that is human sexuality. To engage in sex outside of marriage is to contravene a cherished classification.

In on-campus battles for purity at evangelical colleges, sex becomes the enemy. Outside of marriage, sex is corrosive of a pure body and heart. Sex eats away at your relationship with God and your community. Moreover, the consequences of sex are irreversible. If you have sex outside of a marriage, you are, in a word, ruined.

In dozens of popular Christian self-help books, protecting one's purity until marriage is described as a young adult's number one priority.[6] In the best-selling *Battle* series (*Every Young Woman's Battle*, *Every Young Man's Battle*, etc.), men are taught that they must guard their purity by understanding sex as "the enemy" in a life-and-death battle, by raising a "sword and shield" against it, and even by making an "ocular covenant"—learning to "bounce" one's eyes away from "lustful objects" (i.e., women).[7] Men must allow Christ to take their minds "captive" so nary a thought about a woman enters their imagination, all the while "building a line of defense *in* the heart" against their natural inclination to use women for sex.[8] In other words, because men are by nature sexual predators, their pursuit of purity revolves around doing battle with their very nature.[9]

Women have their own war to fight. Since God made women emotionally inclined, as early as middle school, evangelical girls are taught to protect their purity on four levels: mentally, emotionally, spiritually, and physically. But they also must fight the urge to use sexuality as a way of trying to "capture" a lustful man. This means dressing conservatively, no flirting, and no romantic fantasizing.[10] Women are encouraged to go on what is called a "starvation diet,"[11] purging their lives of all things improperly romantic, emotional, and sexual. They too must do battle. "The only way to kill a bad habit," according to *Every Young Woman's Battle*, "is to starve it to death."[12]

Occasionally, this fight is literally framed as a fairy tale, complete with Disney imagery, quotations, and frequent mention of Prince Charming. One popular book—Lisa Bevere's *Kissed the Girls and Made Them Cry: Why Women Lose When They Give In*—even frames its chapters accordingly, with prince and princess rhetoric: "Awakening

Love," "Sleeping Beauty," "The Original Cinderella," and "Breaking the Curse." In one extreme passage, Bevere instructs her readers:

> When it is not the right time for love, sexual desire is the wrong thing, no matter how pleasurable the sensations. When awakened at the wrong time, desire becomes lust, and lust is restless and shrouded in shame.... We want to *put lust to death* [my emphasis] and in its place resurrect love without a trace of guilt or shame to rob from her beauty.[13]

Living up to this version of the romantic ideal is very difficult. Most youth are more sexual than the quest for purity allows them to feel and acknowledge, much less actually act out. Because of its extreme restrictions, the chances of realizing romantic hopes within the purity paradigm are slim. This can create terrible angst and disappointment for young adults, who are often shattered by their failure to live the fairy tale. Purity culture has a powerful hold within evangelical youth culture. Though the evangelical students I interviewed broke almost every liberal preconception about them, proving to be diverse in their politics, nuanced in their expressions and beliefs about Christianity, and perfectly willing to swim in a sea of doubt and life's gray areas, their pursuit of purity is the one area where almost all of them could see only black and white. Falling short of ideal purity can jeopardize not only a young adult's standing among her peers but also, as these young adults are taught through purity culture, her relationship with God.

UNUSUAL WEDDING PRESENTS: JESSICA MARIN

Jessica Marin is a shy 19-year-old sophomore at an evangelical university in the Midwest. Initially in our conversation, she presents a nervous demeanor, but after a few minutes she warms up and becomes more animated. Jessica considers herself both spiritual and religious and had a strong Christian upbringing. She comes from a military family, and her father is a highly decorated member of the U.S. Army who served as the uncontested spiritual head of his home. During our conversation, Jessica recounts how her father was prone to spontaneously deciding such things as who would conduct the evening's prayer before dinner. He demanded unquestioned and immediate obedience from everyone in the room. It should not be surprising that Jessica's description of her relationship to God is one of ultimate authority and utter submission, with God playing the role of the authoritarian father and her the part of the dutiful daughter. This idea of God is comforting to Jessica. She expresses relief that "God is in charge" of her college experience so she does not have to carry this burden.

On the purity meter, Jessica tilts heavily to one side. She has never dated anyone. She has never so much as kissed, touched, or been touched by a boy. Jessica is working to "keep pure" until marriage; she plans to receive her first kiss at the altar. She says that her friends do, too. "We all want to be [pure] when we get married and . . . we're all working at keeping that as a gift," Jessica explains.

Talking about her purity (which for Jessica means both "physical virginity" of the body and "spiritual virginity" of the mind) as a "gift" prompts Jessica to laugh nervously. She says that although guarding their purity is serious business for her and her friends, there is also something "silly" about the notion of a girl's purity as a "present" for her future husband. She shifts uncomfortably as she ponders what feels "off" about this common expectation for evangelical young women. "It's the . . . here you go! Happy wedding!" part that Jessica says she finds weird, as if on her wedding day she *literally* becomes a gift for her husband. "I *do* think it is a gift that we can give to our spouses," she says, her voice more hesitant now than confident. "But just tossing it around, like, 'I'm his present,' I guess it's just kind of silly to imagine what that could look like. Like, 'Untie me! Unwrap me!' "[14]

The "it" that is "tossed around," making Jessica so uneasy, is, of course, herself. *Jessica* is the untouched body, the unblemished heart, and the innocent mind that becomes the present that shows up "wrapped" in a white gown at her wedding; it is her duty to finally allow a man, her spouse, to "unwrap" her later that evening. Jessica leaves little doubt about the sincerity of her belief in the God-given responsibility to remain pure for her future husband. But her talk about the "silliness" of this duty points more to the discomfort she feels when thinking about her wedding night than to something she and her friends find genuinely amusing. Her body language, the starts and stops in her speech, the nervous pauses, the eyes that refuse to look straight ahead—all reveal anxiety about the idea of sexual intimacy. Her mannerisms say what her words do not: after a lifetime defined by a battle to remain pure, she will suddenly be expected to give up the fight and let go into a previously forbidden realm.

Over the course of our interview, Jessica articulates the classic challenge that young evangelical women face. God has a husband already picked out for her. One day, God will reveal to this man what wife he is to marry, at which point the man will start a chaste courtship.

In the meantime, she is to wait patiently, submissive to God's will. Her only real job is to guard herself from missteps that could derail this romantic ideal—like dating the wrong guy.

"I want to give him [God] complete control," Jessica says with confidence now. "I want to marry who *he* wants me to marry. And I don't need to think about it because at this point God already knows, so why should I mess with it? . . . He knows when I'm ready. He knows so much more than I do, and I could screw it up if it's up to me, and I don't want to screw it up."

Jessica elaborates on this ethic of total self-surrender to God and what it takes to be a "good Godly girl." "We talk about doing things that God wants us to do, have the job, the career that God wants, be at the college that he wants—but *dating*—we never talk about that," she says, shaking her head, about conversations with her girlfriends. "Although we want to marry who God wants us to . . . I think we need to be consistent. If we say we're going to let God choose where we go to school or be where he wants us to be, I don't think we give God enough control of our dating life."

Despite this confident talk, Jessica still worries that she might defy God's wishes by dating the wrong person and/or kissing her betrothed before they walk down the aisle:

> I don't think I'll know right away [who I'll marry]. It's not like they'll have an arrow over their head saying "they're the one" so I don't think I'll only date one person. Right now I think it would be great to be in that situation [to have the first kiss at the altar]. I don't know. Right now I can say I'd be strong to just kiss them and do nothing else but I don't know. So right now I might say that I'd kiss someone and that would be it. It would be nice to wait until I'm married and be like, you're the only boy I've kissed or done anything with.

Though Jessica is committed to living the fairy tale in much the same way as Bevere's *Kissed the Girls and Made Them Cry* describes it, for most young evangelical women the pursuit of purity exacts a high price. The purity ideal sets a nearly impossible standard, requiring a girl to remain utterly "asleep" or "starved" when it comes to desire, romance, and sexuality—until of course a prince comes along (at God's command) to "wake her." Missteps range from "giving the first kiss away" to someone you will not eventually marry to having sexual intercourse before marriage.

The kind of romantic ideal that Emily has lived and for which Jessica hopes resembles a glass castle—beautiful, but a terribly fragile place to live.

THE DAMAGED HEART AND THE PURITY QUOTIENT

"It damages you," says one young woman, Danni, about being sexually intimate before marriage. Nineteen years old and in her first year at a Catholic college, this Presbyterian-raised student is one of the few individuals I met at the spiritual colleges who is acquainted with purity culture. Danni is reminiscing about attending, while in high school, the "Silver Ring Thing"—one of the most popular, faith-based, abstinence pledge programs in the United States and the recipient of considerable federal funding.[15]

Danni went to this "purity party" with a bunch of friends on a Friday night. Those who put on the party made it both fun and funny, thanks to some skits performed by the Silver Ring Thing staff, Danni explains. "They did some illustration where—it was like a piece of fruit [and] . . . every time you do something with a guy, it rips a piece of your heart away, and like, he has a piece. . . . By the end, it's just, like, ruined."

Danni is one of several women (all others were at evangelical colleges) who, during interviews, described the Silver Ring Thing performance, where staff request that a volunteer hold a piece of fruit or a "puzzle-piece" heart, while a string of members of the opposite sex from the audience come up, one by one, and rip off a part of the fruit or remove a puzzle piece until nothing remains. This skit represents what happens to your heart if you date people before marriage and engage in illicit romantic intimacy or sexual activity. The message? Dating people depletes your heart so that when you finally meet your future spouse you have little (or nothing) left of your heart to give. The volunteer whose heart is "ripped apart" is almost always female—implying that it's primarily the woman's responsibility to protect her heart from a man's natural inclination, to resist exchanging her heart for what men want most: sex.[16]

At the time of our interview, Danni no longer wore the ring she received after this performance (it turned her finger green, she tells me, laughing sheepishly). But she is still a virgin (technically, according to her definition of virginity), is hanging on to some semblance of her purity, and is planning to save sexual intercourse until marriage. "I've waited 19 years of my life, [and] I think I can wait a few more," she explains. But she has engaged in oral sex with multiple boyfriends—missteps about which she expresses deep regrets many times during our conversation because she sees these activities as having turned her into "partially damaged goods." In the past, Danni has decided repeatedly that she "wasn't going to do it [have oral sex] again." But then she would "because it was just hard not to." Even though Danni has at least something left of her innocence, she has let a number of boys cut off pieces of her heart—pieces that, according to the Silver Ring Thing purity program, she can never get back.

Though the Silver Ring Thing and other abstinence programs may present a rather disturbing illustration of how to stay pure and what happens when you don't, "staying pure" means different things to different people inside the evangelical community. Among the students I interviewed, purity standards included various permutations of the following:

- Waiting till the wedding ceremony for the first kiss.
- Waiting till the engagement for the first kiss.
- Trying to avoid all lustful thoughts or feelings of sexual desire prior to marriage.
- Dressing modestly (especially for women).
- Restricting kissing to public places as a way of preventing further sexual intimacy.
- Kissing only while standing up.
- Kissing while lying down but avoiding any other "sexual contact."
- Kissing and touching but never achieving orgasm.
- Engaging in "everything but" intercourse, including oral and anal sex (some said they thought anal sex was OK in theory, though none of the evangelical students whom I interviewed acknowledged having had anal sex).

Obviously, these interpretations of the purity rules encompass a wide range of possible behaviors. The last one—the "everything but" view of staying pure—tracks closely with the typical notion of virginity expressed by the students I interviewed at all four college types. The majority of evangelical students, however, understand purity on the more conservative end of the scale. I met many students who had never kissed anyone and hoped to "give their first kiss away" to their future spouse, and most interviewees were alike in their commitment to fighting sexual desire and lustful thoughts and whatever romantic or sexual behaviors are, in their view, illicit and ungodly. I found very few students who believe that a person could do "everything but" and still claim both spiritual and bodily purity. Students who had "already ruined themselves" rarely tried to pass themselves off as still pure, at least according to its strictest definition. Not surprisingly, the signs of this battle for purity were worn disproportionately by women, since the burden of remaining pure falls heaviest on them.

PURITY DREAMS, DUPED PARENTS,
AND PITFALLS OF PROMISE RINGS

Like Danni, Jessica has taken an abstinence pledge through her involvement with "True Love Waits," another of the more popular abstinence programs discussed during my interviews.[17] This organization's pledge typically occurs in a partylike atmosphere, with a worship band and lots of socializing. When questioned about what she remembers about the pledge party, Jessica falters—it was a long time ago and now seems a blur—a reaction common among the evangelical students I interviewed, 18 of whom had formally taken an abstinence pledge as early as middle school. Many of them only vaguely recalled taking the pledge and said that they had no idea where the accompanying certificates were today. Jessica is the exception: she has carried the certificate with her for years.

"I signed a little card and I still have it in my wallet," Jessica says. "For me, that was it. [I decided] I'm not having sex till marriage. And since I got older it turned into 'I'm not having intercourse until marriage,' and that has evolved into 'It's not just intercourse that I refrain from.'"

More meaningful to Jessica than the True Love Waits certificate is the promise ring, given to her by her father, that she wears proudly on the ring finger of her left hand. "My Dad gave it to me after taking the True Love Waits pledge," Jessica says. "It means I'm already taken and I don't know *who* takes me, but even though I don't know who is going to be with me it doesn't mean I can do what I want with my body."

As Jessica's story implies, the role of the father is key within purity culture. Almost every woman I interviewed who wore a promise ring had received this gift from her father as a token not only of her responsibility to remain pure until marriage but also of *his* responsibility to see to it that she does so—a public sign of his duty to keep his daughter pure for her future husband. Upon a woman's engagement, this manly duty is passed down, in some measure, to the fiancé. In other words, promise rings are as much material symbols of a woman's vow as they are of a man's duty—of the father's pledge to serve as a sort of sexual watchdog, standing guard between his daughter and any potential suitors, or of the fiancé's pledge to resist his sexual urges and not take advantage of a woman's willingness "to do anything she can"—even give in to sex—to capture his heart.

A description of one popular "purity ball"—typically a father-daughter formal affair—vividly captures the father's responsibility:

> The Father Daughter Purity Ball is a memorable ceremony for fathers to sign commitments to be responsible men of integrity in all areas of purity. The commitment also includes their vow to protect their daughters in their choices for purity. The daughters silently commit to live pure lives before God through the symbol of laying down a white rose at the cross. Because we cherish our daughters as regal princesses—for 1 Peter 3:4 says they are "precious in the sight of God"—we want to treat them as royalty.[18]

That young women "silently commit" to purity and accept protection from their father until they are found by a husband (the woman's role is to wait for a man to court her) expresses the passivity of women in these purity programs. This father's pledge also shows how a girl who is successful at staying pure becomes "royalty"—a purity princess—in her Christian community.

During our conversation, Jessica confesses something about her promise ring that reveals ambivalence. Because promise rings are worn on the left ring finger, where a woman traditionally wears an engagement ring, Jessica has taken to wearing the promise ring on her other hand (though during our interview, it was on the left). "I was thinking maybe no guys talk to me because I have it on my left hand," she admits. "So I move[d] it to my right hand." Whether this form of resistance violates Jessica's vow to wait passively for God to choose her future husband is not clear. But it reveals something about Jessica that was also expressed by other women I interviewed: she fears that no men are interested in her, regardless of how cautiously she has guarded her "prize." Like Emily, Jessica may be a purity princess, but this sort of royalty is fraught with insecurity. She worries that her success at purity is not simply due to the fact that she is an especially good, Godly girl, but instead because nobody wants her. Waiting for Prince Charming is not only emotionally difficult, it is lonely. Yet if Jessica loses her purity, she may well find herself rejected by her evangelical community.

I ask Jessica what she will do with her promise ring once she gets engaged and find out she has a rather complicated fantasy about it. "Well, when I am wearing it on my left hand, I would have him take it off when we get engaged," she begins:

> But I would still wear it [on my right hand] because I'm not his yet. And I think in our wedding it would be really fun for him to take it off as part of the ceremony and he can just keep it. Maybe we'll have a daughter and he'll give it to her, and it'll be something he can have, symbolizing I saved myself for him, and he can take it and have it.

These statements—"it'll be something he can have [as] I saved myself for him" and "he can take it and have it"—operate on several levels of meaning. The "it" refers to the ring as an object her husband can literally have and hold onto, but also to Jessica's purity—in other words, to her body and herself.

A number of women I interviewed had detailed fantasies about the role a promise ring would play during her engagement, on her wedding day, and throughout her marriage. One young woman explained how one of her friends "melted down her chastity ring and put it into her husband's wedding ring," which she thought "was pretty cool." Another had moved her promise ring to her right ring finger when she got engaged, and had plans to present it to her husband after the marriage ceremony as a special token of how she'd "saved herself" for him. This same young woman also spoke of her promise ring as a kind of "purity heirloom" that her husband would someday pass on to their daughter.

The occasional student who declared she didn't need a ring to remember that her purity was something that she "carries every day in her" was the exception to the rule. Several women did confess, however, that the real reason they wanted a promise ring was that it was pretty and expensive. They simply liked the stone or the band (or the price tag) and knew that telling Dad they wanted it as a promise ring was a sure way to persuade him to buy it. That the rings are a public sign of a girl's commitment to chastity seems enough to get parents to fork over lots of money.

Although the majority of the women I interviewed took these symbols of purity fairly seriously, I did encounter one who laughed at the whole business of promise rings. She said that she had been given a *key* in lieu of a ring when she was in the seventh grade, and she rolls her eyes when I ask her why a key and not a ring. "It was like, the key to your heart that you give to the person that you are going to spend your life with [because] that was the context in which sex was OK," she says with intense sarcasm. When I ask whether she has given the key to anyone or if she plans to in the future, she rolls her eyes again, laughs, and exclaims, "No way!"

One student, May Young, expresses anger at her parents for giving her a promise ring. She sees it not as a symbol of a freely offered promise but as a kind of shackle clamped on her by Mom and Dad. Oddly enough, she still wears it.

"My parents gave me a chastity ring, and I was actually really offended," May begins:

> I was 16, and I still have it and wear it. And I haven't done anything to give it back. In a way I was kind of mad because it gives you boundaries ... I'm not really sure how to phrase it. This [ring] says that I can't have sex of any kind. But it doesn't mean that I can't grope someone, I can't make out [with] someone, or that I can't see someone naked. And that kind of bothers me. I felt almost like my parents didn't trust me. Which, looking back, it was kind of good, but I just wish my parents talked to me more about their expectations of me.

May is unique in her attitude about the ring. She resents her parents' handing her a ring because what she really wanted was a conversation with them about sex. May believes that her parents gave her the promise ring in lieu of a sex talk, even as a way to avoid it. To May's parents, it seems, the promise ring says it all.

A WORD FROM PRINCE CHARMING: MARK JOHNSON

"Sometimes I think it's incredible that I'm still a virgin," says the 18-year-old first-year student sitting across from me.

Mark Johnson comes from an "ultraconservative" Christian household, but in high school, he tells me, he was a really "bad kid." Before coming to his evangelical college, Mark hung out with drug users, punks, and people who had sex—and lots of it. He was a punk himself, and traces of this past still linger: his hair is spiked every which way and dyed at the tips, he wears a belt with spikes, and a chain hangs from his waist. A tall, lanky boy, his answers are animated, his hands and voice expressive, and his manner earnest. He's invested in our conversation and gives me the impression that this interview is part of his penance—a chance to confess past sins and convince an outsider of his recent transformation from bad kid to reformed Christian guy. He's eager to tell his story in all its gory details.

Mark's parents forbade him to date until he moved out of the house. But in high school, he dated a girl behind their backs. He also got heavily into a habit considered hazardous to a guy's purity quotient: pornography—a topic that a number of the evangelical students discussed as a big problem for Christian men. Almost all the evangelical dating and sex manuals geared toward men address pornography as a major issue, and teach that getting into porn is one of the surest ways a man can ruin his purity.[19] Mark and his friends used to troll the Internet for porn and steal "girlie magazines" from stores. And though he's over that now, this part of his past still makes him ashamed.

Mark describes high school as living life with a "dualistic face." He maintained two sets of friends: the "really bad" kids who stole porn and had sex and the Christian friends with whom he pretended to share morals and values. Attending a Christian college has pushed Mark "closer to Christ," something that consoles him. But it hasn't stopped him from dating. He has tried to date four women over the last eight months and actually went out with two, though only briefly. The second relationship started off really well, but then "started getting really physical"—"to the point of making out"—really fast, so they ended it.

Mark struggles with what he describes as his own "really legalistic" attitude about what is OK and what is not OK physically. He constantly worries about boundaries—about "how far he can go" without "harming his spiritual life," about "how far is too far." Mark tries his best to stick to biblical standards:

> There's a lot in First and Second Corinthians that talk[s] about [sex] in the Bible. . . . Probably one of the best verses that is more obscure, but I got the most from, was in Second Corinthians 5. It says it's good for a man not to touch a woman. And I think that's a really wise statement in the most general sense. If you're in a relationship that is not physical at all, you probably won't have much of a problem with [sex]. [The verse to which Mark is referring is actually 1 Corinthians 7:1.][20]

Mark believes it is best for men to steer clear of touching women—another teaching affirmed in virtually all the Christian self-help dating/ sex manuals geared at Christian men. One popular book—*When God Writes Your Love Story: The Ultimate Approach to Guy/Girl Relationships* authored by a young Christian married couple, Eric and Leslie Ludy—has sections that deal directly with Mark's core concern: How far can a man go with a woman who is not his wife? The answer is *nowhere*. "The secret to heavenly romance is to begin practicing purity and cherishing her with your thoughts, actions, and words *long* before you even meet her," Eric Ludy writes. "And I realized I could do that by choosing, in every situation life brought my way, to think of her as if she were right beside me and to consider how my decisions would affect her. . . . Give her your heart, mind, and body *now!*"[21]

Mark is still conflicted about how far to go with this kind of mandate for purity. Mark has never engaged in any sexual activity other than making out, but he is worried that this has *already* gone too far, already damaged his purity. He expresses concerns about people who were "promiscuous" before they got married and then had to deal with all sorts of terrible consequences. Yet he isn't convinced that total sexual restraint—not touching at all—is such a good idea either. Though Mark knows a lot of people who have had lots of premarital sex, he also knows one couple who not only waited to kiss at the altar, but who had never even touched until their wedding day. According to Mark, they lived the romantic ideal for real. One evening, Mark got up the courage to ask this couple how they felt about the path they had taken. Their answer worried him.

"I said [to them], 'Hey, you know when you got married—having had no physical activity—what was it like having sex for the first time? . . . I want to know what it's like,' " he tells me. "And they said, 'You know, if you're not physical until that point when you get married, then generally one of the two people feels used because they're feeling emotion that they've never felt before, or shared with another person. So, on their wedding night, one of them feels used.' " When I ask him to clarify what they meant, he explains that one of them "didn't get fulfillment but their partner did."

This was not the answer for which Mark was hoping. This couple's confession that living up to extreme purity standards ends with one person—likely the woman, Mark thinks—feeling used and unfulfilled is anything but romantic, and it contradicts all the things the books say about what happens if men really *do* practice purity by "giving" their future wives their "hearts, minds, and bodies *now!*" Eric Ludy promises male readers that if they can just manage perfect purity now, endless delights await them in the bedroom once they get married. "I guarantee you," writes Ludy, "the rewards of such a decision are off-the-charts amazing. And she'll love you like a man longs to be loved."[22] After talking to this newly married couple, however, Mark has become skeptical.

"I don't want that to happen to me," Mark says. He doesn't want to disappoint his wife sexually on their wedding night. "But I want to be able to hold the biblical standard to my life. I want to be able to stand before Christ and say, 'I really tried in a lot of my relationships, or most of the time in my relationships to honor you, and still have an enjoyable relationship.' I don't want [my relationship] to suck."

Like many evangelical men, Mark believes that you have to be very careful around women because they can "really mess up" your spiritual life. Women don't just tempt you to walk away from the godly path. They can destroy you spiritually with their sexuality. Guys must be ever vigilant in resisting temptation, lest they lose their way. With other evangelical men I interviewed, the subject of sexual boundaries and the question of "how far is too far" before one's purity gets damaged came up again and again. Men told me repeatedly that because women tempted them sexually, they considered women a distraction from their spiritual well-being and growth.

"I find that I'll get caught up in a relationship, whether it's emotional or physical, [and] it'll be easy for me to lose sight of valuing her as a person," Mark says.

> It's so hard for me, like, as an 18-year-old, having been in relationships that are either really physical or not physical at all, to know where to go. But I think as long as I'm keeping Christ the central focus of my relationship, then together we're separately growing towards him. That, like, if I'm holding hands with her, and it's not something that is going to distract me from my faith, and the Bible doesn't say it's wrong, then I think it's OK.... But I know that inappropriate contact—whether it's, you know, petting or some kind of massage—anything like that that will invoke guilt or conscience is not a direction that I need to be heading because it's not going to promote a spiritual lifestyle for me or for her.

Another biblical standard that guides Mark through the thickets of sexuality also comes from Paul, he thinks, though he can't recall exactly where. This passage, which is actually from 1 Corinthians 7:38 ("So then, he who marries the virgin does right, but he who does not marry her does even better"), prescribes an unspecific but difficult standard that Mark struggles to understand. It too requires that the guy summon up a rather heroic resistance to the sexual temptation of women.

"I don't remember which book but [Paul] talks about relationship, family and marriage—a father giving his virgin daughter in marriage is blessed, and [the] other who doesn't give his virgin daughter in marriage is even more blessed," Mark paraphrases as best as he can:

> [Paul is] just addressing...how it's really good that you hold your daughter back. To me that means I need to be worthwhile for some guy

to give his virgin daughter to be married to me. And whatever that means—[not] being physical, preserving my virginity—it means that I want to try and be worthwhile to whatever guy's daughter I want to marry.[23]

The idea that the virgin girl is passed from father to husband is widely accepted in evangelical college culture and underlies the symbolism of the promise rings. Many young evangelical men spoke just like Mark about expecting this gift of virginity from their future wives and about how they would find it hard to marry a girl who hadn't saved it for them. But concerns about *being* a "virgin gift" fell disproportionately on the women. Only once did a young man describe *his* virginity or purity as a gift for his future wife. Perhaps this follows from the popular notion in evangelical youth culture that men are sexual beings without much feeling and women are emotional beings without much sexuality.

Mark comes close to describing his virginity as a gift, though, saying that as a virgin he will be "worthwhile" to his future wife. I did not often hear this from young men, though a few male students mentioned that they felt obliged to make themselves worthy for their future wives—a duty that mirrors the responsibility of fathers to guard their daughters' purity.

While evangelical women grow up learning the values of patience and passivity, evangelical men are raised to believe they are *active* when it comes to sex, purity, and romance: they *guard* their women, they *prove* themselves chivalrous by heroic restraint, they *take* a woman's gift as their birthright. Women by contrast, *submit* to their guardian, and they *wait* for their prince to come along and for their purity to *be taken* on their wedding day. Not all the evangelical women I interviewed were comfortable with this passive role. A number complained of being nothing more than "ladies in waiting," of not being allowed to do anything to get guys to notice them or ask them out. But hardly any of these young women would cross the line and do the asking.

Among evangelicals, the quest for purity is always a religious quest. While students at Catholic, nonreligious private, and public colleges and universities disassociate romance from religion, romance *is* religious for evangelical students; purity is an explicitly Christian ideal. This is a boon for the chosen few who are able to live up to the close-to-impossible standards of this romantic ideal. But for those who fail in this quest for purity and thereby forfeit the Christian fairy tale, it is a terrible burden.

FIVE

Wanted

A Little Romance

A lot of people come into college expecting to meet their husband or wife ...
once you get here you realize that it's really just not that easy to do.
Like, finding love just isn't that easy. Sex is probably a lot easier.

—*student at a nonreligious private university*

THE PERFECT FIRST TIME: MARIA ANGELO

Maria Angelo, a sophomore at a Catholic college, is not exactly a
member of the party crowd, but she does participate now and again.
Tall, with dark curly hair and big brown eyes, Maria is a serious young
woman. Her answers are thorough and thoughtful, as if she's determined to give as detailed an account as possible of life on her Catholic
campus and her own place within it.

"People on weekends pretty much drink in the dorms then go to
[other on-campus locations]," Maria says about the party scene on
campus, about which she expresses a lot of ambivalence. "It's pretty
much exactly the same every weekend, and ... I don't really like the
whole drinking scene here. I find it boring."

That doesn't stop Maria from participating.

"If all your friends are doing it, you know it will be fun once you go," she explains. "So I just do it because they are doing it. . . . You get to see different friends who you don't get to see during the week, and you get to socialize with everyone. And it's a nice way to meet new people even if you don't remember them."

Maria is acutely aware of how women are perceived by both their male and female peers, especially when it comes to attire. In high school, Maria went through a phase where she "dressed slutty" to get attention, but since coming to college she's given up that act. For many of her friends it's a different story. "It's still girls who want to get attention [by] wearing less clothes and taking them off," she says. "You never know what you are going to see [at parties]. . . . I think the main reason [girls] do it is for attention from boys . . . that is what is going to get them attention."

Theme parties are a regular staple of Maria's weekend life, but she's never dressed the part of the whore. She thinks it "kind of stupid" that whereas boys wear normal clothes, girls are expected to wear short skirts and dress as "ho's." Although Maria may have outgrown the "slutty dressing" phase, she is still hanging out with the attention-getting girls. In fact, she's hanging out with them more than she did in high school. "The group of friends I am friends with now, I would never have really seen myself being friends with," she says. "It's not that I have changed to be friends with them, but I think [they are] not really academic. You obviously want to fit in when you first come to college."

Maria seems like the typical student I have met at this Catholic college: a sometime party girl who gets good grades and is relatively popular and prone to going along with the crowd. But it is soon clear that Maria is different from other women at her school. And she knows it.

Maria is a purity princess of sorts, but of the secular variety. When the conversation shifts to the topic of love and sex, there is a kind of pride and even excitement that suddenly washes over her. Maria's cheeks flush, and she smiles.

Maria feels lucky because she has a boyfriend at home so she is exempt from the dating worries to which her friends are subject. More specifically, she is exempt from hookup culture and the shame associated with it. Because she has a boyfriend, Maria gets to go on real dates, such as dinner and a movie, something she feels is almost unheard of on her campus. She also gets to act like part of a couple in public. Finally, she gets to have sex, and not because she's using sex to try to persuade a guy to date her, but because she's in a mutually reciprocated loving relationship.

Maria realizes that her situation is "odd," or at least this is how she's learned to understand it. She has only one friend on campus who is not unattached. This friend "has a boyfriend, and they have been together since October but they have never gone on a date outside of campus," she says. The fact that this campus couple never does anything that Maria sees as romantic confuses her about what an on-campus dating relationship is supposed to entail. She thinks this sort of behavior is "weird," but when Maria raises this possibility with her friend, the friend gets defensive and insists that her situation is perfectly normal and not weird at all. "I don't know if they like each other that much," Maria tells me. "It seems like he's a weekend kind of thing. Like, he is there in her bed Friday, Saturday night, but he does not come around any other times to hang out with her."

Maria attributes the hookup culture first and foremost to a lot of drinking. This enables students to do things they won't remember the next day. "I know that some girls have hopes that it will turn into more if they hook up with a guy," Maria says, expressing a common opinion about why women are willing to hook up that I heard repeated many times by both the men and women I interviewed. But "some girls just do it because they are drunk and they think it is fun, and boys just go along with whatever girls want to do, and [the boys] obviously want to say they hooked up with a girl that night. Guys are into that."

As far as the morning after goes, Maria thinks that "guys just brush it off and say, 'Oh whatever,'" but her girlfriends react differently. Often they regret it, but most of all they want it to turn into a real relationship. "If it went well," Maria explains, "they'll be like, 'Oh, I wonder if he'll call me? Does he like me? I wonder if it will turn into anything more?'" Usually, he doesn't call. But when he does and the relationship does turn into "something more," it usually entails nothing more than a string of consecutive hookups, which, as Maria observes, puts the woman in a vulnerable social situation:

> If you have a pattern of doing certain things, then that kind of becomes noticed. Everyone is like, "Oh, she is a slut. She hooked up with that guy, that guy, that guy." Even if it only happened for like a month, like she went through this rebellious stage for like a month, like that will stick with them: "Oh! That is the girl who did this and this with that guy."

Maria sees this same Catch-22 regarding what girls are willing to do during hookups. Women are more likely to give a guy oral sex without expecting it in return, according to Maria, not only because "they want the guy to like them" but also because it's something of an unspoken rule. Women just believe that when they hook up, they "have to give oral sex."[1]

When Maria arrived at college, she and most of her friends were virgins, but only two remain. Women are ambivalent about this, seeing sexual experience as something of a loss. But guys are different, Maria says. They don't value virginity as much as women do, and it's really difficult to find a guy on campus who's still a virgin—or at least one who will admit it. For guys, virginity is "something you want to get over with." Women want something else. They don't want to "waste" their first time having sex. "They want it to be with the right person. . . . It's supposed to be a romantic thing that they'll remember the rest of their lives," Maria says. Guys don't care whether their first time is with someone they love, but girls care a lot about being in love when they have sex for the first time. "With girls, it's something more special," she says.

Maria is lucky because her first time *was* something special—really special—and it was with her first love, who was also her first "real" boyfriend. When Maria lost her virginity, her experience included all the ingredients of the secular romantic ideal—a list of characteristics that many young women mention as essential to what I came to recognize as "the perfect first time":

- She was in a committed relationship with a person whom she considered her boyfriend and who considered her his girlfriend.
- She trusted him.
- They were in love with each other and professed that fact to each other.
- She was confident that, though he was not a virgin, he respected her very much, not least because he waited patiently until she was ready to have sex.
- When they first had sex, because they had discussed it at length and waited until they both felt ready, sex was a meaningful— even *spiritual*—experience for them as a couple. It brought them closer together.

Like Emily, who waxed eloquent about her marriage, Maria is effusive about how "positive" an experience this first-time sex was:

I always believed in waiting until I was in love. That was my criteria [*sic*]: I didn't ever want to do it with someone random. . . . I think [sex is] very sacred; it's a way of connecting with someone on a whole different level. . . . Especially the first time [I had sex], it was definitely a sacred thing. . . . I'll always remember, and it will just be very special.

One way that Maria knows her first sexual experience was special is because most of her friends' experiences were so awful. In fact, horrible is so much the norm that after Maria lost her virginity and told her best friends, their initial response was to ask, "Didn't you feel horrible about yourself after?" "I was, like, 'no,'" Maria tells me. "'Was I supposed to?' And [my friend] said, 'Well, when I had sex the first time, I felt horrible about myself after. I just felt dirty, and I think definitely if people are not doing it with the right person, and they are not ready for it, they will feel, they'll definitely regret their decision.'"

Unlike her friends, Maria is proud of her sexual and romantic history and, like Emily, she wishes that everyone could talk about her first time like she can.

THE SPIRITUAL PURITY EQUIVALENT

Students at evangelical colleges see their quest for purity everywhere, in the mountain of available books on the topic and through promise rings and abstinence pledges, among other things. But at the spiritual colleges, it was the rare student who had even heard of promise rings or purity pledges. "Purity talk" was like a foreign language. Yet the broader quest to fulfill some version of a romantic ideal is of concern to virtually all college women, and experiencing romance in some form is important to most men, too. Students at Catholic, nonreligious private, and public schools do not avoid purity standards altogether, either. They have their own version of purity talk and their own fairy-tale romantic ideal. But the purity culture they have created and continue to sustain is complicated; the male students rarely express a wish (at least publicly) to "save themselves" for anything, because the male culture on campus forbids them to—not because men do not harbor any romantic aspirations. This situation creates an unfortunate chasm between what women are both supposed to want and do want romantically, and what guys may want privately but are not allowed to pursue.

Whereas evangelical students use both positive and negative language when they talk about purity—keeping, prizing, guarding, saving, ruining, spoiling, and so on—students at the spiritual colleges almost always use negative terms when discussing their romantic aspirations. Theirs is a language of *avoidance*—in which women voice their wishes to elude being labeled sluts or ho's by their male and female peers, rather than explicitly expressing a desire to be loved, feel cherished, or sexually fulfilled. Because "getting a reputation" is a woman's problem, it is her responsibility to successfully dodge being labeled a slut. The main concern men expressed is to avoid hooking up with a girl well known to be a "ho." Because most men keep whatever romantic feelings they have to themselves, fulfilling the romantic ideal at the spiritual colleges is, for the most part, a woman's quest.

At Catholic, nonreligious private, and public schools, I had to dig a bit to uncover the romantic ideal woven—hidden almost—in the students' stories. The hookup culture at the spiritual colleges ran at cross-purposes to the romantic ideal. The students' romantic hopes came out in conversations, but, as with religion and spirituality, they were far more explicit about romance in their journals. While the strict and traditional romantic ideal I found at evangelical colleges calls for young people to remain virgins until their wedding day, according to the less strict and less traditional romantic ideal operative at the spiritual colleges, students (mostly women) hope for the "perfect first time." Many young people (especially men) see first-time sex as "something they are supposed to just get over with," and there are many (especially women) who recall losing their virginity as "an awful experience." The purity alternative among students at the spiritual colleges, most of whom are not willing to wait until marriage for sex—or do not even consider waiting—is to hope that their first sexual experience will be wonderful and loving, as opposed to disastrous and shattering. Women adhering to this secular version of the purity ideal tend to evaluate their romantic success and failure against whether or not their first time occurred during a committed relationship with someone who loved them and whom they loved in return. It was in the stories of *women only* that I came to recognize this idea of the perfect first time as the epitome of the romantic ideal. Not one man I interviewed at the spiritual colleges idealized first-time sex or recalled his experience in a way that said he measured romantic success or failure against it.

Overall, at the spiritual colleges, the practice of this purity alternative for most women involves the following:

- Women are not committed to the ideal of saving themselves for marriage, but they have a vivid narrative about what their first time should be (or should have been): the perfect first time.
- Women must somehow navigate young men's contradictory desire for them to be at once virginal and sexually experienced.

- Women are keenly aware of what activities, conducted in which situations and with what frequency, will get them labeled a slut or whore, and they avoid these activities and circumstances at all costs, sometimes by perpetuating gossip about "dirty girls" and distancing themselves from these individuals.
- In public, women maintain a lax attitude about no-strings-attached hookups, but in private, they express ambivalence and even dismay that they allow themselves to be pressured into sexual behaviors that often make them feel used and unhappy.

Success in romance for women at the spiritual colleges is complicated by the reality of being immersed in a social scene that emphasizes some frequency of random hooking up without getting labeled a slut or "ho" in the process. Party too little, and you are a prude; party too much, and you are a whore. Though evangelical young adults can pick up a purity manual (or 10) that describes in excruciating detail how to live out and live up to the evangelical romantic ideal, their counterparts at spiritual colleges have to infer their ideal from movies, television shows, novels, and rumors among friends. Students at these schools don't line their bookshelves with self-help manuals on "how to live the romantic ideal at college" or "why you should save first-time sex for the perfect guy," because there aren't many. More likely than not, women at the spiritual colleges have books with more depressing messages displayed, like *He's Just Not That into You.*[2]

BROKENHEARTED AND HOPELESSLY ROMANTIC: JAMIE WOODHOUSE

When Jamie Woodhouse walks in the door, he oozes charisma. Athletic and handsome, his demeanor impresses me the moment we shake hands. Jamie's smile is genuine and warm and talk flows easily from one topic to the next.

When I first ask for religious affiliation Jamie answers "none." But I later learn he grew up Catholic, was confirmed during high school, and even served as a peer minister for his local parish, leading retreats and other student events when he was a teen. He's lately begun to study philosophy during his time at college—he's 22 and a senior now—and considers himself spiritual but not religious. To be religious, according to Jamie, is "to completely accept the teachings" of a tradition, allowing a religion to answer all questions. "Being spiritual," on the other hand, "is something that allows for thought and allows for critical thinking." Critical thinking, being a "thoughtful person," doing some "serious moral reflection," and "becoming a better person," this idealistic young man tells me, are what college is all about. As our discussion hops from one subject to the next, Jamie expresses concern about social inequalities between men and women and about the human rights of people of different sexual orientations. His sincerity, eloquence, and intellect repeatedly burst stereotypes about jocks on campus. Jamie is the star basketball player at his small Catholic college. He is also a hopeless romantic and not afraid to admit it.

Jamie loves romantic poetry. The Sufi mystic Rumi is his favorite, and in his journal Jamie writes of regularly consulting *Rumi: The Book of Love: Poems of Ecstasy and Longing*[3] as a "way of reconciling his feelings for another." A second book that features prominently on his shelf is the *Kama Sutra*, but not for the obvious reasons. Jamie says, "The *Kama Sutra* has been helpful when it comes to the more intimate parts of a relationship, in that it speaks of proper ways of treating each other, not just in a sexual way."[4] Reading Rumi is helping to heal Jamie's broken heart. His girlfriend of two and a half years broke up with him not long before our interview.

"I was absolutely stunned by the presence she had," Jamie recalls. "She is absolutely beautiful. . . . Just from talking to her, I knew she was a person that I could very much hang out with and not worry about anything. I was very comfortable around her from the very beginning."

It's difficult for Jamie to talk about his former girlfriend, who is without a doubt his first love, so I ask whether we should switch topics. He tells me no, it's OK to talk about her. Because he is still in love with her, he welcomes the opportunity to tell someone about their relationship. He continues, wistful:

> There was something intangible about hanging out with her, or just looking into her eyes—there was always something more that wasn't, you know, I could never put it into words. . . . I guess the glue [of our relationship] was the fact that every time I either hung out with her, or got to talk with her, I just completely understood why I felt the way I did about her. It wasn't ever anything that became mundane.

Jamie says that people should engage in sexual activity only if it's "*completely* right." "What makes a situation right?" I ask. He lists these ingredients: commitment, respect, a deep intense connection, and a whole lot of love. Jamie may not have experienced the perfect first time, but his third sexual partner—his most recent girlfriend—transformed his attitude about sex. Jamie doesn't want to judge friends who have sex all the time with just about anybody. That's their business. But having sex while deeply in love has altered what he wants from sex and from women. Jamie doesn't just want a partner for a night; he had a one-night stand with someone shortly after the breakup, when he was trying to get over his broken heart. It was a disaster. It depressed him to be that intimate with someone with whom he didn't have any connection. He won't do it again, he says.

"It was *very* much a spiritual experience," Jamie says about sex with his former girlfriend, "because of the sentiment attached to it." Jamie wishes people put more thought into their sexual encounters—having sex with his girlfriend wasn't just sex, it was making love. From now on, that's what Jamie wants sex to be.

THE PRESSURES TO BE A PLAYER

Although Jamie waxes romantic about the meaning that sex has come to have for him, he is like almost all the other young men I interviewed at the spiritual colleges in that aspiring to a perfect first time wasn't even a blip on his radar. Jamie was fine admitting he'd had four sexual partners and that it was girl number three who had really opened him up to love and the joys of having sex within an intense, long-term, and committed relationship. Still, Jamie was the only male student at a spiritual college who was so expressive about loving his girlfriend, so vivid in his description of how he felt about her, so open about all she meant to him, and so vulnerable in describing how much he had been hurt by the breakup. Jamie was an open book emotionally, and this was unusual bordering on unique among the young men I interviewed outside the evangelical world.

Several men fit the "frat boy" stereotype with disturbing accuracy, although they were not, by any means, in the majority. Most men I interviewed would not have felt at home in the movie *Animal House*. Although most were far less concerned than the women I met about virginity and the perfect first time, having sex—though certainly a goal—was not a regular part of their lifestyle. In fact, I talked with plenty of men who expressed dismay about the sexual-predator-like expectations for guys on their campuses. Whereas college women worry about getting labeled as sluts, the men I interviewed complained that expectations to display their masculinity through multiple sexual conquests—to be "players"—were cramping their ability to develop a romantic relationship with just one woman. Admitting you want a girlfriend, some men told me, makes you seem weak and effeminate. Though many seemed to share the desire that Jamie expressed so openly—to find someone to love, care about, and have sex with—most don't dare talk about this openly with other guys or even women. Men feel they need to hide this desire for fear that their male peers will find out. Whereas women told me that girls tend to tone down their number of sexual partners, since a little deflation makes them seem less slutty, guys told me that they inflate their numbers, claiming far more sexual partners than they have actually had in order to impress other guys.

"Guys are expected to go out and get as drunk as [they] possibly can and not remember who [they] slept with the night before," says one young man, a first-year student at a nonreligious private university. If "you want to fit in [and] feel like one of the guys," he says, you have to be active in the hookup culture. During his first semester at college, this particular student was hooking up all the time with random girls, but by the spring semester he had stopped. "I felt like I was betraying myself, like this isn't really what I like to do, this isn't who I am, this isn't the kind of college experience I want to be having," he says.

Another young man, a senior at the same school, said that girls have it easier if they want to show more restraint about the hooking up, almost as if he envied their ability to say no. "If a guy doesn't do it, I feel that people are like, 'Why is he not doing it? He should be going out there and doing that kind of thing,'" he says with frustration. "Whereas, girls, I think if they didn't want to do it, they could get away with it a little easier. But for guys, if you don't do it, socially, people will look down on you for it." A first-year student at Jamie's Catholic college sums up this double standard: "For guys to be promiscuous is kind of cool, . . . whereas girls will be labeled as sluts."

This may sound like a good deal for college men—that they can be as promiscuous as they want and get away with it. Although some men revel in this "no repercussions" free-for-all, many think hookup culture hurts their ability to form healthy friendships and romantic relationships with women. Many men also told of going on what could be called "hookup binges," only to end up feeling so empty and unfulfilled that they swore off any further behavior of the sort. I left these interviews wondering: What if these young men knew how many other male students felt this way? And what if the women knew that most guys aren't too happy about hooking up, either?

SEXUAL MINORITIES: SEARCHING FOR
ROMANCE AND AFFECTION

Although most men and women I interviewed had some version of a romantic ideal that guided their aspirations—evangelical or otherwise—one group certainly wanted a romantic ideal to which they might aspire but seemed confused about what this ideal might be. Students who are gay, lesbian, or bisexual can find themselves longing for the heterosexual fairy tale vicariously through friends because they don't quite know how to find their own way in love and romance.

Of the 111 students I interviewed, 12 identified as lesbian, gay, or bisexual. They came from every type of institution I visited: 4 from evangelical schools, 4 from Catholic colleges, and the remaining 4 from nonreligious private and public schools. Some were out, and some were not.

When answering the questions about sex and romance during the interview process, these students spoke of a need to "remove themselves" from the typical ideals about romance on campus in order to "be sexual." This was true whether perspectives about sexual orientation at their colleges were conservative and relatively unaccepting or more liberal and accepting. These students were most concerned with what having sex did to their identities as gay, lesbian, or bisexual. Rather than trying to attain their ideal romantic fantasy, they were struggling with something more basic: what it means to be a sexual being with a minority sexual orientation.

Molly Bainbridge, a student at one of the evangelical colleges, says that for her to be sexual, she has to "step outside of whether or not what I was doing was wrong and say, Do I really want to do this whether it's wrong or not?" Though she has dated only men, she feels attracted to women and is uncertain whether this makes her lesbian or bi. But in between comments about wanting to be romantically involved with women, she occasionally steps back into a more traditional romantic paradigm, expressing the wish "to get married one day." "Sex is something that you should keep to as few people as possible because it is so emotional, . . . so spiritual, . . . so intimate, and it's so open," she tells me. Ideally, you should experience it first "with someone you are bound to." Whenever she speaks about sex in this light, she is imagining it with a man. She can't seem to apply this romantic ideal to sex with a woman.

Both Molly and a young woman I interviewed who also identified as bisexual had a hard time coming by this identification. Like Molly, this second woman—a student from one of the Catholic colleges—has had boyfriends in the past and isn't quite sure if she will eventually choose one orientation over another. But, unlike Molly, who has never been with a girl in any sexual way, this student kissed a girl once and is effusive about the experience in her journal. "I think my favorite experience thus far was the first time that I kissed a girl," she writes. "Or rather she kissed me. After hooking up, we just fell asleep in each other's arms and it was just very comfortable."

Christina Marsden is a pastor's daughter and an out lesbian at an evangelical college who is deeply involved in founding a club at her school for sexual minorities and for students questioning their sexual identities. She says she enjoys a lot of student and faculty support about both her sexual orientation and her efforts to start this club, but when Christina is being realistic, she just hopes the group will be officially recognized "within her lifetime." The traditional evangelical romantic ideal is strong with her also. Though she has only had girlfriends in the past and is currently in a committed relationship of three years with a woman, she says, "I think part of me wants to . . . get a good Christian spouse." The part of her that wants this is that part that sees people all around her aspiring to a life of being the good Christian wife to a good Christian man and her dream of taking up her rightful place both on campus and in her hometown. In the next breath, however, she affirms that "being gay is part of who I am."

Christina lost her virginity to a guy she said treated her "really poorly." This experience helped her to realize that she had never felt comfortable with men. She says this is something of a cliché—becoming a lesbian after a terrible sexual encounter with a man, and rolls her eyes, trying to hide her embarrassment, muttering, "How lame is that?" Still, it is her personal cliché, and she seems secure about her sexual identity for most of our interview. Nonetheless—and here is the power of evangelical purity culture—one reason she is so sad about losing her virginity in this way is because it "is a sacred thing to save yourself until your future husband."

Taneesha James, a lesbian who is a junior at a nonreligious private university, expresses intense confusion about her sexual identity and romantic hopes, despite the fact that hers is by far the most liberal campus I visited. "I feel like no one knows what to expect," Taneesha says, when it comes to being a lesbian. Is this identity about actually having lesbian sex or about falling in love with another girl? One of the intense "emotional dramas," as Taneesha puts it, with which she and her lesbian friends must grapple if they hook up with someone is:

"Does she really think she's gay?" Taneesha and her friends have learned from experience to assume that a girl is probably straight and just interested in trying out lesbianism for a night.

Taneesha's lesbian friends share with heterosexual women the worry about whether the person with whom they just hooked up will call the next day. They too speak regularly about the anguish of un-requited love. But Taneesha has an additional issue to tackle. "Some-times when I'm out with my lesbian friends, I feel like I'm not a real lesbian because it's all based on sex, but I've never had [sex]," she says. "Maybe I'm not really gay because I've never had sex with a guy or a girl. But for me, it's about my sexuality and my emotions and who I like and who I don't. But ... it makes me feel guilty and like I'm not a real lesbian."

Taneesha says that she wants to wait until she is in love to have sex; she is holding out for the perfect first time. Yet, for Taneesha, having lesbian sex is what makes you a member of the lesbian club. She is caught in her own dilemma. If she holds onto the ideal of losing her virginity to a woman she loves (and, for now, she is), she jeopardizes her standing as a "real lesbian." Like college men who feel their masculi-nity is defined by having sex with people indiscriminately, Taneesha feels that becoming a "real lesbian" involves similarly random, sexual encounters with women. Once again, living the romantic ideal is not only very difficult, it's confusing.

A gay young man named Gabriel Firth also talks of "saving him-self" for the right person. "To me, [sex is] something very sacred," says Gabriel, a senior at the same private university as Taneesha. "It's giving my body to someone else, and it's a very close connection, and it's something that I would only do with someone that I was in a very serious relationship with, someone that I thought I was going to spend the rest of my life with, or someone that was a candidate for that."

And Gabriel did wait for the right person, he tells me. He has just had sex for the first time, with his current boyfriend of six months. It was his boyfriend's first time, too. Gabriel has had several other boy-friends in the past, all of whom wanted to have sex with him, but he always said no. He said in the interview that he knew instinctively that none of them was the right guy. Looking back now, Gabriel says that he "would have been devastated had he lost his virginity" to someone other than his current boyfriend. And it means so much to him that his boyfriend had saved himself, too.

"My whole dream in the back of my mind was that I wanted to lose my virginity to a guy that was also a virgin, but at the same time everybody was like, 'Are you kidding me? That's never going to happen,'" Gabriel says. One reason that people advised him against having sex with a virgin was that it would be a horrible first time; he should lose his virginity to someone who knew what he was doing.

> But I thought more of someone that had also been saving themselves, someone that also really wanted this intense physical connection with one specific person. I totally, like, found that in [my boyfriend now], and I feel we *knew* because we talked about it in the beginning. I was like, "You're the one I feel like I want to lose my virginity to," and he was like, "Yeah, I totally feel that way, too."

According to Gabriel, it was worth the wait. "I love him so much," he says, his voice dreamy.

> I have such, like, a spiritual connection with him, and I'm glad I gave that to him, and I'm glad that he gave that to me. It was a perfect exchange. We just totally fit together like puzzle pieces; we get along so well. I'm totally going to move in with him after graduation, and we have a future together. My family loves him, his family loves me. It's just the perfect scenario. And I feel like we knew from day one.

Among the gay, lesbian, and bisexual students I interviewed, Gabriel Firth was the only person who seemed to have lived out his romantic hopes. In that regard, he seemed similar to Emily and Maria. He was not waiting until heterosexual marriage, as Emily had, but, like Maria, he had a perfect first time. He too is living the fairy tale that has eluded the overwhelming majority of his friends, despite the extra angst that most sexual minorities experience.

WHY ROMANCE ISN'T SEXY AND SEX ISN'T ROMANTIC

There are many differences between students at evangelical and spiritual colleges, but they shared similar views about how sex relates (or doesn't) to romance. The number one romantic experience among the students I interviewed was "just talking"—"talking for hours":

- "We spent a great deal of that night sitting outside and talking."
- "We lay on a blanket, watched the stars, and just talked."
- "We went to the lake and walked for hours just talking and laughing."

- "We went for a walk on a warm evening, sitting and talking in a café for seven hours."
- "We picked up a pizza and a bottle of wine and headed to the beach around sunset. We had a picnic-style dinner and simply hung out and talked."
- "It got colder and colder as the night went on, so [he] enveloped me in his arms and [we] watched the stars, sang songs, and talked about anything and everything."

As these examples indicate, students are looking for communication. Talking *without* sex. Without even so much as a kiss. Romance, to them, is chaste.[5] Some students made the innocence here explicit, underscoring the point that there was no touching whatsoever. "We walked to the [river] and skipped stones before going back to her room at 3:30 A.M. We didn't do anything physical at all, and it was still incredibly romantic."

In their journals, students were invited to write about romance and describe what they understood as "the most romantic night of your life so far." Occasionally, their narratives moved beyond just talking, but not far:

- "A boy... came to my window throwing rocks at it. I came down and we sat outside late one night in summer and talked and then kissed."
- "After dinner at my favorite restaurant, we walked... and talked forever. Next he drove me home and kissed me goodnight."
- "We had a picnic dinner and a ride in a boat on a river and look[ed] at the stars, and a long kiss in the moonlight."
- "We were gone for hours. We walked, and eventually sat down on a street corner and talked. I finally told him how I felt about him, and he told me that the feeling was mutual. Before I knew it he had leaned over (like in all the movies) and pulled me in by the back of my neck for a kiss."

Kissing came in second—a distant second—to "just talking," but even these stories included talking first, and spending time, often lots of time, in each other's company. Hardly ever did a student story about romance include any suggestion of sexual intimacy.[6]

At all the participating colleges and universities, women and men alike, regardless of religious affiliation, tended to disassociate romance from sexual intimacy. They understand romance as "pure"—chaste. Seventy-nine percent of the students who responded to this romance question left sexual intimacy out of the picture altogether—save the 14% (included in this figure) who mentioned kissing.[7]

Sex did creep into some of the romance narratives, however: 13% of students included a sexual encounter in their tales. One of these was an evangelical married student, and two others were gay men speaking of their first sexual encounters. Sometimes what made the sex romantic was the fact that the participants weren't drunk or stoned. "We watched a movie," wrote one young woman. "Went up to his room after the movie. He lit candles by his bed. We had sex for an hour. No drugs or alcohol involved, just love." Other students who mixed sex and romance here took pains to indicate that the sex was "passionate sex" or "making love"—again, not just the garden–variety drunken hookup. One of the gay men emphasized that the experience took some time and involved some commitment. "I met his family, and then we drove an hour together, holding hands, and talking about each other," he wrote. "We went home and spent the night together. For the first time, both of us experienced a sexual experience."[8]

TABLE 5.1.   Perceptions about Romance

	Women (55)	Men (44)	Total (99)
Students who identified romantic experience as having no sexual intimacy	38 (69%)	26 (59%)	64 (65%)
Students who identified romantic experience in conjunction with a first kiss or kissing	8 (15%)	6 (14%)	14 (14%)
Students who identified romantic experience in conjunction with having sex/more than kissing	5 (9%)	8 (18%)	13 (13%)*
Students who reported never experiencing a romantic encounter	4 (7%)	4 (9%)	8 (8%)

Please note: only 2 of the students included here were from evangelical colleges. One of these was a gay male, and the other was a married woman who talked of "romantic sex" in the context of her wedding night.

What these stories and these data show is that, at least in the minds of the majority of these college students, once you start having sex, you are no longer being romantic.

After my first school visit—to one of the Catholic liberal arts colleges—I realized that very few of the people I interviewed (only 5 out of 17) even mentioned *love* in a romantic context, or as a concern of theirs. Yet almost all of them said that sex was a popular topic of conversation on campus. So I began asking students at other institutions whether love was a popular topic, too. The answers were revealing. Of the 81 students whom I asked, 36 (44%) said no. "Sex is just more interesting," one student told me, and another said it is much "scarier" to talk about love than to talk about sex. Of the remaining students who said that love was a popular topic, only 17 (21% of the overall pool) indicated that this conversation was robust. Some added, however, that it was only OK to talk about love among women, and one young man said that men had to be careful when discussing love lest they "get shunned" by other guys. Finally, 35% said that they talked about love on their campus but only nominally, as in "Oh, I love her," or "Are you in love with him?" or "I wish I could find someone who loves me." These students were using the word "love" but were not really talking *about* love. Love talk, in short, seems to be getting edged out by sex talk at the spiritual colleges and by marriage talk at the evangelical ones.

The distancing of romance from sex, and of love from sex, seems consistent with evangelicalism and its purity ideal—evangelical youth spend vast amounts of energy attempting to eliminate all sexual desire and dissociating sex from every relationship that is not a marriage. But sex is equally estranged from romance and love at the spiritual colleges. Students at Catholic, nonreligious private, and public schools are having lots of sex, but apparently, it's not very romantic or very loving. They talk about sex all the time. But what are they getting out of it? What is hooking up *for*? And what, if anything, does religion have to do with it?

THE TRUTH ABOUT SEX ON CAMPUS

It's like, being a virgin is a negative thing. It's like, something to be corrected.

—*student at a nonreligious private university*

SIX

Where Dating = Marriage and a Kiss Means Everything

It's like a shoe factory. I've heard it described like,
you come in single, and they box you up paired.

—*student at an evangelical college*

THE SENIOR SCRAMBLE: RING BY SPRING
OR YOUR MONEY BACK!

Hookup culture may dominate the student social scene of spiritual colleges, but students at evangelical schools face unique pressures of their own. They are preoccupied with finding a spouse for life, not with finding a sexual partner for the evening.

This reality was underscored for me by a spiky-haired young man who happened to be the first person I interviewed at an evangelical university. What he had to tell me made it sound as if he had been teleported from the 1950s—a time when women went to college not to get a B.A. or a B.S., but to get their Mrs.

"You know what they say," he tells me with a wry smile. We are talking about whether men and women value relationships differently at his school.

"No, actually I don't. What do they say?" I respond, perplexed by what to me appears to be a private joke.

"Ring by spring or your money back!" he exclaims, laughing and leaning back in his chair so far that it tips and rests against the wall behind him.

No wonder he has all the confidence in the world, I think to myself. Men have it easy. If the imperative is "ring by spring," it's up to them to do the ring giving, the choosing, the asking out on dates. At least in evangelical youth culture, a woman's job is to be patient and to pray to God not to end up as one of those pathetic senior students without a ring on her finger at graduation. So many students delivered this same line—ring by spring or your money back!—that I had to wonder why the spiky-haired boy thought he was so clever. Some delivered the line with sarcasm, some rolled their eyes, some felt annoyed by the expectation, and some treated the idea as a joke. These were mostly men. When women delivered the line, most often they did so with anxiety, and some expressed the fear that they would end up as "one of those girls" who had failed at college.

Failing college for these young women is not about grades or jobs. Failing college is about graduating without a husband, or at least a fiancé.

"I think that a lot of the girls just want to get married, and they came to college to find a husband," says a 21-year-old junior. "It seems like every spring there are a lot of people that get engaged," she says, before singing the money line: "Ring by spring!"

"Did you go to college to find a husband?" I ask.

"I'm a girl, so a part of me is like, 'I'll find a Christian guy at a Christian school, narrow the field down a bit,'" she says. "I don't think it was necessarily one of my main reasons to come here."

The real problem for women, she tells me, is that they are expected to be passive in the ring-by-spring game. They have to wait for the men to decide *everything* when it comes to relationships. Apparently, that's just the Christian thing to do—not a surprising view given the many popular dating and sex manuals geared toward evangelical youth that preach this in spades. This young woman says she thinks it's "kind of odd" that on a coed campus, the men are the only ones allowed to "do the asking"—and not just in terms of marriage, but throughout the entire dating scene.

Another young woman I interviewed, a senior in her spring semester at this same evangelical university, was visibly stressed out by her relationship status. Not only is she not engaged, she has yet to date anyone during college. The clock is ticking and, as we talk, she seems to move from stressed to depressed.

"Once you get to be a senior, it feels like dating is even more of a big deal, more serious," she begins, trying to make sense of her predicament. "A lot of seniors that are in dating relationships started dating their freshman or sophomore year, and they've been together ever since and now they're making marriage plans. It's always tongue in cheek, you know—'ring by spring or your money back!'" She looks up at me when she says this, her voice almost angry. Until this moment, she has been staring into her lap, wringing her hands, and mumbling. "There's this big pressure to find somebody, and if you haven't found somebody, then there's something wrong with you."

This young woman worries that there is something wrong with her. But what can she do about it? Not much.

"Girls are expected to *not* make the first move—the guys are expected to," she says, rolling her eyes. "But then the girls get frustrated with guys for not wanting to make the first move, so there's that tension."

I press her on this issue, asking, "What happens if a girl discovers she likes a guy? Can't she at least tell him?"

"I don't think it's very encouraged for the girl to vocally be, like, be the first one to express those feelings," she says, irritated.

Some of the young men who mentioned the "ring by spring or your money back" motto—and the money-back offer was almost always tagged on—talked about it with a dose of fear in their voices, rather than with the angst and frustration displayed by the women. One was rather smug about his privileged position as the man—the person with the power to decide, to choose, to do the asking, and to require the woman to do the waiting. But many other young men were afraid to even ask someone out because, if they do, the relationship automatically becomes serious. You can't really date, in other words, without dealing with the marriage question from the start.[1] This makes some guys afraid, so afraid that it stops them from asking women out altogether. So the culture creates a formidable impasse.

Happily, however, there is a way around it. At this evangelical university, the makeshift solution is called *frugaling*.[2]

Frugaling is not dating, but it's not *not* dating either. It's something in between: a boy and a girl start hanging out together all the time; they are seen talking in public, just the two of them, regularly, but the man never declares anything. There is no DTR (determine-the-relationship) conversation. There are no PDA (public displays of affection). There is no private physical intimacy either. But *everybody knows* when people are frugaling, students tell me over and over. It goes without saying. Since most men and women at evangelical schools hang out—when they do hang out—in groups, it just isn't common to see a guy and a girl, just the two of them, together in public unless they are already a couple. As soon as people notice this very noticeable behavior, they also know that the guy and girl must be frugaling—even if the two don't admit to it.

The term *frugaling* in this context has no simple etymology—not surprising, given that most students don't even know how to spell it. But it seems to come from the slang word *frugaling*, which refers to frugal people going shopping on the cheap—at thrift stores, for example. The frugaling these students are doing is "shopping" of a sort, and it too is done on the cheap—without the hassles and complications that students "pay" for officially "dating." Frugaling seems a smart option to evangelical students caught in a culture that values female passivity yet hamstrings men from asking women out by linking dating and marriage so closely. It gives them a way of getting to know one another without all the pressures that come with outright dating in a culture so intimately tied to marriage. It is interesting to note that, when women at these schools talk about marriage—and on average they are far more gung-ho about this prospect than the men—it often seems their concern is less about marrying than about graduating without a ring. They want to save face. They want to prove to their peers and to themselves that they are desirable, worthy Christian women, and the ring is the thing that proves it. But between the relative calm of the first year of college and the storm that comes during the senior year, students frugal.

At the other evangelical school I visited, students employed all sorts of parallel terms for the dating and marriage scene on campus. "The freshman frenzy" might sound like hooking up, but it is really about how first-year students (mostly the women) act once they are suddenly faced with an entire community of (allegedly) good, marriageable Christian guys. The "frenzy" part is pretty chaste, involving the rush to find someone to whom to attach yourself early on, with the presumption that this will be the person to whom you will get engaged in four years. In reality, there is little "frenzying" on the part of the women, however, since the guys are supposed to be doing both the attaching and the engaging.

Dating rituals at this evangelical college include "campus walks," which are a step *toward* dating and in some ways like frugaling. Guys do the asking, literally, "Do you want to take a Walk?" he says, and she replies yes or no. The capital *W* is there because "taking a Walk" around campus isn't the same as "taking a walk." If a guy asks you on a Walk, he is asking you to step outside the typical guy/girl friendship group to spend some time Alone. Students get to know each other while walking the long loop on campus that meanders from the heavily populated residence halls and classroom buildings to more private woods and garden spaces.

Emily Holland had first introduced me to the "senior scramble," this school's push toward marriage. Here again, the term "scramble" refers mainly to women—though they are not scrambling too actively, since they are expected to mainly do a lot of waiting around. When I spoke with seniors, the pressures of the scramble were palpable. One student, a senior who proudly informs me that she got engaged in the fall, explains that the senior scramble refers to "when the seniors who are still single and want to be with someone all hook up." By "hook up," she is not referring to "hooking up" in the standard, sexual sense as at the spiritual colleges, but instead to finding someone to date and possibly marry. What I found interesting about this young woman was how unabashedly she seemed to be looking down her nose at the unlucky girls who had failed to "hook up." Like Emily Holland, who was smug about already being married, this senior was smug about having scrambled well. She was one of the girls who had "made it," and as a result she could breathe a sigh of relief and give thanks that the despair of the other girls would not be visited upon her.[3]

Men, by contrast, showed almost no concern with this scramble, senior or otherwise. Their worries were more centered on girls' efforts to trap them into marriage, and most seemed content to graduate without a future wife. Men at this school focused far more on what they were going to do professionally than on whom they would marry. One man I interviewed, a junior, gets quite jumpy when talking about a woman with whom he has just gotten involved. "Well, she's a *senior . . . ,*" he explains, as if this says it all, his voice trailing off. By now I have heard enough about the senior scramble to understand what this statement is supposed to convey. These two students may be recently dating, but this does nothing to relieve the cultural pressures they already face about their relationship, especially because of timing. The possibility that she might be expecting him to soon ask her to get married petrifies him; though he likes her a lot, he confesses that he might have to end the relationship because he isn't ready to think of marriage, and he can't take all the anxiety.

For women on evangelical campuses, it is as if a ring signals your self-worth. Initially, it is the promise rings that, by symbolizing your purity, attest to your value. But by senior year, the engagement ring is the measure of a woman's value. If you don't have one, you begin to feel worthless. This failure—and women *do* experience it as one—is jarring. Not finding your future husband at college is not only a social failure but also a religious failure. A woman begins to fulfill her role as a good Christian woman when she becomes a wife. Until then, she is simply *waiting*.[4]

WHEN A KISS IS *NOT* JUST A KISS

Aside from the intense pressures around marriage, evangelical colleges seem to be shelters from the kind of hookup culture so prominent at Catholic, nonreligious private, and public schools. Apart from a very occasional dinner or movie with friends, students at the spiritual colleges report that their campus social life is dominated by partying, drinking, and hooking up in residence halls, where all bets are off. Students at evangelical campuses, by contrast, usually engage in social activities that have nothing to do with drinking or hooking up, and they live in communities where all rules—including parietals, which bar men and women not only from living in the same residence hall but also from being in each other's rooms—are strictly enforced.[5]

"There are always things going on, on campus," one woman tells me before ticking off a list of activities that I had heard from many others at her evangelical college:

> Every once in a while there's a dance party on campus, there will be concerts on campus, there will be movies or lectures or just get-togethers in the dorms. Your [residence hall] floor might have a game night, or your floor might decide to do something together. People will take the bus downtown and go ice skating in the winter, or go get coffee. People go to the movies and go bowling, do things close by around here.

Before my first visit to an evangelical school, I wondered whether I would hear students talk about drinking and partying just like everywhere else. Though some did, they were a tiny minority. And the others don't even see that type of activity enough to report on it. I interviewed only one young man at an evangelical institution who moved in and out of the party crowd, and he too said that partiers were a rare breed on campus.

It may be surprising to read about men and women who are seniors and have never dated or even kissed anyone, or about girls who think it is a big deal to have kissed almost a dozen boys—but that's exactly what I found at evangelical colleges. Kissing is the activity people gossip about, and kissing defines the level at which much of the "sexual recreation" occurs among evangelical students. One young woman tells me that "kissing is really acceptable" at her school. But it is still something to talk about. Another young woman, when we get to the topic of her sexual history, lowers her voice, smiles as if we are some-how conspiring together, and exclaims in an excited whisper: "I've kissed like ten guys—*all of them with tongue!*"

Students at evangelical colleges use the term "hooking up," but almost always to refer to a kiss or some fairly chaste making out. Many claim that although it isn't their style, they know of people who hooked up. At one school, the popular name for this activity was NCMO (pronounced *nick-mo*) or NCMO-ing (*nick-mo-ing*), which stands for "noncommitted making out." When I asked students how they under-stood "hooking up," they often responded by asking me, "You mean NCMOs?"

Of the 36 students I interviewed at evangelical schools, 5 men and 2 women said they had never kissed anyone. Several of these same stu-dents had been in serious, long-term romantic relationships, and a number of them were seniors. Those who had kissed someone before often talked at length about what went into the decision to "give their first kiss away." But many students who talked about NCMOs did so playfully. Some students said that they had had NCMOs once or twice, but they usually discussed these experiences with humor and a smile. It didn't seem as if this behavior commonly led to a negative reputation on campus.

Yet, in the online survey, there were students who, upon reflection, expressed anxiety and remorse about these random kisses, in much the same way that students at the spiritual colleges expressed regrets after one-night stands. Only 62 evangelical college students (as opposed to 495 students at the spiritual colleges) chose to answer the optional, open-ended question inviting them to discuss hooking up on a personal level—describing how it felt to hook up and what they thought the next day about the experience. Many of these same answers indicated that the evangelical students understood the term to refer to sexual experi-ences occurring within a committed, long-term relationship, in sharp distinction from students at the spiritual colleges: not a single student at a Catholic, nonreligious private, or public institution regarded "hooking up" as an activity occurring within a committed relationship. For the evangelical students, a hookup was typically equated with any sexual intimacy that occurs between a boyfriend and girlfriend.

But there was also evidence of students who have a more "traditional" understanding of the hookup at evangelical colleges—though the sexual intimacy usually stops at kissing (though not always).

Only 14 (23%) of the 62 evangelical students who responded to the open-ended question said they felt OK or "fine" about hooking up, and several of these expressed the "thrill" of transgression—hooking up was a walk on the wild side that felt exciting, even liberating. "It feels good," one young man writes.

> Usually we both just had some sexual energy to blow off, and knowing that it won't cause drama between us or that the relationship needed to be defined gave us a sense of freedom. Knowing that I could express myself with a girl with no strings attached was wonderful and really gave me a sense of fulfillment and joy.

This kind of attitude was rare, however.

The lion's share of evangelical students who chose to answer this question (40 of 62, or 65%) fell into the "regret" category, describing hooking up as making them feel bad and, most of all, "dirty." "Regret, something pure spoiled, *taken*," writes one young man, adding, "Innocence lost, innocence taken."

Another young man gives a detailed and heartfelt description of his regretted sexual experience, which was with his girlfriend. Even as he regrets what the two of them did—which was to have sex, though he makes an unusual distinction between sex and intercourse—he tries to justify it somehow (presumably because he did not reach orgasm during their limited time engaging in intercourse), and even to hang on to both his own virginity and his girlfriend's:

> I want to clarify that the one time I have had intercourse has been with my girlfriend who I am more than close with.... We are both devoted Christians who are devoted to virginity until marriage. We fell to temptation and for ten minutes we lay together, me inside of her. We did not move or create physical pleasure for it hurt her too much to move. We stopped before we had sex but we did engage in intercourse, at least this is how we have come to see it. We are devoted to virginity now stronger than ever as a result.

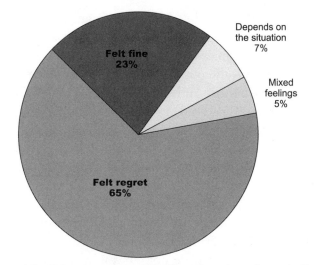

CHART 6.1. The Morning after a Hookup: Reactions from 62 Evangelical Protestant School Respondents. A total of 79 students from Catholic, private-secular, and public schools filled in a response to this question, however 12 answers were thrown out because the responses either lacked enough information to categorize them or simply said "not applicable."

Many of these remorseful evangelical students also talk about "failing" or "betraying" God by hooking up. "Extremely guilty, praying to God for mercy," writes one student, repentant about his behavior, and "like I broke another commitment to God," says another. One clear dividing line between students at evangelical colleges and those at the spiritual ones was the evangelicals' determination to bring divinity into the sexual equation. With one exception, *only* evangelical students mentioned God when they wrote about hooking up. Students at Catholic schools do not talk this way, despite their presence at colleges with religious affiliations, and neither do students at the nonreligious or the public colleges. The most interesting answers from the evangelical students in this "regret" category came from two students who reported asking God for forgiveness for hooking up *and receiving it*.

"[I feel] [v]ery convicted, knowing that I was a flat-out sinner for doing something so sacred out of marriage," says one woman about how she felt after her version of a hookup. But then her story turns abruptly in a different direction. "Jesus has forgiven me, and I don't have to worry about feeling guilty anymore," she says. The second woman begins, "I feel empty, like what I did just made me lose all the morals I thought I had re-built up until that point." But then she adds, "I feel slightly bitter, but I don't let it get me down. I've only had vaginal sex with one guy a few years ago, and I've gone through counseling and many times of prayer to be healed of that." It is this important possibility—the possibility of being "forgiven" for past injuries to God or to another, of being "healed" of injuries to oneself—that gives some evangelical students an edge over others when it comes to dealing with their sexual experiences emotionally.

Asking for forgiveness about regrettable sexual behavior for students at spiritual colleges is not even a thought in their minds—most of them wouldn't have any idea whom to ask for forgiveness in the first place, and they do not live in communities where someone would likely suggest this possibility (it would be an imposition). Even engaging in a process of discernment about sex—taking time to assess and reflect on experiences that were not enjoyable or that a person feels shameful about, to try to discover better, more satisfying ways of being sexually active—does not seem to occur to students at the spiritual colleges. If it did, they would probably keep it to themselves. For evangelical students, having a lifelong, deeply intimate relationship with God helps some of them (certainly not all) through the pain of regret and onto the road to healing and better future decision making, even if they never tell another soul about why they asked God for help in the first place.

WHAT EVANGELICALS THINK THEIR PEERS THINK ABOUT SEX

As a group, evangelical students were far and away the most expressive when asked about faith across all the interviews. But conversation about sex was another story. Occasionally, I met a young woman like Emily who barreled right through the questions about sex with a smile on her face and without the tiniest change in her cadence or demeanor. But Emily was the exception. Even students still on the purity track displayed considerable anxiety. One obvious source of this stress is that evangelical college students live in a community that—though it allows faith to provide a sacred canopy for classroom and student life—subscribes to a particular style of Christianity that idealizes sex within marriage and villainizes not only sexual activity but also every hint of sexual desire unless talk of marriage is on the table. But another source of anxiety is student-generated and has to do with fears that your peers are purer than you are or, in some instances, anger that your peers are not pure enough.

Generic talk about virginity, sexual restraint, and purity flowed freely among evangelical students during interviews. So sex talk, at least in this sense, is about as popular on evangelical campuses as it is elsewhere. But talking about their own sexual desires and sexual experiences is something very few of these students do; the revelation of sexual exploits is taboo.

Sure, sex happens, most students I interviewed at evangelical colleges said. But you can't talk about it.

Evangelical students will freely talk about sex, however, on paper (so to speak).

All students who took the online survey were given the option to answer an open-ended question about how they perceive their peers' attitudes about sex on campus. From the evangelical colleges alone, this question produced almost 500 responses, which fell into six major categories. Thirty-seven percent of the students who volunteered answers felt their peers valued chastity, reporting that attitudes about sex on campus focused on "chastity," "staying pure until marriage," or "keeping to biblical standards." Students who fell into this category typically reserved judgment about whether this attitude was good or not, though some tagged their answers with comments such as "and I believe that's right," or "and I am happy that my peers feel this way." As one student put it, "I think most of my peers view sex as a God-given gift to experience intimacy with a loved one within a committed relationship; I strongly agree with this view, and am glad I'm surrounded by others who generally approach sex in this way."

There was a similar feeling, small group of students (6%) who observed both that their peers emphasize maintaining sexual purity and that their campus fosters an atmosphere where students can talk openly about sex and ask questions freely among peers, faculty, and ministers. "I believe there is a relatively open, positive view of real sex at [my college]" was a typical response in this category. One student commented about the "healing" that is possible when students fail to live up to the chastity ideal. "On campus sex has happened but there has been spiritual healing," this student writes.

> [My peers] all stress purity in physical and spiritual forms. However, situations do occur when one feels it is right to engage in sexual activities. They know this. They are forgiving and offer encouragement to better oneself. It's a strong support system. They don't judge, they just love and accept. However, they do hope that the right decisions will be made when concerning sex.

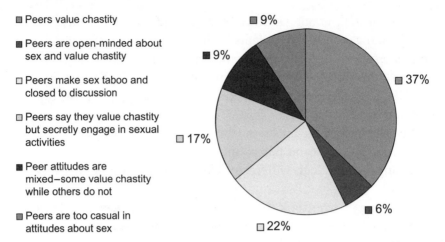

■ 9%

■ 9%

■ 37%

☐ 17%

■ 6%

☐ 22%

CHART 6.2. Peer Attitudes about Sex at Evangelical Protestant Schools: 479 Responses

These students were a minority, however. A much larger percentage of students (22%) agreed that the campus ideal is chastity but said that sex is a "closed," "taboo," or "feared" topic, and they complained that their fellow students are overly judgmental, even watchful about sexual behavior, as if they are trying to catch people in sinful behavior, and that this is a dark mark on the community. Some students even wrote in anger about what they see as a pretense of chastity that distorts everyone's sensibilities about sex—and most in this group wished that sex could be discussed more openly, honestly, and in a more "realistic, less naïve" fashion. "There's a strange balance between being open, talking generally about sexuality and sex, but then being 'hush-hush' about what we really do," says one student. Others complained about peers "shoving their beliefs on others" and about people who feel sex is evil— the "ultimate sin"—and ostracize those who are sexually active. "They do not understand and are cruel to me because I have sex," one student says. "I feel like many of [my peers] are erotophobic," says another. "They are afraid that sex will eat them alive." Another respondent writes, "If some of the people on my campus knew that I wasn't a virgin, I would lose friends. A lot of people on my campus would assume that because a woman has had sex before marriage, she's committed the worst sin there is to commit."

The fourth group of students (17%) identified a disconnect between what people *say* they do and what they *actually* do. This group believes that publicly everyone holds to the party line that "sex outside marriage is always wrong," but behind closed doors people are doing all sorts of things, including having lots of oral sex and even intercourse but still claiming that they are "holier than thou." Within this category are students who suspect that people lie and keep secrets about sexual activity—especially women, since the common view is that more of a stigma is attached to women who have sex. "I think most people are virgins and believe that sex before marriage is wrong," one student in this category writes. "However, I know for a fact that there are several of my peers who have sex on a regular basis."

The last two groups each tallied 9% of the total responses. The first group said that there is a range of attitudes about sex: most people value chastity, but others do not. Many of these students expressed considerable confusion about sex, saying that nobody really knows where the lines are between what you should and should not do.

The remaining 9% complained that the sexual ethic on campus is too lax. One student protested about those students who have not had intercourse yet who "think it is still okay to have oral sex, and they think they're virgins." But even as she is judging her peers, she worries about doing so. "Keeping virginity until marriage is very important for me, and I want my future husband to be the same as me," she writes. "However, I must not have a prejudice or condemn people who are not virgins as Jesus did [not condemn] a prostitute."[6]

Overall, evangelical students agree that maintaining one's purity, chastity, and virginity is the dominant sexual ethic at their colleges, but their perceptions vary widely concerning whether their peers are open to discussing this ethic, and to what extent it is embraced. When students were simply asked to express their perception of their peers' attitudes about sex, it is interesting to note that most students took it upon themselves to state both their perception *and* their feelings about it—expressing dissonance between what they value and what they think others value. These students are caught in a communications void and feel alone if and when they fail to live up to the perceived expectations of their peers. Given the close, communal atmosphere fostered at these colleges, they also are anxious about the possibility of failing the expectations of faculty and administration.

Evangelical students may be leaps and bounds ahead of students at spiritual colleges when it comes to talking about and actively practicing their faith. But because sex is such a high-stakes religious issue for their communities, it is often a painful, frustrating closeted topic for many evangelical students—the one area where integration and openness just doesn't seem realistic.

SEVEN

Hookups, Ho's, and Losing It

[Hooking up] can be the worst, like, "Oh my god, what, how did I get here!?"...
I know people who have been like, "Dammit! I left my earrings there
and they were my favorite earrings but I was so freaked out
that I had to get out as quick as I could."

—*student at nonreligious private university*

SEEING THINGS FROM THE (ALPHA) MALE'S PERSPECTIVE

"I wanted this girl to give me head," Aaron Bleiberg says. He looks right at me, his expression blank.

I stare back. By now I have mastered a poker face. Students have told me all sorts of graphic stories, many of them vulgar, about their sexual exploits. Before I began this study, I had thought that maybe because I am a woman some of the men would hold back with the language and the details. They didn't.

Aaron Bleiberg is movie-star gorgeous. He possesses the dazzling good looks that makes girls stop and stare and hope he might simply glance in their direction. As soon as he walks in the door, I find myself concluding that he is one of the most sought-after men at his nonreligious private university. His olive skin is smooth and tanned—he's just back from spring break during his junior year—and his dark eyes are framed by long lashes. I wonder whether he'll be as charismatic as

Jamie Woodhouse, the good-looking, brokenhearted basketball star who waxed romantic about his old girlfriend. As soon as Aaron begins talking, however, the dazzle wears off. He has about as much personality as the sterile conference room in which we are sitting. And less tact.

"She thought about it for, like, five minutes," Aaron continues:

It was kind of weird. So then she's like, "OK." But then *I'm* like, "I don't even like this girl, and she thought about it for this long, she must *like* me so she wanted to do it." So when she said yeah, I was like, "Actually, never mind." That would just make it hard because I knew I didn't like her—*like her, like her*—so that would just make it harder.

Hooking up is Aaron's preferred mode of interaction with women. He likes no-strings-attached encounters, the less talking the better. He enjoys regaling his buddies the next day with details about the night before, which generally also involved imbibing large amounts of alcohol.

"Well usually we're, like, 'Yeah, I got some *ass* last night!'" Aaron says enthusiastically, chuckling a little, the first sign of emotion he's shown during our conversation. "Or we'll, like, make fun of it if it was no good or if something funny happened. But usually it's just, 'Yeah, I got laid last night,' and just bragging about it a little bit. But not *too* much."

Aaron complains that women typically aren't as casual as guys about hooking up, which according to Aaron means anything from kissing to engaging in oral sex and sexual intercourse (he plainly prefers the latter). Girls usually pretend they are cool with things, but really they're hoping that the one night will somehow turn into a long-term, committed relationship, he tells me. Aaron does observe that a lot of hook-ups turn into what he calls "steady hookups," but these are not the same as relationships. They involve two people who keep hooking up physically every weekend until they move on to other people.

Aaron doesn't hook up as much as he used to during his first couple of years at college. He doesn't like all the complications of dealing with a girl who said she was OK with getting together for the night but really wanted something more from him. In fact, he hates that. It always seems to happen to him, too—the girls end up liking him for real. So now, Aaron hooks up only when he feels absolutely comfortable with the situation—which means that he and the girl have both been totally up front about how this goes no further than a one-night encounter.

Even then, it can be risky.

Aaron's description of the first time he had sex is almost clinical. "I wanted to have sex. My friends were having sex," he says. "I had a girlfriend. We had sex. It wasn't that big of a deal to me." And no, he tells me, he didn't love her. And he doesn't say anything about whether it was a big deal for her. He doesn't seem to care.

Aaron thinks sex is easier for girls: they can have it whenever they want it because guys are always looking for girls to have sex with them. Guys don't have it so lucky. "If you're a girl and you wanted to get laid, I don't think it would be too difficult," he adds.

As for oral sex, Aaron observes that girls more often offer it to guys than vice versa. He isn't quite sure why. "Maybe girls just feel it's been going on, their friends do it, so they think, 'Well maybe I should be doing it too,'" he speculates. "Maybe they have more insecurities, that maybe the only way to get a guy to like them is to give him oral sex." Aaron is not averse to giving oral sex to a girl, it's just that he wouldn't do that during a hookup. "I wouldn't give oral sex [to] a girl unless I really liked her, unless I dated her," he says. "But I would have sex[ual intercourse] with a girl if I didn't date her."

So girl-on-guy oral sex and intercourse are both casual? A big yes to that, says Aaron. "I don't have to know them for a while," he explains about his rules for having sex with a girl, which are pretty lax. "I have to like them, or *think* I like them. Or if they're really good looking and they know it's just a physical thing, then I'd probably have sex with them too."

Again, Aaron says he wants girls to know that he's not interested in anything but sex with them. I can't tell for sure if it pains him to hurt someone or if it's simply a pain to deal with women who are hurt, but I get the impression it's the latter. He doesn't want to waste time when women come begging for something more than a one-night stand. "I'm much more focused on my schoolwork; it's my most important thing," he says in the same monotone he uses throughout our conversation. Aaron did try having a girlfriend once. It didn't work out.

"So, recently, I almost got into a relationship. I started talking to this girl and seeing her every day for three weeks, and then it was like, *whoa*, this is a huge time commitment. So I kind of just backed off and stopped talking to her. School is very important to me. Midterms came around and I had all this stuff coming due." Later, Aaron adds, "I know that was kind of a dick move. But I [had] to stop to do things that are more important to me."

This gorgeous young man, someone whom women would surely trip over themselves trying to please, has yet to fall in love. Oddly enough, the one department in which Aaron has so far struck out is love. "I know I'd like to find [love]," Aaron tells me, despite his commitment to sex without commitment. "But I've had no luck."

Like a lot of guys who are into hookup culture, Aaron puts virginity and girls who "save themselves" on a pedestal. But he's not interested in worshiping them. "I perceive it as noble," he says. "But would I get into a relationship with someone who was a virgin? I don't know. I would have to *really* fall head over heels for her. So probably not."

TOM BEECHER: ALPHA MALE

"I'd say it's a reproductive thing," says Tom Beecher, a 20-year-old junior at another nonreligious private university. Tom has just told me that girls idealize sex, and that boys don't. He explains why this is.

"If you've fertilized [them,] then hanging around isn't going to benefit you," he says.

On every campus at the spiritual colleges, I interviewed at least one "alpha male." Alpha males tend to be good looking and charismatic. They are popular, some of them are athletes, but most of all they are big on the social scene. Alpha males can get girls with a snap of their fingers. They tend to talk disrespectfully about women without knowing (or at least caring) that what they say is degrading, and they set the tone for sex rhetoric and partying on campus. At small colleges, they are the barometer for the entire school when it comes to hooking up, sex, romance, and relationships; at large universities, they control this culture only for their particular cohort or clique. They are the guys whom parents hope their daughters will avoid.

Alpha males are by definition few in number, but their influence is great. There are what some would call *alpha females*, too—but even these popular, party-going women take a backseat in terms of influence to their male counterparts. Alpha males set the bar for other guys, to be sure, but their behavior also determines what women should expect for themselves when it comes to sex, hooking up, romance, and relationships. Alpha males show other men what they are *supposed* to want, what they are *supposed* to do, and what they are *supposed* to avoid if they want social success.[1] They have the power to silence dissent among their peers, so that even the majority of students—both women and men who long for committed relationships—have little way of knowing that they are not alone in feeling this way. Aaron Bleiberg is a classic example of the alpha male. So is Tom Beecher, who seems completely unaware of how shocking and offensive his language is, perhaps because the way he talks about and treats women is normal among his friends. Tom prides himself on living in one of the biggest party houses at his university, and one of the coolest. They throw at least five "ragers"—the kind of party where hundreds of students show up and the cops likely get called to break it up—a semester.

Tom has been to lots of theme parties, which he sees as "an excuse for girls to dress up like sluts." Tom believes that theme parties have gotten so popular because the regular raging party is old news—been there, done that. "So you have to have the party again *with different clothes*," he says.

Recently, Tom went to a "lingerie party."

"All the girls wore really put-together lingerie stuff," he says with enthusiasm. "The guys were supposed to wear bathrobes or boxers. I was like, 'I'm not doing that.' So I got there, and everyone ripped my shirt off. Everyone hangs out without their shirt on and stuff, so it was cool."

When I ask whether hooking up with girls is a priority, his face lights up.

"Hmmmm," Tom answers. "Yes it's a priority. *Yes. It. Is.*"

Tom started having sex at age 13, and when I ask about the appeal of the random hookup, he tells me that "it's a natural urge." But people don't hook up, he adds quickly, "nearly as much as they should"—especially women. Girls talk a good game about sex, Tom complains, but they don't put their words into action. "I mean, they say they want it and then don't do much about it."

"I would like a girl around more often," he continues. "You know, like, *for me*."

Is Tom talking about a girlfriend? Probably not. I'm fairly certain he means that he'd like a regular sex partner. "I think that guys don't want to worry about having a girlfriend so much," Tom explains. "It's, like, somewhat of a burden."

Tom divides girls into two types: girls he might date and girls he would have sex with, but not date. He tells me he's pursued "both kinds of girl" at different points during college, but he's unsure which he'll pursue over the coming months. The problem with this division of women is that women generally don't know about it. A woman whom Tom would only want for sex isn't told she is a sex-only girl. If the woman's desires line up with Tom's and she's in it just for sex, too, then fine. But if she wants more out of the hookup—and chances are she does if the many women I interviewed who see random hooking up as the surest way to a boyfriend are telling the truth—this can create problems for the woman. She is set up for disappointment, and Tom isn't about to enlighten her before the fact. Tom is far more concerned about how the fact that all women want relationships (as he sees it) creates problems for guys like him, who have to deal with the sex-only girl's wish to be treated like a dateable girl.

"They want you to call back and to call them up and to hang out, and it's not just after a party and that sort of thing. Like, *during the day!*" he says.

All girls—both kinds—want to spend time with guys *during the day*, Tom says, as if this were a shocking expectation.

"I think it's easier for guys to just forget about the emotional stuff," Tom continues. "The girls will idealize, maybe make expectations that the guy won't reach, like that it be a steady relationship thing. And the guy will be like, 'Well, we did this, and now I'm free again.'"

Tom reports that oral sex is common during hookups, "because you can't get pregnant from it," and girls see it as a way to "get around losing their virginity." He claims it is definitely more common for girls to give rather than receive. "The guy wants more to be satisfied, more than the girl does," Tom says in an effort to explain this imbalance. "I just feel like guys want to have more orgasms in a month."

Though this method seems to keep guys from getting a reputation, girls aren't so lucky. Tom has a special name for girls who have lots of sex: "dirty girls." By "dirty," he means diseased—the kind of girls whom everybody wants to avoid. "There's this girl I know that has sex a lot, and her friends were saying that she was into me," Tom explains. "And I perceive her as being tainted. Like possibly dirty to me. Like she could have an STD [sexually transmitted disease] that she doesn't know about that I wouldn't want to get just because I slept with her."

A woman who has sex with lots of guys is a potential health hazard, though for some reason Tom doesn't believe that men have to worry about this problem. But having sex with a "dirty girl" is also *worth* less, according to Tom, in the economy of campus sex. If you have sex with a woman who everybody knows is easy, then it means less "to everybody involved," by which Tom means him and his friends.

In Tom's world, it's "more acceptable for girls [than for boys] to be virgins," because girls are "a more docile gender." But it is terrible to date a virgin because she can lead you on forever but never have sex. This happened to a friend of his, and they were all frustrated with the situation, thinking, "*Geez.* Why won't that girl *loosen up?*"

For guys, being a virgin is a sign that something is wrong with you, rather than something valuable: "If you're a guy and a virgin it's like, '*Geez*. Get your priorities straight!'"

After all this, Tom surprises me by confessing that he was in love once. He met her on his third day at college. As he tells the story, this alpha male type, who doesn't seem to have a romantic bone in his body, suddenly became wistful and wide-eyed.

"She was the most beautiful girl," Tom says.

> We went on walks, and we checked out the city, went to museums. And I started seeing her and really loving it. We just totally melted together. When you first get to college, you don't have many friends, and we found what we were looking for in each other. . . . I mean, we went out to parties and stuff, but we were just really satisfied with each other.

Tom was not merely satisfied with her. He fell madly in love with her—his first and only love.

"It was, like, very, very serious," he says. "We were totally in love. It just really felt like the right thing to be doing, you know, with our time here on earth." It taught him a lot about good sex, too. *Meaningful* sex. "I think that sex, when done for the right reasons and sincerely, can be the most beautiful thing," he says.

The relationship lasted through his first year at college and continued into his second. But in her eyes, their relationship took an irreparable hit over summer break. Tom was willing to try to make it work during sophomore year, but she was always too busy, and he found himself trying over and over to persuade her to make time for him—*for them*. He doesn't notice the irony in this—that he was so dismayed that his ex-girlfriend wouldn't make the time to be with him just minutes after he had complained about how annoying it is when girls want to spend time with guys "during the day."

"She had so many extracurricular activities, so many hours of [sports] practice a week, and she was never around any weekends," he complains. "We were living two totally separate lives, and I wanted a lot more from her than she could give time-wise."

Finally, Tom's love broke up with him. He was heartbroken but persuaded her to stay in the relationship. But soon Tom got a taste of what many guys (himself included) dish out to the girls with whom they hook up: after she agreed to stay with him, she promised to call him but never did. They haven't talked since.

"I was miserable," he confesses, laughing cynically. "It was January, it was cold and dark all the time," he adds.

When I ask Tom whether he is looking for a relationship like the one he had with his former girlfriend, he says, "I would love a relationship like the one I had before, but I've been looking for that type of girl for a year and a half now, and I've gotten pretty much nowhere." He laughs uneasily. "I met one girl that seemed like a sure bet, but I couldn't get past the fact that she had, like, an extra 20 pounds on her. I still see her now, and she gets mad because I only come home with her when we're at a party." She settles for hooking up with him, and that's as far as it goes.

GETTING IT OVER WITH

"I'd just turned 18, and it was at prom. Well, it was after prom. It was really stereotypical."

I am talking about first-time sex with a tall, 21-year-old woman with a long, blonde ponytail and a friendly, upbeat demeanor. A junior at the public university, Chloe Miller is also an Episcopalian who goes to services every Sunday with friends. She wears a purple track suit and her voice is hoarse, but I can still detect a southern accent. She grips a cup of coffee in one hand and raises it occasionally to her mouth for a long gulp between answers.

"It was really weird," she says, choosing her words carefully, as if wanting to get things just right. "It was with this guy I had sort of dated off and on since maybe second grade. It was, you know, puppy love when we were younger. I think he had never done anything."

Both he and she were inexperienced sexually, and their experience having sexual intercourse was disastrous. It wasn't about love. It was about "getting it over with."

"It was one of those things where he didn't want to tell his friends that he was still a virgin so it was kept under wraps. Before prom he was like, 'I'm going to college, I haven't done anything, we've got to do something,'" Chloe explains.

> So it was kind of forced, I guess. We were both like, "We *have* to do this." We were there getting ready to, and then I was like, "Maybe I shouldn't do this," and then I was like, "Oh, just, you know, it'll be all right, let's just go ahead and do it." But afterwards I wasn't just, "Oh, no," and crying—I thought my life was *ruined*. It really didn't work out how we thought. It was *awful*. It was a one-night thing.

Chloe is not the only student I interviewed who talked about losing her virginity as something she had wanted to "just go ahead and do."

Because so many students at the spiritual colleges feel pressured to put an end to their virginity, I heard from a lot of women and men who decided one night to rid themselves of this stigma, this "mark" (as Amy Stone regarded it) that kept them from being "normal" adults and from having a "normal" college life.[2]

But many of these same students eventually regret this decision.

Chloe's friends haven't changed much since she was in high school. When they were first-year students, they hooked up a lot. They still do, though now she sees many of them going the "friends with benefits route"—hooking up regularly with a friend without expectations that the "friendship" will turn into a romantic, committed relationships.

"They won't talk to this guy for a while and then they'll have sex, and then they won't talk to him for like a month or so, or they'll be on the phone a couple [of] times, then they'll have sex," she says, laughing, trying to explain the back and forth of how it all works. "I wouldn't want to have a relationship like that, but a lot of my friends do. I guess they're really busy, or the guy is really busy. They just don't have time."

Many students said hookups and one-night stands are easier than steady relationships because everyone is so busy with schoolwork, part-time jobs, volunteer commitments, extracurricular activities, friendships, and of course partying. Committed relationships can drain a person's time, and most students just don't have room (or don't make room) in their schedules for hanging out regularly with a boyfriend or a girlfriend. So squeezing in no-strings-attached sex after hours seems more efficient. At least, this is one way that girls rationalize their hookups and the disappointment they feel when someone with whom they have had sex does not call.

Chloe *says* she "wouldn't want to have a relationship" of the friends-with-benefits kind, but in the next breath she tells me that this is exactly how she got together with her current boyfriend. It started as a hookup, then another, and another, and they have been dating for six months now.

"It was kind of weird," she begins, trying to recall how they've gotten where they are now, living together off campus:

I think we had gone to a party, and we got back and we had sex. Then it was this weird feeling. I didn't know if I wanted to do anything with him. Then we were like, "Well, we'll just have an open relationship." After a while, I realized I cared about him, and he moved in after I had a roommate move out. The main reason he moved [in] was that I was kind of afraid, living by myself.

When I suggest to Chloe that it sounds like this relationship started out as friends with benefits, she laughs a bit awkwardly before conceding that, yes, that *is* how it happened.

Between her disastrous prom date and her current boyfriend, Chloe has had sex with four other men—a couple of them one-night stands. Once Chloe got first-time sex "over with," this left her open to being freer about hookup sex. Several young women told me that, once they lost their virginity, they felt as though they might as well continue. After all, once you've done it, what's the point of stopping?

Chloe tells me about one of her one-night stands. "I had a couple of drinks, and I was hoping to create a relationship with this person," she said. "I think he thought that since we did have sex that it was easy and that he'd be able to get with me any time," she continues. "And after we did have sex, I realized that person wasn't for me. I felt a lot of regret about it. I felt that I kind of just gave myself."

Not everyone is embarrassed by being a virgin at college, however, or looks down on students who are saving themselves for someone special or even for marriage (at least not much).

One young woman told me that, at her Catholic school, by the end of the second month in her first-year residence hall, students had developed a kind of catalog about who was experienced at what and who was not experienced at all. At the time I interviewed her, students were about to enter into a lottery for on-campus apartments and residence hall rooms for the following year. A group of five women from her hall, all of whom were virgins, stood out among everyone else.

They call themselves "Virgins 'R Us."

"They came up with the name themselves—I think it's cool," this young woman explains, emphasizing how these women chose to advertise their sexual status proudly rather than allow others to look down on them. The woman telling me the story is not a virgin herself, but she is quick to argue that virginity is a perfectly legitimate choice for some people. "They have signs in the hall. They brag about it," she continues with a combination of amazement and respect. "I have a friend in the hall who has been with her boyfriend for three years, and she wants to wait for marriage, and I think that is an amazing decision. I think people really respect people that make that decision," she says. But then her attitude changes, and she talks of virginity not as a personal choice but as a sign of feeling unwanted and of lacking self-esteem:

> At the same time, I think it's a confidence issue. I think people get extremely—they feel like they are left out or something. . . . People that

want to have sex and haven't, they feel unconfident about it. They don't want to talk about it. I don't, I don't want to say people look down on them. I guess they feel like they should have it.

Virgins 'R Us makes sense only at the spiritual colleges. Calling yourself a virgin is a provocation only at institutions where virginity is—or appears to be—a rare condition. If a group of girls did the same thing at an evangelical college, it wouldn't make sense.

Of the young men I interviewed at the nonreligious private schools, only three answered that they were virgins. One of these men told me a story about the extraordinary lengths to which his roommate had gone to lose his virginity. "He actually traveled to Washington, D.C., to have sex with one of his friends from high school," he begins, chuckling:

> They both thought that coming to college as a virgin was a mistake because to them sex wasn't a really big deal. But it was kind of a big deal, and they didn't want to start having sex with someone completely unknown. So my friend traveled how many hundred miles just to have sex with his other friend and get it over with. Being a virgin is a negative thing—it's like, something to be corrected. Growing up, you get these vibes that if you're not having sex, you're not cool, and part of that is still there in college.

THE "FIRST HOOKUP" VS. THE "FIRST DATE"

One young woman I met, a 21-year-old senior at one of the nonreligious private universities, managed to stay a virgin *and* hook up "all the time" during her first year of college. Claudia Muñoz loved every minute of it and felt empowered by the experience—she was giddy discussing it.

Claudia informs me about what to her is an obvious fact: dating is simply not an option at her school. "I've never gone on a date here," she says. "I don't feel like people date anymore. I just don't hear, 'Oh, I went on a date with so-and-so last night.' You either meet up at a party or you hang out at their house. It's not as formal."

Just because people don't date doesn't mean that people don't want to.

"I think girls want to be taken out on dates, I really do," she says. "My friends and I have talked about this before. I really want to go on a date to see what it's like. We don't think it's any different than just hanging out, but just the fact that you get dressed up to go out on a date—it seems like such an odd idea in our heads just because we don't do that."

The alternative to dating, Claudia tells me, is hooking up. Students see it everywhere they go—at parties, in dark corners of a bar—it's all around, people meeting and then going home together. That's where the guy has the power, Claudia says. The girl always goes to the boy's house. He gets to determine the hookup location, and it's never the girl's apartment or room. Since everyone was doing it, Claudia decided to do it too, just as long as it was understood up front that sex, including oral sex, was out of the question. She may have hooked up a lot, she tells me, but she always made sure to stay a "good girl."

"It's almost like a conquest," she says, giggling again. "It sounds awful, but it's definitely for fun. I wasn't looking for any kind of relationship. I was just like, 'Oh! There's a cute guy, let me hook up. I never hooked up with people I didn't know, and I wouldn't go to a bar and find some random hookup."

Why was this empowering for Claudia? How was it a "conquest" (a term a few other girls used in our interviews, but none so effusively as Claudia)?

"For me, it was more to see if I could hook up with that person. If it was someone I really, really liked or thought was really cute, then it was like, 'Oh yeah! I hooked up with so-and-so last night. Go, me!'" Claudia continues, adding that it must sound awful, talking this way. But to me, it sounded refreshing because most women I interview talk about past hookups with such angst. Claudia said that out of all the times she hooked up, she can recall only one when she later felt uncomfortable. She stayed over at a guy's house—something she usually never did—and the next morning she felt terrible about it, even though (as she assured me), they "only made out, nothing else." What made Claudia feel terrible was "the walk of shame." "I feel the situation is a little more awkward because you don't go out with the intention of something happening, and then if you happen to wake up there the next morning, you have to do the walk of shame back to your place in the clothes you wore the night before," she explains. "That's where the embarrassment part comes in."

Claudia's hookup rules are simple: kissing only, and no going home with anyone. Follow those rules and a hookup is guaranteed to be fun, *and* she gets to keep her good-girl reputation. At least, she thinks she does.

"I never heard anything," she says with some hesitation, wondering whether her hookups might have given people something to talk about and she just hasn't heard the gossip yet. "I don't know if people were just talking behind my back or what. But I don't think so. I hope I didn't get a reputation," she says, giggling one last time.

Most of the students I interviewed at the spiritual colleges admitted to having at least one hookup. Yet the random hookup after an alcohol-soaked party does *not* happen regularly, they say. More likely, it happens once or twice a year, if at all. Equally important, almost none of the students to whom I spoke see the random hookup as anything approaching an ideal. The overwhelming majority of students say they prefer romance and relationships. But in public, students are complicit about hookup culture. They make a concerted effort to laugh just as loudly as everyone else during weekend cafeteria conversation about the exploits of the night before, and participate in similar banter in online social networking sites like Facebook and MySpace, even if they are only pretending that all this talk of hooking up is great fun.[3]

Many students had elaborate theories about how and why committed relationships often arise *from* hookups. A single random night becomes a not-so-random series of nights, or a "steady hookup." Then, feelings may develop and the two people may decide to become a couple. In fact, *most* relationships at college seem to begin as hookups. How else are relationships to begin if students are largely unacquainted with what they see as the quaint, old-fashioned practice of dating? Numerous students I interviewed said it was almost unheard-of for one person to ask another out on anything approaching a traditional date, for several more dates to ensue, and then for the two to become a sexually active couple once a committed relationship was established. You might go on dates after you have hooked up and become a couple (though even then it seems rare), but the "first dates," insofar as they occur, likely occur after two people have been sexually intimate for quite some time.

Jake Stein, a student at a nonreligious public university, describes hookups as a testing ground to see if you want to hang out with someone. "People hook up to try it out and see if they like the person, to see if it's worthwhile to do it again or to go on a date," Jake explains. "I feel like hooking up is kind of like a trial run. It's like, 'All right. We're going skip all that first date stuff and see if it [is] worth going and actually having the first date.'"

A first-year Catholic college student told me how all the students in her residence hall came to learn fairly quickly that the kind of behavior that would have been considered "slutty" for high school girls was "just normal" for college students. In a similar vein to the "trial run" idea, she warned that people who may *intend* not to care when a first date or a phone call does not materialize after a hookup may nonetheless realize later that they are hurt. "Some people go out and don't have any intention of doing anything with anyone. Then it just happened, and they don't really know the person. Then the entire hall knows about it, and it's not a good scene if one feels uncomfortable about it. Usually I know of too many girls that cry," she explains. But not every girl gets hurt. "There are plenty of girls that went out with the intention of it, and they were happy with it," she assures me. "They knew the person, and it was fine. It wasn't a big deal for them. I guess it depends on who it is and what their intentions originally were."

According to students at the spiritual colleges, most relationships develop like this: one night after a party, two people hook up, then it happens again, then it becomes a regular thing, and eventually they find that they are in a relationship. A number of students I interviewed who were in relationships said they started with late-night encounters in a residence hall. After some additional late-night encounters, the two people involved realized that they had feelings for each other, and they decided to become a couple. If any coffees, dinners, or "just talking" romantic encounters occurred with these students, these experiences typically happened *after* multiple hookups and the decision to become a couple. Dates just aren't a common way *into* a relationship. Students don't see many avenues into committed romantic relationships aside from hooking up.

At the spiritual colleges, the first hookup seems to have replaced the first date. Perhaps this is why so many women who talk about wanting committed relationships are willing to hook up even though they would rather spend a weekend evening just talking with a guy—and the guy would most likely prefer to do the same. After all, hookups sometimes do turn into committed relationships. Odds are, however, that one-night stands will be just that, leaving disappointments and hurt feelings in their wake for *both* men and women—even if the men don't express it.

Many students also told me that drinking and hooking up went hand in hand. But answers to an online survey question about the relationships among sex, hooking up, and drinking or doing drugs—from a total of 1,138 respondents across the four institution types—show this behavior to be less common than students assume.[4] Of the 923 students at spiritual colleges who responded, only 7% say that they either engage in this combination—random hookups/sexual activity with drinking/ doing drugs—"frequently" or "all the time." An additional 9% say they are "usually" drinking or using drugs when they engage in casual sexual activity. These numbers go up even more, however, when it comes to the middling response to this question. Approximately 33% percent answer that they are *equally* as likely to have been drinking or under the influence of drugs during sexual activity than not. A much more common response to this question is that the student is "never" or "rarely" drunk during hooking up—a whopping 51% fell into this category.

Unless students are underreporting their behavior, these figures indicate that the relationship between random hookups and sex while drinking to excess is *not* the norm according to about half the student population surveyed at the spiritual colleges. These figures contradict the widespread student perception that getting drunk is virtually synonymous with socializing. For now, however, the perception that drunken hookups have replaced the romantic first date prevails on most campuses.

PROVING YOUR SEXUALITY: WHY GAY GUYS ARE "SLUTTY"

"Straight guys can do what they want, but gay men are like girls," Jeremy Kim, a sophomore at a nonreligious private university, says. "If you sleep around, you build up a reputation, and rumors fly."

Getting a reputation sounds like a woman's problem to most. But, as this young gay man informs me, it's not confined to them.

Jeremy sighs a lot during our conversation, bats his eyelashes, and occasionally runs a hand through his jet black, spiky hair. His tone is animated, alternately playful and sarcastic. The sarcasm comes on especially heavy when he describes growing up as an "extremist" evangelical Christian who used to "sit up front in church and sing the loudest" until one day he just decided he was "sick of it and quit" playing the good Christian boy. Now, he's spiritual rather than religious, he says. Sometimes when he's feeling really low, "some of him" misses the church community in which he was once so involved. But that part of him is small and fading. Jeremy is still not out to his parents, and he's not sure when he's going to break the news. He does wonder, however, how his Mom and Dad haven't figured it out, since (according to him) he's "so obviously gay." For now, he's glad because, unlike his sister, who knows and is accepting of it, his parents think that being gay is "satanic" and "would react very violently."

His parents aren't Jeremy's only problem. His efforts to find romance within the gay scene at his university have been spectacularly unsuccessful, and he thinks it might be because he's Korean American. He seems resigned to his lot as "unlucky in love."

"Basically, the majority of the gay men here are white, and I'm not, so I'm excluded," he says with a heavy sigh. "And they all hang out together, and I feel like, 'Don't you want to hang out with me?' and I see them more since we're at the same parties, and I'm like, 'Why won't they be friends with me?' I think since I'm Asian they look down on me."

As far as dating goes, if you are gay, there is no dating. At least, that is how Jeremy sees it. It's all about lust, attraction, physical appearance, maybe money, "if you're into that." Gays hook up far more often than do straight people, Jeremy is convinced. But the frequency of it doesn't forestall the "reputation" problem.

"Oh, gay men are *a lot* sluttier. And rumors fly like *that*," Jeremy says, snapping his fingers in the air. "They want someone pretty who's good in bed and don't want anything else. The people who don't want [random sex] don't get anything because no one else really wants that."

People like Jeremy, for instance.

"I'm still a virgin, which kind of blows," he says. "When I was at the place where all the gay people hang out, we were playing a drinking game, and I said I was a virgin and everyone was surprised because they assume you won't be by college. What can I do about it? I'm not going to lie." Some of the people who found out Jeremy was a virgin tried consoling him, saying that it's good he "hasn't given it up to someone he doesn't like." But he thinks that consolation was "bullshit."

"My personal love history kind of sucks," Jeremy continues:

> By senior year, I was out [of the closet]. Pretty much everyone knew. I wished for meeting someone, but it didn't happen. Then that summer I hooked up with my first guy, and it didn't go far. My freshman year, I started seeing this [other] guy. I really liked him, but he said he worked two jobs and didn't have time, so I was upset. Then I met another guy, and we hooked up one night, and I was sick so we couldn't do much. Then that Friday, we went on a date, and it was really romantic. Then I went home for Thanksgiving, and he was like, "Let's just be friends," and I was heartbroken. That [relationship] was only one and a half weeks and that's it. It sucks.

Jeremy is at his wit's end about his love life. He doesn't much care anymore what he gets from someone or who it's from as long as he gets *something*. He'd just like to get this virginity thing behind him.

"I don't care," he says emphatically. "I'd like a long-term relationship but, honestly, if it lasted three weeks, that would mean a lot to me. I just want to meet someone who is interested in me longer than a week and a half."

Students in the LGBT (lesbian, gay, bisexual, transgender) community who are not sexually active worry that their identity is tenuous at best among friends of their sexual orientation because many perceive that sexual activity is what proves your identity. Given these circumstances, it should not be surprising that public displays of affection are particularly significant for gay and lesbian students. Another gay man I interviewed from a private university said that one of the best nights of his life was "when a boy I fell for kissed me in a crowd of people at a parade and then held my hand for the rest of the night." The gay, lesbian, and bisexual students I interviewed described experiences of being affectionate and romantic in public as highly meaningful. These experiences provided two thrills: publicly *proving* to others one's sexual orientation and getting to be *openly sexual* in public.

In short, although the hookup game is as common in the LGBT community as it is among heterosexual students, because of its implications for sexual identity, the stakes are higher. The double standard applies to all sexual minorities, too, whether male or female: being sexually active proves your sexual orientation, while at the same time sexual promiscuity risks your reputation. Like heterosexual women who try to walk the fine line of just enough sex to please but not too much to get labeled a slut, gay, lesbian, and bisexual men and women seemed damned if they do and damned if they don't.

YES GIRLS, DIRTY GIRLS, AND FEARS ABOUT GETTING LABELED A SLUT

Mandy Mara, the young Catholic woman who is active in campus ministry, is talking to me about who gets what reputations and why when she tells me about an infamous clique of girls at her Catholic college.

"They were called the 'yes girls,'" she says, "because they would do *anything* with *anybody*." Like others who tell me about the yes girls, she has some trouble separating fact from fiction. "The rumor is . . . I think they were having sex. . . . I don't know," she says.

> Personally, I think it is disgusting having that many different people who you are doing things with, so I don't agree with it. The people in

my class know them now as the yes girls even though they don't do that anymore. It's definitely going [to] stick with them. But they all supposedly have boyfriends now.

One boy begins his commentary about the yes girls by saying, "I wouldn't say that I know many of them." He laughs as he speaks:

But it's definitely something that I learned about within the first month of coming here. They tend to pack together. I notice them at lunch, or dinner, at a meal because they all sit together. To some extent, you can pick them out. It's basically a group of girls that just say yes to whatever they're asked. They are the group of promiscuous girls or the group of slutty girls, I guess you would say. They're just a group of girls that I guess aren't looking for the relationship thing, [or if they are,] they are going about it the very wrong way.

"Well, *everyone* knows about the yes girls," adds another woman. "One of the yes girls got in a fight one weekend, and everyone was like, 'Who was it? Who was it?' and we're like, 'It's one of the yes girls,' and everyone knew who it was."

"I haven't heard anything about yes guys," I say, pushing her a bit.

"I never thought about how there's no yes guys," she responds, pondering the idea. "I don't know. I don't know. You just think of the girl, I guess. I don't even think, 'That guy kisses girls all the time,' or anything like that. I think girls just notice it more and, just talking to girls, I think girls gossip a lot, and I don't hear the boys gossip."

Although the yes girls were famous, I never met anyone who was friends with a yes girl, or who simply hung out with one on occasion. Neither did I speak with anyone who had any firsthand proof that these girls were as "slutty" as everyone made them out to be. That didn't stop anyone from sticking a derogatory label onto them and gossiping about what they supposedly do, and with whom. Sexually active heterosexual men are exempt from this scrutiny.

But I do learn another label attached to girls at this same Catholic college: the "ho train." For some students, the ho train is synonymous with the yes girls. For others, it is a more generic term used to describe *all* first-year women as they make their way to weekend parties.

"The freshman girls on Friday and Saturday nights—they all go in a big train to junior and senior dorms to drink because the guys give them alcohol," one woman informs me. "The girls just go over there because they want to flaunt themselves, and they think it makes them popular."

"It's just, they will pretty much say yes to anybody," says another, who seems to conflate the ho train with the yes girls. "I personally don't even know if that's really true. I know they go to parties, they dress provocatively, and they are six good-looking girls. I've heard the [term] 'yes girls,' and I've heard the 'ho train.' It's kind of mean and kind of bad, but I'm guessing they did something to get that name."

"Are the yes girls and the ho train the same group?" I ask.

"Yes, it's the same girls," she confirms. "I'm sure any girl that's completely innocent that goes around dressed in little short-shorts and little shirts—they are going to call her a ho or a whore."

A young man at this college says that he feels "like you're labeled if you hook up a lot," but when he says the generic "you," he doesn't mean himself and other men. "You definitely get the reputation, and you're part of the [college] ho train," he adds. Only women get reputations. For him, this label is not restricted to first-year women. "It's not just the freshmen, it's just more visible for the freshmen because you can always see them moving together in packs from dorm to dorm. Upperclassmen girls are [no longer] in those dorms, so it's not as visible."

The yes girls may be restricted to this one Catholic school, but references to sluts, ho's, whores, dirty girls, and the theme party culture that promotes similar images of young women are widespread at the spiritual colleges.

Many girls live in fear of getting a bad reputation. One way they ward off this stigma is by attempting to affix the "slut" label to others. A lot of young women I interviewed said this was a major problem; they think women gossip more than men do and are more likely to start rumors.[5] Given the tremendous fear among women of getting a reputation—regardless of whom the label comes from—you would think that women would steer clear of theme parties that explicitly cast them in the role of whore—but it seems that women find safety in the fact that, as many explained, at theme parties everyone is just *pretending* that women are ho's.

SEXY DRESSING, SEXUALIZATION,
AND THE HO-THEMED COLLEGE PARTY

Theme parties were very popular campus-wide at several colleges and universities, and at the remaining schools students were typically aware that these types of parties were popular within certain campus cliques, if not within their own. A number of students looked at me quizzically when I asked about theme parties in interviews, and to a survey question, some responded simply, "What's a theme party?" But many more responded with stories.

"There are some frats, and they'll have something called a pajama party," explains Chloe Miller, the churchgoing girl from the public university, "but it's basically girls come in with very minimal to no clothing and they get drunk and then [guys] have [their] way with them." Chloe and her friends stumbled upon theme parties during their first year of college. They were walking into what they thought was an ordinary party at a fraternity when some boy blocked them from entering. "They were like, 'This is a pajama party. You have to take your clothes off. You can't come in with clothes on,' and we were like, 'We're leaving.'"

In my education about this new college ritual, I heard about "lingerie parties," "naked parties," "maids and millionaires," "jock pros and sport ho's," "professors and schoolgirls," and the more traditional "toga party" (where women are now known to craft the two-piece toga—basically a bikini made from a sheet), among others. Some students also told me about innocent-sounding themes like "ugly sweater" parties, "middle school" parties, or the more familiar "decades" parties that I attended in college. But more often, the themes seem driven by guys' desire to get women to show up wearing "next to nothing" *and* the girls' desire to "dress sexy" for the role.

At these events, men are given all the power positions. They are CEOs, millionaires, professors, and athletes. Women, by contrast, serve as their whores. It is not difficult to make the leap (or small step) from these parties to the male fantasies of pornography. In fact, these parties' themes mimic classic porn scenarios, now widely accessible on the Internet. Instead of simply watching porn, however, college men get to re-create these fantasies live, in person, and among women with whom they go to class during the day.[6]

Women are divided at most college campuses when it comes to how women are supposed to dress. Where exactly is the line dividing "sexy" from "slutty"? Is it OK to wear super-short miniskirts and teeny tank tops? Some women talk with disapproval about how women at their school dress when they go out. Men and women alike snicker about how absurd it is for women to go out "virtually naked" in the middle of winter, wearing high heels and no stockings, tottering through the snow to parties in below-freezing weather.

But I spoke with plenty of women who find theme parties empowering. They get to dress as sexy as they want—a rare and exciting opportunity according to some women, who complained that sexy dressing for class or for a "regular" party would get them a lasting reputation as a slut. Dressing sexy for a party with a ho theme gives women the freedom to express their sexuality, many explained, without long-term repercussions—something lots of women long to do, but find that other acceptable outlets for sexy dressing are almost nonexistent on campus. One woman defined sexy dressing as wearing "outfits that include short skirts and halter tops or high heels and tight jeans . . . [clothes that] show skin." These outfits she then carefully contrasted with "really slutty" attire: shirts that are "really, really low or skirts that are really, really short." Many women students talked about dressing sexy when "feeling rejected by guys and [wanting] to attract male attention," as one puts it in her journal. "In every instance it has made me feel a lot better about myself, confident in my femininity," she writes. "Whether it was the particular outfit or the fact that I held myself with more confidence in those outfits, people definitely noticed me more, pursued me, wanted to talk to me."

Many others, however, express mixed feelings about dressing sexy to get the confidence boost that male attention brings. They feel beautiful at moments, but at other moments they feel slutty, even embarrassed by their decision to dress as they did. One woman writes about how she "dressed in a manner inconsistent with the level of attention [she] wanted to receive, particularly from the opposite sex." Another says it is difficult for her *not* to dress sexy because of her "C cup bra size." "If I wear a low cut shirt, it always attracts attention," she writes. "Doors are opened, drinks are offered, and smiles are flashed. Sometimes I feel empowered, sometimes I feel cheap. I suppose it depends on the manner of attention I receive."

"I would describe my dress as flirty sexy," writes another.

One particular outfit that comes to mind was an extremely short black "skort" (a skirt with shorts attached) and a midriff baring top that I wore on Halloween when I went as one of the Pussycat Dolls. I was a little nervous about the outfit because if I show skin in one area, I will usually try to cover up in others. In this outfit I felt very vulnerable and uncomfortable because I thought it attracted too much attention. In the end, my friends were surprised that I wore such a provocative outfit. I doubt I'll ever wear something that revealing again, because I didn't like the image it portrayed. I am usually more "classy" with my dress and I felt as though this outfit portrayed a more "loose" image.

Other young women talk of periods of "experimenting" with sexy dressing on spring break when they are away from circumstances that might get them a reputation that lingers. One woman reports how, on spring break, she and her friends "all dressed in slutty little outfits and went out to the clubs every night." "I thought that I looked good at the time," she writes. "But now looking back I'm embarrassed. I definitely got attention, but that attention was not positive. It was attention from boys wanting to hook up with me, not boys that respected me at all." Young women at evangelical colleges, where "modesty" is valued, railed regularly against women who "bare it all," or at least a substantial portion of it.

"Culture has this thing where [people] are completely focused on sex, which in turn tells women to dress very sexy," an evangelical woman tells me.

> This bugs the crap out of me. Don't get me wrong, sex is and can be such a great thing. But again, it shouldn't be disrespected. I don't particularly like walking in the mall only to see a girl's thong from beneath [her jeans]. I just want to say something like: Wouldn't you rather have a man respect you? Why are you parading around like this? Do you realize that you're sending the message of, "I'm easy, come pick me up?"[7]

Between the parties and the degrading language, the objectification of women is clearly present on campus. Women are being socialized into a culture that sees dressing up as secretaries, maids, and "ho's" as the epitome of a good time.[8] Many psychologists today refer to this kind of socialization of girls and young women as "sexualization."[9] Sexualization begins as early as the "tween" years—between the ages of 8 and 12—and continues throughout high school and college. According to the American Psychological Association's Task Force on the Sexualization of Girls, which released results of a major study in February 2007, *sexualization* is distinct from *sexuality* in four important ways: (1) a person's value is equated with "sex appeal or behavior"; (2) a person is submitted to a "standard that equates physical attractiveness with being sexy"; (3) a person is "sexually objectified—that is, made into a thing for others' sexual use"; and (4) "sexuality is inappropriately imposed upon a person."[10] Sharon Lamb, a psychologist and member of this task force, discusses the sexualization of young American girls in her book (coauthored with Lyn Mikel Brown) *Packaging Girlhood: Rescuing Our Daughters from Marketers' Schemes*. Lamb and Brown focus on music, movies, magazines, and, perhaps most relevant to theme party culture, how the clothing industry merchandises "sexy dressing" to young girls during even the pre-tween years.[11]

The sexualization of America's girls and young women accelerates once they leave home. Women make up about 58% of the college population—and growing.[12] From the moment that a woman walks onto a spiritual college campus, the message that "to be a girl is to be sexy" is reinforced in all sorts of ways, implicit and explicit. As Lamb and Brown attest, American culture writ large does not help teen girls to navigate the highly sexed culture that beckons them. So many young women have no idea how to draw lines between what is and is not acceptable to them, what they are willing and not willing to do, and when whatever is being asked of them is just too much. Young women also receive the message that they must not only be sexy but also be overachievers academically because they have to work harder to get the same things that boys do.[13] For many girls entering colleges and universities, achievement on a social level often requires a certain amount of sexual expenditure.

There is an emerging cultural trend where many young women learn to trade sex and its allures—sexual favors and/or sexy dressing—for popularity, long before they step foot onto a college campus. Young girls and women as early as middle school and certainly by high school barter their sexed-up bodies for status. Eventually they come to believe that, by allowing college guys to objectify them in various ways, not least at "CEOs and ho's" theme parties, they can earn enough social capital to become popular, desirable, and perhaps win the ultimate jackpot— a real, live college boyfriend—though they also must take care, of course, to avoid the minefield of getting a reputation in the process. Perhaps most unsettling is how the sexualization of young women seems to be desensitizing college students to sexual assault. Many young women who have been the victims of nonconsensual sexual violations talk of these events without any awareness that they were assaulted. As respect for personal boundaries, including the boundary of the body, dissolves and disappears online, at parties, and in the bedroom, is the boundary between consent and assault—a line that the feminist movement and most colleges and universities have taken great care in recent decades to delineate—vanishing, too?

WHEN SEXUAL ASSAULT BECOMES BLURRED:
JULIA TANNER AND HAILEY NATHAN

"I had numerous conversations with the boy I dated in high school about how I didn't want to have sex," says Julia Tanner, a tall girl with curly dark hair who is a junior at an evangelical college. "I was 18 at the time. And I had conversations with this boy," she says again, emphasizing her repeated efforts to communicate to him her wishes about sex. "And I really didn't want to have sex, and he kept pushing, and he had had sex with one other girl before me."

Julia's older sister had counseled her many times to save sex not necessarily for marriage but at least for the boy she would marry. Her sister hadn't waited for the "right guy." She had sex with various partners and had gotten pregnant in college. Julia didn't want to repeat her sister's mistakes, but during high school she was feeling rebellious. This rebellion led her into the arms of a boy her parents didn't like, someone she would come to regret ever meeting. "I didn't actually say no in the situation, but it just kind of happened," Julia says, recalling the first time she had sex. "I didn't really know that it had happened," she adds, explaining that she was confused about what having sex actually entailed. Julia spoke about how she didn't really feel anything and wasn't sure if her boyfriend had been inside her or not. "I actually called him later that night and was like, 'Hey…did we have sex tonight?' And he was like, 'Yeah, we did,' and he was like, 'Are you angry?' And I was young, and I was like, 'No, no,' and at that point I had already made the mistake, so what was the point of stopping at that?"

They didn't stop having sex. As Julia continues to describe her sexual experiences with this boy, I find myself struggling to think through what she has just told me.

Julia was raped, though she doesn't see it as rape. She tells me over and over that she had told her high school boyfriend that she didn't want to have sex—not that first time when she was confused about what he'd been doing to her that one night. I found myself wishing Julia would get angry about what happened, but she wasn't.

Later, as Julia is talking about her current boyfriend, whom she has been dating for several years, Julia's denial begins to lift. "I just knew I wanted to be committed to the next person I had sex with, and I wanted to be engaged to be married," she says with some emotion.

> So my [current boyfriend] had never had sex before, and that was a
> really, really, really, *really* hard thing for the two of us to work through

together. He just felt like he had been saving himself for me, in the sense that I was going to be the person he was going to marry and have a committed relationship [with], and I hadn't saved myself and [had] done it in a noncommittal, casual kind of way. We talked about it a lot, and it was a big issue for us. And I told him the story about the first guy and about how I told him I didn't want to do it, but I don't feel like he raped me, but it *was* against my will the first time. I don't really know all the definitions of those types of things.

The only time Julia uses the word *rape* is to disassociate it from her experience, even as she acknowledges that what happened was against her will.

Julia told her current boyfriend she would consent to sex only if they were engaged, but they did not end up waiting. "He said he knew he wanted me to be his wife someday," she explains. "So at that point, we sat down and talked about it. And it wasn't just in the moment that I was like, 'All right. I'm willing to have sex with you because we are going to get engaged and get married someday.'" But then she *did* have sex with him—once—before he left for a long trip abroad. When he came back five months later, she was still stressed about the decision. She says, impassioned:

He came back and I said, "Look: I know we did this before you left, but I am not willing to do this all the time unless you come to Planned Parenthood or whatever with me and get contraception with me."...
But I'm unwilling to do this as just a casual sort of thing again. I want this to be something that we talk about and are proactive about.

With the help of her older sister, Julia did eventually persuade him to go to Planned Parenthood, and they've "been having sex since." This time, it has been a positive experience for her. But the effects of the assault linger in her language of "willingness" and "unwillingness" and in her fear that, once again, she had somehow "given in" and allowed sex to "happen to her" under circumstances that were not ideal.

Julia Tanner was not the only young woman I interviewed who recounted being raped without calling it that. Four other women described their first sexual experiences as being forced, being unwilling, saying no, or *not* saying yes, and then having men proceed to have sex with them anyway. Hailey Nathan, a sweet, soft-spoken student at the public university, wonders years later whether she lost her virginity by being raped. She says the word so quickly, so quietly, as if racing on to something else, something more tolerable perhaps, that she almost swallows the statement as if she never said it at all.

Hailey was 14 when it happened. Since then, she tells me, she has had 53 sexual partners.[14]

"I wonder if my sexual experiences are partly due to the fact that I lost my virginity so young," she says, her voice shy. It's difficult for me to reconcile how this timid girl has had so many sexual partners, especially since she was heavily involved in her family's Pentecostal church as a child, and cared enough about religion to convince her parents, when she was 10, to become Episcopalians. She had "absolutely" planned to "save herself for marriage," she says.

"I was 14 and I hung out with older kids, and I was at a friend's house at a party and there was alcohol," she recalls. "I guess I feel that I was taken advantage of. I didn't pass out—I remember it—but I don't know."

I press Hailey about whether she really consented to have sex. "Well, I don't think I made a clear decision," she responds.

> I was taken into a bedroom two times with two different guys. The first guy was nicer because I wasn't ready, and he was like, "OK." And the next guy—we had sex—and I remember it because it hurt. But I didn't really want it to happen. But he was just a normal guy, a typical 15-year-old guy. I don't think he cared about me. He just knew I liked him, and [he] thought that's what I wanted.

A "normal guy," as Hailey understands teenage boys, seems to be someone willing to force a girl to have sex, especially if he knows a girl likes him.

"I don't feel like I had much say in the situation because why would I say no only to say yes?" she explains, alluding to the fact that she said no to the first boy. But as she tries to figure out exactly what happened, she goes back and forth. Like many victims of sexual assault, she is confused, anxious, sad. She was so young, she tells me again.

"I don't think I've ever really discussed the sketchiness about how I lost it," she continues. "Sometimes I wonder if it was rape or if I really wanted it and wanted acceptance. I'd be lying if I said I wasn't struggling with it, but I feel a lot of it is [my] intent."

Only one student explicitly described a sexual assault. This first-year student, 19, also from the public university, did something unique when our discussion turned to personal sexual experiences: she differentiated between the first time she had sex and the time she lost her virginity. This is because she was raped when she was 12. After several years of struggling with this traumatic experience, she decided to take back control over her sexual identity, particularly what it meant to lose her virginity. She decided that she was a virgin until the first time she had sex as a matter of choice, not as an act of force. So during our interview, she told me that she lost her virginity at age 18 with a boy she really liked.

DEALING WITH DASHED HOPES THE MORNING AFTER

Beyond the stories of those students who hook up for fun, those who later regret their actions and the reputations attached to their behavior, and those who don't seem to know the difference between consenting to have sex and being sexually assaulted, there are a wide variety of opinions floating around about hookup culture at the spiritual colleges.

Of those students who took the online survey, 557 chose to answer an open-ended, optional question that invited them to describe how they felt the morning after a hookup. Of the students who answered, 495 (89%) were spread fairly evenly across Catholic, nonreligious private, and public schools.[15] These responses provide abundant evidence of what I call the "dashed hopes" hookup, with 41% of these students expressing such emotions as feeling awkward, used, dirty, empty, regretful, ashamed, alone, miserable, disgusted, duped, and, in the words of several, abused. One common reason provided for these feelings was "because it didn't turn into anything more."[16] "I have felt

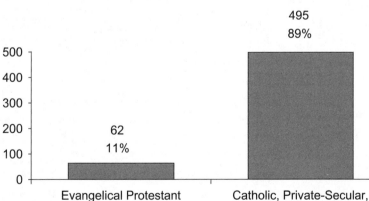

CHART 7.1. The Morning after a Hookup: Percentage of 557 Respondents by School Type

The Truth about Sex on Campus

disconnected with myself, as though I were a person I wouldn't talk to," writes one student. And "dirty is the best word for how I feel about myself," writes another. Some write of betrayal and insecurity. "I often feel as though I've betrayed myself and my values by being physically intimate with someone I do not share an emotional intimacy with," one young man writes.

> I sometimes feel as though my partner has taken advantage of me, even if I first approached her. I feel my actions arise more from a desire to please my partner and a desire not to spend the night alone more than anything else, and I look at hooking up as signs of my own insecurity.

One young woman who has managed to remain a virgin while hooking up reports that she feels "really lucky not to have been taken advantage of." Other students say they felt stupid or upset about putting themselves in situations where "something bad" could have happened to them. Some students write extensive evaluations of the morning after the hookup, as does this young woman, who catalogs her post-hookup feelings:

> Feel bad about myself (like a sleaze). . . . Disgusted with my decision (not consistent with what I believe). Feel empty. I wonder: Does the other guy really want more? Was it just sex and if it was, [was] I . . . just an object? . . . I degraded myself. Even if it was meaningful, I should have waited until we were in an intimate relationship.

Students who felt this way often mention alcohol and how getting drunk complicated the hookup experience; some participants simply couldn't remember anything the next day. "Sometimes I don't remember what happened due to intoxication," writes one student. "I usually take a shower to rid myself mentally and physically of the actions I did the previous night, and say I never want it to happen again."

However, 62 (13%) of these 495 respondents report that how they feel about a hookup depends on the situation. Were they sober or drunk at the time? Was it with a friend or someone they did not know? Was the person with whom they hooked up really OK with the lack of commitment in the encounter? Might the hookup turn into "something more"? "I feel that as long as it was consensual and that we both enjoyed it and were safe that it was a good experience," writes one student. "I don't think any less of myself or the other person, as long as both of us are free of any committed relationships."

Another student, a young woman, explains the morning-after dilemma this way:

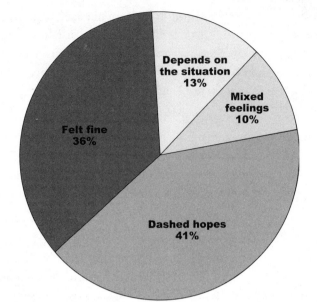

CHART 7.2. The Morning after a Hookup: Reactions from 495 Catholic, Private-Secular, and Public School Respondents. A total of 589 students from Catholic, private-secular, and public schools filled in a response to this question, however 94 answers were thrown out because the responses either lacked enough information to categorize them or simply said "not applicable."

> It depends on whether you liked the person before or if it [was] some random person from a bar. . . . If it's someone you had a crush on, who knows? It might turn into something. And if not, you can at least say you hooked up with that person. . . . But if it is a random person who you don't even remember their name—things could be awkward, thus making you feel a bit like a slut.

Yet another student writes, "I always wish that I weren't 'so drunk' or 'so carefree' during the experience."

Sometimes, these evaluations of a hookup depend on far less emotional matters, such as the attractiveness of the person with whom they spent the night. "If she's attractive and there's evidence that I used protection I feel extremely positive about my actions," one man writes.

> If she decides to hang out too long, wanting breakfast or cuddle time, this begins to make me angry and I feel less positive. If she is not good looking and/or friends or acquaintances with someone that knows I have a girlfriend, I regret my actions and wish I had shown more self-control the night before.

A third group of students—50 (10%) of the 495 respondents from the spiritual colleges—express mixed feelings about their hookups. On the one hand, they feel excited by the night and think it was fun, but on the other hand, they express worry that they shouldn't have let themselves do "something like that" outside of a committed relationship. "Sometimes I feel like the world is teeming with brightness and all things good," writes one particularly articulate student, who continues:

> Most of the time my stomach is in a knot and I try to suppress memories of the night before, misplaced guilt wells up, and I am somewhat miserable. But I think this is a good thing—I think that is life: the night of beauty, wonder, and arousal, the morning of destructive thought and regretful recollection.

Another student with mixed feelings writes in a more sarcastic vein:

> A series of thoughts. . . . Sometimes I feel really proud of myself. When I look at my partner, I often think (dependent on partner): I did *THAT?* Pretty! [or:] *Eh.* This again. Should I leave now? Should I write a thank you note? "Thank you, I can hardly walk, now." Quite often, I suppose, I just feel a bit empty. This isn't how Disney raised us to believe. As for my actions, well, they were always clumsy and stupid, but that's what makes the humiliating grin fun the day after.

The final group of students, 179 (36%) of the 495, reacted either positively or indifferently to hookups, saying things like they felt good, fine, indifferent, nothing, whatever, mostly OK, happy.[17] Some in this category state explicitly that they have no regrets. "I usually feel proud of myself," one young man writes. "I feel that I accomplished something impressive the night before. I respect the woman I was with, because it was effectively her decision to be with me, and I typically do well in not hooking up with girls I later regret." Another student in this cohort is rather clinical. "I feel fine," he begins. "I have had three or four one night stands with vaginal sex. Humans enjoy sex. Of course, these 'relationships' lack substance or a future, which makes the sex actually worse. I do not feel that remorseful however. I am still respectful of the opposite sex." One person affirms that hooking up is part and parcel of what college is all about: "I feel that it is an experience of being young and spontaneous—I also think it has a lot to do with the situation of being in an experimental environment (college), academically and socially." Still other students say that they feel "fine" about their hookups, as long as everyone follows the "nothing more" rule. "As long as I don't have to roll over and introduce myself," says one student, hookups are just fine, while a final student, who talks about his casual sexual experiences as "great," laments that the next morning, he "need[s] the girl to get the fuck outta there."

WHAT EVERYONE THINKS HIS OR HER PEERS
THINK ABOUT SEX

Since students at spiritual colleges are immersed in a culture that, at least outwardly, praises no-strings-attached hooking up, and most students can attest that they have hooked up at least once—most students also think everyone else is far more participatory in hookup culture than they are. When pressed, few students express a desire to hook up randomly on a regular basis—though most accept that hookups are the most likely way to find a long-term romantic partner. Instead, most students distance themselves from what they regard as an overly casual attitude toward sex. Some even wonder privately whether their peers are more conservative about sex than they acknowledge. An even greater number wish for more respect and awe about sex among their peers. Only a handful of students express any desire for greater sexual freedom or a more casual student attitude toward sex.

More than 700 students from the spiritual colleges responded to the open-ended question about how they perceive their peers' attitudes about sex on campus. As with the evangelical students, I sorted these comments into six major categories. But, for the spiritual colleges, I had to add one additional category—students who saw sex as a personal decision and said it was not their business to comment on other students' choices—and I also had to take one category away: chastity.

The largest number of students at the spiritual colleges believe their peers are "casual" and "open-minded" about sex. A small group of evangelical students felt the same way, but the meaning is different at the spiritual colleges. When evangelical students say that their peers are open, healthy, and *casual* about sex, they are talking about attitudes, not behaviors. At the spiritual colleges, "openness" and "casualness" about sex have to do not only with how easy it is to discuss but also with what they believe other students do sexually. Thirty-five percent at the Catholic schools and 42% at the nonreligious private and public institutions responded simply and with little or no judgment that, on their campuses, the peer attitude about sex is "open," "positive and healthy about having sex," "no big deal," "casual," "accepted," and/or a "normal part of what goes on at college." These students' answers were typically brief and nondescript when it came to comparing this peer attitude with attitudes of their own. Occasionally, these students added that the peer attitude was casual but also put a major emphasis on "safe sex."

The responses get more complex in the next major grouping, which includes students who said that their peers have casual attitudes about sex but who also offered, unsolicited, that they have problems with these attitudes. Forty-five percent of respondents at Catholic schools and 36% of respondents at nonreligious private and public institutions are unhappy about their peers' attitudes about sex. This group said that students on campus "put overwhelming, unwarranted emphasis on sex"; they are "*too* casual," "careless," and even "hurtful" in this regard. This same group added comments about how this overly casual and careless attitude makes it difficult both to be and to admit to being a virgin. It makes people "treat sex like a game," and as a result students "don't think enough about [the] emotional and physical consequences" of sex.[18] One student bemoans how women in particular are hurt by hookup culture. "I think people are too lax about who they have sex with and how often," she writes. "People here hook up way too often, and guys especially have no problem hooking up with more than one girl in a night and not thinking anything of it." "I feel that the attitudes of my peers on campus towards sex are much different than mine," another student, a young man writes:

> I believe in being committed to a person and being in a monogamous relationship before getting sexually involved with a person. I believe that most of my peers on campus don't believe that you should be committed to a person before you get sexually involved. I think this is too bad, because sex isn't just a game, it's a serious matter that should be cherished between two people that love each other and hope to be with each other for a long time, not just a one night stand.

Some respondents in this category, both women and men, do suspect that most of their peers are *less* casual about sex than they pretend. "I feel like there are more of my peers with conservative attitudes toward sex than are normally perceived," writes one student. "I feel like there is a relatively small group of my peers that is extremely sexually active and attaches little meaning to sex, but this is not representative of the majority that consider it only appropriate in a dating relationship."

Another student comments similarly: "I think the general attitude is one of casual carelessness on the surface, however, I do think that people are searching for something meaningful, and at times may feel degraded or undervalued." This view comes the closest to those evangelicals who believe that their peers say they value virginity on the surface but are sexually active in secret—though it's also strangely opposite: one group of students want to appear more promiscuous than it is, and the other wants to appear more virtuous than it is.

At the spiritual colleges, there was not a single student response that fit the "my peers value chastity" category. I did encounter a small minority, however, who said that, within their group of friends at least, people value sex within a committed relationship. I created a new category for these respondents. At Catholic schools, approximately 3% of student respondents fit this category, and only 11% fit it at the nonreligious private and public schools.

Another small minority of students at the spiritual colleges comment that there is a range of attitudes about sex and/or that their campus is "divided" between those who treat sex casually and those who don't. Eight percent of students at Catholic schools and 5% of those at nonreligious private and public schools fit this category. A paltry 1% of students from Catholic schools and 2% of students from nonreligious private and public schools say that their peers are "not casual enough" or are "too uptight" about sex.

Finally, there is the category that I had to add—one that showed up only at the spiritual colleges but was relatively significant there: respondents who say that what other people believe or do about sex is personal and private and "not my business." At Catholic schools, 7% of respondents fit this description, and 12% did so at nonreligious private and public schools. This is in sharp contrast with evangelical college students' views of the relationship between religion and sex. For these students, sex is *never* a personal decision. It is *never* simply a private matter, even for those who don't make their sexual histories public. Sexual morality is ordained by God and mediated by the larger community. It's not anyone's personal, private right to decide what kind of sex is right and what kind is wrong. That is God's job.

Though the definitions and prominence of hooking up vary widely between the spiritual colleges and the evangelical ones, most students at all schools indicate dissatisfaction about campus culture when it comes to peer attitudes about dating, hooking up, and sex—and they disassociate themselves from the problems that are creating it.

TABLE 7.1 Student Survey Responses: Qualitative Assessment of Peer Attitudes about Sex on Campus

	Evangelical Schools N=479*	Catholic Schools N=340**	Private-Secular and Public Schools N=411***
Peers value chastity	37%	0	0
Friends value sex in committed, loving relationships	0	4%	3%
Peers are open-minded about sex	6%	35%	42%
People *say* they value chastity but secretly engage in sexual activities	17%	0	0
Peers make sex taboo/closed to discussion/peers aren't casual enough about sex	22%	1%	2%
Peers are too casual about sex/suspect that people act "care-free" about sex in public but feel otherwise in private	9%	45%	36%

Peer attitudes are divided between those who value chastity and those who do not/those who are casual and those who take sex seriously	9%	8%	5%
Sex is personal/not my business to judge others	0	7%	12%

*This indicates the number of respondents who chose to answer this optional question on the survey—factoring out students who answered "I don't know" or in whose answer not enough information was given to categorize them appropriately. The number of total respondents from evangelical schools for this question was actually 525.

**This indicates the number of respondents who chose to answer this optional question on the survey—factoring out students who answered "I don't know" or in whose answer not enough information was given to categorize them appropriately. The number of total respondents from Catholic schools for this question was actually 373.

***This indicates the number of respondents who chose to answer this optional question on the survey—factoring out students who answered "I don't know" or in whose answer not enough information was given to categorize them appropriately. The number of total respondents from private-secular and public schools for this question was actually 453.

SEXUAL ACTIVITY, WHO'S REALLY DOING IT, AND THE VIRGIN GAP

As table 7.2 indicates, at spiritual colleges, almost three-quarters (74%) of students report that they have been sexually active in some way. The percentages of sexually active men and women are almost identical.

Some people may find these figures surprisingly high. I suspect, however, that many college students will find them surprisingly low, since most of them assume that just about everybody is having sex. When you split the data by school year, however, the picture becomes

TABLE 7.2 Sexual Activity at Non-Evangelical Colleges (Overall and by Gender)

	Women*	Men**	Total***
Students who answered yes, they consider themselves virgins	232/733 (31.7%)	105/311 (33.8%)	342/1,050 (32.6%)
Students who answered no, they do not consider themselves virgins	501/733 (68.3%)	206/311 (66.2%)	708/1,050 (67.4%)
Students who answered no, they have never experienced oral, anal, and/or vaginal sex	165/733 (22.5%)	80/312 (25.6%)	356/1,346 (26.4%)
Students who answered yes, they have experienced oral, anal, and/or vaginal sex	568/733 (77.5%)	232/312 (74.4%)	990/1,346 (73.6%)

*This column includes students who answered both the question in the left-hand column and also indicated their gender as female and did not also affiliate with one of the two evangelical schools listed at the end of the survey.
**This column includes students who answered both the question in the left-hand column and also indicated their gender as male and did not also affiliate with one of the two evangelical schools listed at the end of the survey.
***This column includes all students who answered the questions in the left-hand column but who did not also affiliate with one of the two evangelical schools listed at the end of the survey.

TABLE 7.3   Sexual Activity at Non-Evangelical Colleges (by School Type)

	Catholic Schools*	Private-Secular Schools*	Public School*
Students who answered yes, they consider themselves virgins	175/472 (37.1%)	111/354 (31.4%)	35/188 (18.6%)
Students who answered no, they do not consider themselves virgins	297/472 (62.9%)	243/354 (68.6%)	153/188 (81.4%)
Students who answered no, they have never experienced oral, anal, and/ or vaginal sex	127/472 (26.9%)	74/355 (20.8%)	28/188 (14.9%)
Students who answered yes, they have experienced oral, anal, and/or vaginal sex	345/472 (73.1%)	281/355 (79.2%)	160/188 (85.1%)

*These columns include all students who answered the questions in the left-hand column and who also indicated school affiliation with one of the two Catholic schools, or one of the two private-secular schools, or the public school at the end of the survey.

more nuanced, with 46% of first-year students claiming virginity, 33% of sophomores, 23% of juniors, and 21% of seniors.[19]

If you break down these data by institution type, the picture changes a bit, with the percentages of students who say they are virgins ranging widely: 37.1% at Catholic schools, 31.4% at nonreligious private schools, and 18.6% at public universities. This shows that perhaps religious affiliation *does* matter to a degree. Likewise, the number of students who answered yes, they have experienced oral, anal, and/or vaginal sex varies widely among school types, with 85% of students at public universities reporting that they have been sexually active in one or more of these ways; the figure falls to 79% at nonreligious private schools and to 73% at Catholic colleges.

Which brings me to the virgin gap.

It is common knowledge today that teens and young adults are legalistic about "how far" they can go and "still remain virgins."[20] This is especially true for those with strong religious affiliations, evangelical

TABLE 7.4 Sexually Active Students (by School Type)

	Evangelical Schools	Catholic Schools	Private-Secular Schools	Public School
Students who answered yes, they consider themselves virgins	481/608 (79.1%)	175/472 (37.1%)	111/354 (31.4%)	35/188 (18.6%)
Students who answered no, they do not consider themselves virgins	127/608 (20.9%)	297/472 (62.9%)	243/354 (68.6%)	153/188 (81.4%)
Students who answered no, they have never experienced oral, anal, and/or vaginal sex	394/609 (64.7%)	127/472 (26.9%)	74/355 (20.8%)	28/188 (14.9%)
Students who answered yes, they have experienced oral, anal, and/or vaginal sex	215/609 (35.3%)	345/472 (73.1%)	281/355 (79.2%)	160/188 (85.1%)

Each column includes all students who answered the questions in the left-hand column and who also indicated school affiliation with one of the two evangelical schools, or one of the two Catholic schools, or one of the two private-secular schools, or the public school listed at the end of the survey.

youth in particular. The figures above seem to confirm that a number of students who have had oral, anal, or vaginal sex still consider themselves to be virgins. Some students simply do not consider oral or anal sex to be "real" sex—creating what I call the "virgin gap."[21]

For example, at the public school, 85% of students claim to have experienced oral, anal, and/or vaginal sex, while only 81% claim they are no longer virgins—leaving a 4% gap. This gap increases to about 10% at both nonreligious private and Catholic schools, implying that, at these institutions, being a virgin may be a more valuable claim than at public schools. The virgin gap is highest at the evangelical schools (14%).

Most telling about these data at the spiritual colleges, however, is the huge discrepancy they point to between sexual realities and romantic ideals. The overwhelming majority of students I interviewed—79% if you factor in those who included kissing in their ideal romantic encounter—held to a *chaste* view of romance. Most students are having sex at some point during the college experience. But they also long for romance without sex. How satisfied are students with their sexual experiences? Is it possible that most of the sex that students are having is "nonromantic" in nature? And if this is true, *why* is this sex nonromantic? Student descriptions of romance rely heavily on communication and emotional connection. But the sex they are having appears to be lacking in both. Why are most students failing when it comes to integrating open communication and emotion into the realm of their sexual experience? Where does this divide between romance and sex come from? How might students begin to bridge this gap—presuming they'd like to?

The gap between romantic ideals and sexual reality is narrower on evangelical campuses, and sexual activity is far less typical overall. At the evangelical colleges I visited, 35% of students said that they had experienced oral, anal, or vaginal sex, far below the 77% who said yes to the same question at non-evangelical schools. These lower levels of sexual activity may not have any effect on whether evangelical students are *satisfied* with their sexual experiences, but they seem to indicate an increased likelihood that, when it comes to romance and dating, the experiences these students are having are more likely to be chaste—and therefore more likely to feel romantic.[22]

If indeed there is a vast distance between romance and sex at the spiritual colleges—much more so than at the evangelical ones—then what aspects of campus culture contribute to this divide? What other social structures contribute to such an emotionally and romantically unfulfilling climate? How do religion and spirituality affect students' sexual and romantic experiences? Or, in the end, do they not matter at all?

RECONCILING SEX
AND THE SOUL
(OR NOT) ON CAMPUS

I know the church is against premarital sex—that is the letter of the law.
But sometimes you have to go against the letter of the law.

—*student at a Catholic college*

EIGHT

God vs. My Boyfriend

I'm supposed to be a great Christian guy and I have sexual feelings,
and with God I feel guilty, and I ask God to forgive me,
and I feel that I'm going to run out of grace.

—*student at an evangelical university*

THE RARE SEXUAL SAGE: CARA WALKER

"If you've already had sex, there are ways to repackage your virginity," Cara Walker tells me matter-of-factly, as if people "repackage" their sexual histories all the time.

Cara Walker and I are chatting like old friends. She speaks with a slow, southern drawl, rounding out her vowels, keeping the pace of our conversation leisurely, as if we have all the time in the world. She wears her thick, light-brown hair with blonde highlights in an old-fashioned flip, shoulder length, making her seem older than her 20 years. A sophomore at an evangelical university, Cara comes from a missionary family that lived in Africa for 10 years, bouncing from one country to another. She went to church regularly, prayed at home, did Bible study and youth group—the standard evangelical upbringing. At college, Cara has continued these activities. She "feels tired" if she doesn't go to church on Sunday. Her friends are "really involved" Christians, too. They pray together, go to services together, and even do yoga together—their "meditation time." Cara calls herself religious—which is "the stuff that you do when you're Christian, you know, like going to church." She also calls herself spiritual, which has to do with her "personal relationship with God" and how "she lives her life day to day."

So far, Cara sounds average. When we get to questions about sex I realize Cara is different.

Cara began having sex when she was 18. It was only for a summer—a full year before college—and it was with one guy. After the relationship ended but before she got to college, she tells me, she felt caught between feeling OK about what she had done and regretting it. "I got really, really close to him, and he said he loved me," she explains:

> I never said I loved him, and it did get really serious, and he wanted to continue dating, but I didn't want that. I think it was a positive experience, but I think it's taken a long time for me to heal from it. I believe that when you have sex with someone, you get bound to them spiritually, and there are a lot of emotional things that come along with that. For the most part, I don't regret it because I know it happened for a reason, but in a way I *do* regret it. But I don't *let* myself regret it. I just try to look on the positive side and see how I've grown from it.

Cara is different from her evangelical peers. Not because she had sex: I interviewed a number of evangelical students who had sex, and about 35% of those who took the online survey claimed to be sexually active. What sets Cara apart is that she does not look back on having sex as an entirely negative experience, as something that was simply "sinful." She recognizes elements of this sexual relationship as positive: she and her boyfriend were emotionally connected, he loved her, and, from the sound of it, she found sex enjoyable. Cara's effort to see "how she's grown from it" distinguishes her from her peers at evangelical institutions. Except for Emily Holland, who is married, the evangelical students I interviewed who had sex were torn up about it, hating themselves for falling into it and hating sex because they thought it a wrong thing to do outside of marriage.

But then, Cara does talk a lot about regret—about feeling some regret yet trying to ward it off. And no wonder, since her decision to have sex almost destroyed her faith. Cara finds it difficult to live with the fact that she is no longer pure—that she has given away her physical virginity to someone who is not her husband—though I soon learn that, from Cara's perspective, it's possible to redeem a person's spiritual purity.

"Any physical sexual activity apart from kissing can just kind of tear away at your purity and spirituality as a virgin," Cara explains. "A virgin who has never done anything—I think you're on a completely different level." But Cara cannot aspire to this level of purity anymore. "I definitely felt like I was running from God, trying to hide what I was doing," she says, recalling the summer she first had sex. "It took me a long time to get back to a relationship with God."

"How long?" I ask.

"A year and a half," she answers. What she did during that time was repackage her virginity, at least in spiritual terms, a process that restored her sense of religious and personal self-worth. "I think it means to make a commitment to not have sex again," Cara explains further. "You can't take back what you did, but you can restore your spiritual virginity, I think. I think it's not a complete loss. God does forgive you, and it is forgotten. I don't think you ever forget about it, but you are given a second chance."

According to Cara, repackaging your virginity is well worth the time and effort. Becoming a "born-again virgin," as this task is more popularly known, or achieving a "secondary virginity," was not instantaneous for Cara. It is not as if she woke up one day and vowed not to have sex again until marriage—as if simply saying, "OK, I reclaim myself a virgin" would make it so. You can never restore your physical virginity either, Cara says—once that's gone, *it's gone*. Some critics reduce secondary virginity or born-again virginity to this sort of cheap grace, making the concept itself laughable to outsiders.[1] But whatever grace Cara found during this long and arduous process was anything but cheap. Cara worked hard during that year and a half to reclaim her relationship with God and to regain her "spiritual virginity." During this period, she experienced lots of doubt, terrible regret, and deep alienation from God. At times, she believed that God would never forgive her for having sex and that she would never forgive herself. This period *began* with a vow to not have sex again outside of marriage, but it also entailed many hours in personal prayer and working closely with a mentor—a young married woman whom Cara found through a church, and the only person other than her boyfriend who knew initially that Cara had had sex. Even with a mentor, however, Cara sometimes felt alone and abandoned. "Mainly I did it myself—I didn't really talk to any adults," aside from the mentor, she says. But in the end, she was able to restore her spiritual virginity.

"It took me about another half a year to just forgive myself," she says. "I did wonder, I don't know, 'What if God's going to punish me for it? What if the guy I start dating doesn't want me because I'm not a virgin?' It took me a while to believe in my heart that I could start over."

Cara is now confident not only that God has forgiven her, but also that her past experience was not a complete loss. God has given her a second chance, and part of her responsibility is to use her sexual history to help friends who are desperately seeking understanding and advice about sex—in both its physical and its spiritual dimensions. Cara still has regrets about her summer before college, but for the most part she believes that "it happened for a reason"—that there was a higher spiritual purpose behind her sexual experiences.

When Cara entered college as a first-year student, she worried that no one else would be like her. Everyone else would be "better Christians" because they would still be virgins. But Cara eventually learned that her roommate had the exact same worry. When Cara told her roommate what happened in high school, her roommate jokingly exclaimed, "Hallelujah," at which point she confessed to Cara that she wasn't a virgin, either. As Cara made more friends, she found out that she was not alone. She also discovered that her openness about her sexual history and newfound confidence as a born-again virgin gave her an important role among her many girlfriends. She doesn't tell just anybody about her sexual past, since "you don't want to come across as [bad] because then you won't get the right husband, and once you get a reputation, you have it until you graduate." But the more Cara spoke about her sexual past to friends she felt she could trust, the more she realized that her friends did still respect her. In fact, she explains with pride, her past, and her willingness to talk honestly about it, gives her an important and unique standing among her peers.

Cara has become something of a sexual sage. Her friends respect her for being forthcoming about her sexual history. "They respect the fact that I can help them through things, and I know what I'm talking about," she says. "I've helped a lot of girls reset their morals and helped them realize that they can move on from these kinds of things."

"Reset their morals"? I ask Cara what she means by this.

"If my friend's dating, and she's getting really physical with a guy and she wants to talk to me about it," she says,

> I don't have to be afraid to tell her, "You need to stop doing that because it's going to get too far," because I've had that experience. It's not like I'm talking down to her, because I've done it too, so I can talk to her because of that experience, and I can help her. And my friends,

because they know that I can relate to that and that I've been through it, they listen to me more than I think they'd listen to someone completely pure who'd never experienced anything like that before.

One reason Cara's friends flock to her for advice is that many of her peers do not "feel comfortable" discussing sex with their professors, administrators, and ministers. According to Cara, this is a big problem. She says lots of students are having sex, but it is nearly as taboo to admit this as it is to do it. People worry that the social repercussions will be disastrous if others find out.

It isn't surprising that girlfriends would rely on each other for advice about sex. What's unique in Cara's case is how her sexual experience gives her a special kind of moral authority which she uses to guide her friends through the thicket of sexuality. Almost without exception, the evangelical students I interviewed expressed a belief—even a fear—that they would lose status among their friends and adult mentors if they should stumble sexually. Moral authority resides in those who are "pure." It seemed never to occur to other students who have had sex that being open about their experiences could give them a special and positive role in their community.

"I didn't *try* to take on the role," Cara tells me about her standing as a kind of Dr. Ruth for evangelical girls,

> but I think once they found out, now if they have a question, they'll come and ask me, and I know it's because they feel comfortable telling me because I've opened up and told them about my past. I feel like I've got to make the best of the situation, and I mean, I feel like it happened to me for a reason, and one of the reasons is that now I can help girls understand what it feels like.

Opening up to others about her sexual past has also strengthened Cara's relationship with God as she acts as adviser and moral authority among her peers. The purpose behind all this—God's purpose, according to Cara—was to repackage not only her virginity but also herself, to provide her with an opportunity to step up and own her sexual past for the benefit of others.

At evangelical colleges, when someone's acknowledgment of past sexual behavior is welcomed (rather than rejected or judged harshly), it liberates not only that person but others, empowering them to be authentic and open about who they are as sexual beings. In Cara's case, the fact that talking about her sexual history elicited a "Hallelujah" from her roommate is telling; it helped enable her to be authentic and genuine among friends.

As Cara and I get to the end of our interview, I notice that she is wearing a promise ring. I know that she has restored her virginity spiritually, but still it surprises me to see her wearing this sign of purity.

"My Dad took me out to dinner [during] my sophomore year of high school and bought me a diamond ring, and it was a purity ring," she says, placing her hand on the table and shifting it so the stone sparkles in the light. "I obviously broke that pledge. But since then, I try to remember to wear it. I've retaken that pledge. I'm not going to have sex again until I'm married. I know that I can do it."

TWO TYPES OF STUDENT, ONE TYPE OF DILEMMA

Cara is one of the few students who was able to tell me a story about how she reconciled her sexual and religious lives. This is a tricky task for any young single person, not only for students at evangelical colleges. Cara expressed the kind of pride about her spiritual path that I saw in Emily Holland. But she stands out because she found a way to integrate sexuality and spirituality—sex and the soul—outside the traditional boundaries of marriage. Cara even found a way for her sexual past to *enhance* her spiritual life and her role in her religious community.

Some students do not even try to reconcile their sexual lives with their faith lives because they do not believe it is possible to do so within traditional organized religion. Others, like Amy Stone, seek meaning in and justification for their sexual activities in the murky sphere of the spiritual. None of these students is quite like Cara, however. Cara has managed to pull off what to most college students is an improbable, even a heroic, feat. She has recognized herself as a sexual being with a sexual past and future, without renouncing her faith. And she has recognized herself as a religious being, with a religious past and future, without renouncing her sexuality.

With the exception of Emily, who is already married, these students, evangelical and otherwise, are all sexually mature—at least physically—but they do not occupy the one religiously sanctioned space for sex, namely, marriage. Here again, students can be split into evangelicals and everyone else. As far as attitudes about how religion and sex go together (or don't), students at Catholic colleges share with their non-religious private and public school peers the conviction that faith is faith and sex is sex and never the twain shall meet; the idea of allowing religious beliefs to affect one's sex life is silly if not laughable.

When it comes to sex and the soul, I encountered two main types of students: the godly and the secular, split neatly along the evangelical divide.

The Godly

Godly students, the rarer of these two types, see religion and sex as inseparable, at least on a theoretical level. Sex is a gift from God designed to be experienced and enjoyed only inside a religiously sanctioned marriage. Students who hold this view typically strive to restrict sex to these confines. This norm is communicated, enforced, and negotiated through a person's religious community—in the case of most of the godly, in an evangelical college campus community. Sex for these students is *never* a personal decision left to the discretion of the individual or couple. This is because sex is not just personal. It is designed by God and given by God to human beings for a purpose. Therefore, it is always other-centered, always religious, and always relevant not only to the people involved but also to their broader communities. Both a person's partner and his or her larger faith community have the right, therefore, to demand respect for and obedience to God's laws in these matters. They also have the right—the responsibility even—to call to account those who have transgressed those laws and to assist those who are struggling to follow them. Having sex outside of these acceptable boundaries is a high-stakes affair. It can jeopardize your friendships, your standing in your community, your potential for future happiness in marriage and family, and, depending on the person, your relationship with God. It is rare to find this type of student at a spiritual college.

The Secular

Secular students, the more common of the two types, split sex and religion into two entirely separate spheres. To call this type "secular" is not to say that these students are irreligious or do not believe in God. It simply means that their religious beliefs have nothing to do with what they believe about sex or what they do sexually. In other words, sex is a secular domain to them. For this type, ideas about sex, sexual freedom, and sexual responsibility are largely mediated by popular culture—by television, movies, the Internet, and what their peers are saying and doing. For this type, sex is personal, not communal. It's nobody else's business as long as everyone directly involved consents. And for the most part, what everyone consents to, at least in theory if not also in behavior, is casual sex. Sex is *supposed* to be casual in today's day and age. And if religion says otherwise, well then, religion is outdated and unrealistic. When it comes to contemporary college campus life, sex and religion are irreconcilable. It is difficult even to imagine how religion might have something useful to say about sex. Having sex for secular types is a low-stakes game. It's a normal, even a banal part of the college experience, at least on the level of one's peers. On a more personal level, however, the stakes are higher, not least because whatever personal repercussions sex might involve are not likely to be discussed with others. It is rare to find this type of student at an evangelical college.

This divide may seem unremarkable at first. Of course, secular students do not turn to religion when it comes to sex. Of course, godly students, who try to bring religion to bear on all aspects of their lives, will involve religion in their sexual choices. The surprise is due to the fact that secular students aren't secular throughout every aspect of their lives. They're secular only in the sexual aspect.[2] Given the large percentage of students self-identifying with religion and/or spirituality, one might reasonably expect students to make meaning of their sexual lives via these resources. Yet religion and spirituality have almost no influence on student behavior related to romance, love, and sex at at the spiritual colleges. Evangelical campuses, however, tell a very different story.

In *Forbidden Fruit: Sex and Religion in the Lives of American Teenagers*, Mark Regnerus claims that, though one might expect to find a powerful tie between sex and religion among evangelical teens, they are not much different from other teens when it comes to sex, aside from the fact that they delay first-time sex longer. According to Regnerus, the confusion here lies in the widespread tendency to stereotype evangelicals as devout. "This is a mistake," he writes.

> Affiliating with an evangelical congregation does not make someone devout. There is no shortage of religiously apathetic evangelical adolescents and adults in America. Yet most research conclusions about evangelicals are from studies of affiliation or self-identity alone, not combined with religiosity. Thus, my results may be picking up, in part, on the sexual practices of evangelical youth whose religiosity is average or below average.[3]

Regnerus's claim may hold true for many evangelical teens in America. But I found something different among the godly students. In their interviews, in their journals, and in the online survey, young adults at evangelical colleges almost invariably approach sex and sexuality, anguished or otherwise, with their religious community's teachings in mind. To be sure, they do not always live up to those teachings. As anyone who believes in sin can tell you, they often fail to live up to their ideals. But whether they are succeeding or failing, they are doing so in conversation—deep, though often private, conversation—with the teachings of their religious tradition and with God.

One reason that my study's findings differ from those of Regnerus may be because our study contexts are different. Regnerus relied on conversations with teens randomly selected from across the United States,[4] whereas I chose to interview only college students. Moreover, most of the evangelical students included in my study attended evangelical colleges; they are young adults who were attracted (or have parents who were attracted) to these explicitly religious campus environments.

To put this another way, what may account for these differing attitudes is a difference in *community*. The mission of the tightly knit, evangelical campus culture is to model and to teach young people how to integrate their faith with all aspects of their life.[5] So it makes sense that these evangelical students would stand out against a more random sampling of teens. Going to a Catholic college is unlikely to make an American teenager more Catholic. But going to an evangelical college seems to make a student *more religious* and more reflective about Christianity.

Someone like Cara Walker would likely show up in Regnerus's study as a student whose religious identity has little or no effect on her sexual activities—simply because she has had sex. In reality, however, she has passionately pushed herself to reintegrate her sexual reality and her religious ideals. Becoming sexually active does not automatically mean an evangelical youth must be disconnected from their faith as a result of it. On the contrary, many of them were *anguished* about how they had betrayed these values, which they still hope to uphold. Although it is true that having sex can turn a student away from worship, from faith, even from God—it also seems that these shifts can be reversed. Moreover, the shared campus culture at evangelical schools tends to keep sex and the soul in conversation.

EXTREME BOUNDARIES: CAL SAUNDERS

Cal Saunders and his girlfriend of almost two years are always walking on eggshells. They *thought* that kissing would be OK, that a few pecks now and then couldn't possibly lead to bodily ruin and sexual sin. But lately, they can't seem to stop with just kissing. So they talk endlessly, defining and redefining sexual boundaries, some familiar to their relationship, some new, in a desperate attempt to return to more innocent times, when holding hands was enough to satisfy their physical needs for each other, enough to bring happiness and fulfillment. Cal and his girlfriend will try just about any rule, draw just about any line, in an effort to avoid what to them looks like a road to ruin. They can kiss but only without their tongues; they should not allow themselves to be alone in a room together; they will stop kissing for a specific period of time; they can kiss, even with tongue, but only if they are not lying down; they are not going to see each other at all for a while, or at least until these lustful desires go away or at least lessen. Unfortunately, these conversations fix nothing. Each leads to yet another method for dousing this sexual fire—some more extreme than others, a few too severe to last for any real length of time.

Besides, it is just not possible for them to not see each other. They are in love. Being apart is like torture.

But staying together is torture, too. Neither of them wants to forgo virginity before marriage. Each wants to remain pure, or at least as pure as still possible. Sex is not worth the price of their relationship with God and their standing inside their religious community. So they keep talking. And redrawing lines. And stepping over those lines. And talking some more.

"For the first year, we agreed that there would be no kissing," Cal explains in a serious tone. A tall, good-looking, articulate young man, Cal sits up straight and answers all my questions with ease. He has dark, curly hair and kind eyes, and he rests his arms calmly on the edge of the table between us. His easy demeanor belies his internal struggle. "Waiting a year was a great thing for us," he says with a slight sigh, adding that, when they finally did kiss, it was the first kiss for both of them.

"She hadn't dated anyone before," he says of his girlfriend. He hadn't either. "We talked about what dating meant to us and what boundaries we wanted to set in our own relationship. Probably the biggest boundary was that our relationship was not based on physicality, but a deep and emotional involvement with each other."

This was only during the pre-kissing year, though. After they kissed, the boundaries got looser, and ever since everything about their relationship has changed—has gotten more difficult, more complicated.

"It is almost easier to be more into a physical relationship," he explains. "But, you know, that is *not* the basis of our relationship. We *have* to make sure we are still deep and emotionally involved."

Cal is urging me to believe that their relationship is deep and emotional rather than shallow and physical, but I also hear him trying to convince himself. Cal *has* to convince himself of this, because the alternative—that their relationship is based on sexual desire—is anathema in evangelical purity culture. As boyfriend and girlfriend, they must work overtime if necessary to guard the purity of their bodies and minds, until marriage opens the door to legitimate sexual expression. Until their wedding day, their job is to resist. Their futures and their faith depend on this willpower, this battle against a tide of desire.

"It is very important to both of us to remain virgins until we are married," he assures me, "and not just remaining virgins *physically*, but remaining virgins in our pure minds and pure in our relationship."

Physically, Cal and his girlfriend have proceeded gradually. Little by little, they did this and then that. Increasingly feelings of doubt have crept in, guilty feelings that seem to say that they have pushed the boundary too far. Now these feelings are forming a dark shadow of unease over their relationship. They are ashamed that things are going further than they intended. They worry that, if they aren't careful, they will soon pass the point of no return.

"I think the guy is a sexual being," Cal explains. He never says anything like this about women. "And being 21, there are a lot of hormones and a lot of outside influences that say it really is OK to just go and have sex. But more than I find it hard to wait, I have a desire to wait. I have a desire to please God and to respect my girlfriend more than I have a desire to have sex at this time."

One solution to this problem is to date for only a short time and get married early. Cal and his girlfriend are walking a fine line, almost an impossible one. By staying together for years at a time, they are risking much of what makes their lives meaningful: their faith and their relationship with God, their honor for each other, and their respect for the values in their community. Dating can be disastrous if you aren't careful, but then, it isn't all bad either, Cal says.

"Dating can hinder [your spiritual life] because you can become infatuated with your girlfriend rather than God or living a Christian life," he explains, stress finally seeping into his voice. "But I also think [faith] can better your relationship. I can relate to my girlfriend on a vulnerable level and in doing that we can engage in deeper conversations about spirituality and just get a deeper idea of God."

Despite Cal's angst about jeopardizing his own and his girlfriend's purity, he shares with most of his peers an idealized sense of sex if it occurs in the proper, godly circumstances: within marriage.

> I think sex can be a spiritual experience because two people are being drawn together in the most intimate way; it is more than just physical. . . . You are emotionally, spiritually, and physically involved with this other person. And you feel deep intimacy like you have with God—not that God wants to have sex with you, but God wants to be totally drawn together with you and you with him, so your soul can be one with God.

Cal believes that sexual intimacy within marriage can bring you closer to God, whereas sexual intimacy outside marriage draws you *away* from God. But not only that. This sort of sinful sexual intimacy is also false intimacy. By giving in to it, you are actively trying to replace your relationship with God with a sexual relationship with your partner.

"This falseness will block your vision of God," Cal says with conviction.

DATING: DISTRACTING AND DANGEROUS

Many other evangelical college students tell me the same thing as Cal—that dating can distract you from your spiritual path, turn your focus away from God. This view can also be found in the popular self-help books designed for young evangelicals. Dating "can be sinful and often is," because "even though your desire for romance isn't sinful, your response to these deep feelings can cross God's boundary lines," writes Jeramy Clark in *I Gave Dating a Chance*. "You can date foolishly. You can be drawn into compromising with the world. If you become involved in inappropriate emotional or physical intimacy, you can and will sin against God."[6]

In *I Kissed Dating Goodbye*, Joshua Harris talks about dating as something that isolates you from, among others, God:

> The exclusive attention so often expected in dating relationships has a tendency to steal people's passion for serving in the church and to isolate them from the friends who love them most, family members who know them best, and sadly, even God, whose will is far more important than any romantic interest.[7]

He claims that dating goes against God's will and "rob[s] our ability to enjoy what He *has* given us."[8] In a chapter on fighting romantic "pollutants," Harris warns:

> Any time we allow someone to displace God as the focus of our affection, we've moved from innocent appreciation of someone's beauty or personality to the dangerous realm of infatuation. Instead of making God the object of our longing, we wrongly direct these feelings toward another human. We become idolaters, bowing to someone other than God, hoping that this person will meet our needs and bring fulfillment.[9]

Harris's answer to this sort of idolatry is simply not to date at all. This perspective comes up often in the interviews I conduct on evangelical campuses.

"I think if you're dating solely for the purpose of dating then *that* can become the focus and it can take the focus off of your spirituality," Emily Holland tells me. "It can in some ways be a substitute—if you're looking to fulfill [yourself] with a person instead of fulfilling yourself with God. But if done in the right context, it can actually help you grow spiritually," she adds, as if paraphrasing from Harris's best-selling book.

"If dating is a priority in your life, it is probably going to hinder your relationship with God," says another young woman. She adds the following caveat: "If God is still your number one priority and your relationships are spiritually encouraging and things, then I think that is fine." Dating relationships can be "spiritually encouraging" if they are (a) faith-centered and (b) with a fellow Christian.

Given the taboo against dating non-Christians, the evangelical students I interviewed took comfort in the fact that they lived in something like a Christian bubble. They are surrounded by Christians, so anyone they date would almost certainly be a Christian. But several students spoke of an additional requirement: they "needed to make sure the other person had a strong relationship with God" before agreeing to go on a date—a far cry from students at the spiritual colleges, where beer and a little chemistry are often all that is required before hooking up with somebody. Evangelical students in dating relationships talked about how they pray together, go to services together, study the Bible together, and talk together about God and faith. Religious practices are not simply something these students share, but the foundation on which they build their relationships. Still, even under the best of circumstances, dating is always risky, because sexual temptation is inevitable.

One young man who has been dating someone for more a year tells me that sex is a "big block" spiritually. If you aren't married and you are engaging in anything sexual, then "you're not with God, and you're disconnected, and you're letting God down." Though he and his girlfriend have never done anything other than kiss, he feels lots of guilt and shame about doing even that, since kissing gives rise to sexual feelings. "I'm supposed to be a great Christian guy and I have sexual feelings, and with God I feel guilty, and I ask God to forgive me, and I feel that I'm going to run out of grace. And I feel that I'm messing up sometimes and living a lie."

This young man, 20 years old and a sophomore, talks of grace not as something boundless and inexhaustible but as something he is depleting day by day. His comment recalls the dramas staged by the Silver Ring Thing in which dating rips away your heart piece by piece until you have nothing left to give. In this case, grace is like the sand in an hourglass that slips away grain by grain with every "sexual feeling," every kiss.

Many students tell me that sex is "the worst of all sins." One young man, who had recently endured a pregnancy scare with his now ex-girlfriend,[10] tells me with some anguish that he feels guilty for "corrupting" her in a way that cannot be undone, since after she had sex with him, she has gone on to be "more and more loose" with other guys.

Another young man who has "made out" with several girlfriends but otherwise doesn't have much in the way of sexual experience speaks of how sex can damage your relationship with God so severely that you start to believe that God "hates" you. Like the student who sees grace as running out, this young man detects a limit to God's forgiveness.

"I think [sex is damaging] just because you feel so much shame. In every sexual act, shame is in company with it, so God becomes less of a loving God and more of a God that hates you because you made a mistake," he says dramatically.

The depth and intensity of this stress and anxiety around sex, sin, and shame among students are hard to overstate.

LOSING HER RELIGION: KATRINA TAN

Katrina Tan is really stressed out. She's stopped going to church. She's not sure why. The entire first month of fall semester, Katrina and her roommate went "church hopping." The search was unsuccessful. Katrina throws her silky, long black hair to one side, revealing her flawless, almost porcelain skin. She stares at her hands, clasped tightly in her lap. She and her roommate pray together now, instead of attending services, but that has just happened recently. They do devotions. That's better than nothing, right? The days when Katrina was a good Christian girl—summers at vacation Bible school, assisting her father (a pastor) with mission work in the Philippines—seem far away now that she's in her first year at an evangelical university. Her parents still live in the South Pacific, and she goes there on breaks. She's glad she doesn't have to go home anytime soon, she tells me, looking up.

The worship life that Katrina knew as a child has all but disappeared, though she is not entirely without community. She finds spiritual solace among a small group of girlfriends. "They're the ones that I go to when I have problems spiritually, emotionally," she says. "The period of time when my roommate and I weren't doing the devotional[s] together was difficult for us spiritually. Having that constant reminder of what we're living for—it's really easy to forget even on a Christian campus." When I ask Katrina how long it took to get back on track with some sort of prayer life, she laughs for the first time, but it's a resigned laugh. "Until about a week ago," she says, with some embarrassment.

Katrina thinks that being at a Christian college, in an environment where most people are Christians and are trying to be true to their faith, makes you "want to act more godly." But then, there are people on campus who are really overbearing about their Christianity, who judge people too harshly and "repel" her, she adds. Katrina doesn't want her life to be about going to church or Bible study because she believes these activities interfere with her "personal connection with God," which is "more important to me than following routine, or traditional activities which I associate with religious behavior." Katrina labels herself "spiritual but not religious"—a rare example of this affiliation on an evangelical campus.[11]

As I listen to Katrina, I realize that she is trying to sell these explanations about her lax behavior not only to me but also to herself. She sees a gap between how she thinks a Christian should act and how she is actually living. "I really do want to push myself further," she says, "but right now I'm just trying to focus on where I am and how I can improve myself since . . . *I can't*. I don't know," she says, trailing off. Something is stopping Katrina from being "more openly Christian," but she doesn't know what it is.

Then our conversation turns to sex.

Katrina wishes sex wasn't such a big deal on campus. People feel pretty uncomfortable talking about sex, she observes.

"I just wish it wasn't such a big deal here because there are a lot more important things in life to think about or to focus on," she says. "I know even if I'm, like, talking to someone about how I'm doing spiritually, and something about sex—even the tiniest little bit comes up—the whole conversation will move to be about that instead of what I was focusing on." Sex is "really distracting," she tells me repeatedly, taking you away from your studies and your relationship with God.

Katrina has been in a long-distance relationship for about four months with a guy she met at Bible school in Italy. Dating was forbidden, but by the end of the program, it was clear they liked each other. He made repeated trips to visit her at her grandparents' home where Katrina stayed the rest of the summer, despite the fact that she was "kind of scared of committing to a relationship just then," she says. "But he kept being persistent about it. I really did like him, and I liked spending time with him, and he came to visit me at other times, like while I was living with my parents, and when I lived with my grandparents, and finally I said, yes, that I would date him."

Katrina and her boyfriend are both Christians, but her spiritual life has taken a hit since they've been dating. So has his. Again, she's not sure why. "My boyfriend and I have been trying to, like, revitalize, I don't know, what is it called?" She is stopping and starting again, trying to find the right words and frustrated with herself that she can't. "Trying to bring back to life our spiritual lives, get back on track or whatever," she continues. "At least, I've felt like my life has been so stagnant recently, and he's noticed a change in me, too, so he's kind of helping me along with that."

The source of Katrina's spiritual decline and rising anxiety soon becomes clear to me: she and her boyfriend had sex. Just a couple of weeks ago.

"Initially, I tried to keep my virginity until marriage," she says, after telling me that she is no longer a virgin. It all happened so quickly. Again, the words are hard to find:

He came down to visit for a weekend, and before he left it was just a really emotional time or whatever, and it was against our better judgment that we did that. And it's just strange because, because he was here for such a short period of time, and it was the first time that he was visiting, and it was just—it was a strange situation. I don't normally see him, and after he left it was almost like it didn't affect me a whole lot because it didn't feel like it really happened. It just didn't feel real when he was visiting. And also because I had told myself from the very beginning that I was going to save my virginity until marriage. It just seemed really weird.

As with so many other young women when we spoke about sex—not all of them evangelicals—Katrina refers to having sex as "it," as if the best way to talk about sex is without referring to sex directly, as if a pronoun can distance her from the unsettling fact that she is no longer sexually pure.

They didn't even talk about having sex beforehand. Maybe that is why Katrina feels like "it" didn't really happen. Like Cal and his girlfriend, Katrina and her boyfriend were already having all sorts of difficulties patrolling their sexual boundaries. They would set them, then break them, then set them again. Before this visit, they pledged to have "more self-control." At first, they did fine. But he was staying at a hotel this time; he couldn't stay with her on campus because of the strict visitation rules in her residence hall.

The hotel was what did them in, she says.

"We weren't planning on having sex, we didn't talk about it, but just being in a secluded area together and him leaving," she says, obviously anguished about the night she spent with him. "It was easy to just let things keep going."

Katrina hasn't seen her boyfriend since the night they had sex, and she isn't sure she wants to. She regrets what they did, but she realizes that she "can't go back and change it." And what makes it worse is that it wasn't even pleasurable. It was painful, awkward, and awful, she tells me. There were other complications, too.

"My biggest stress after he left was that we didn't use any protection," Katrina says. Many young Christians who end up having sex find themselves sweating out the aftermath this way.

> He didn't wear a condom and I didn't take birth control because neither
> of us was planning for that. I wondered whether or not I was pregnant,
> but then I got my period fairly soon afterwards, so it was OK. But it was
> a really big strain on our relationship. I guess I was upset at him because
> he had told me that we weren't going to do anything, and he was upset
> at himself, and he was kind of distancing himself from me for a while
> because he felt really guilty about what we had done. Then, after a
> while, we talked to each other a lot about it because it was really
> stressing me out, and he told me that he wanted to be there for me no
> matter what happens, so we just reconciled ourselves.

Katrina shrugs her shoulders after this lengthy monologue, takes in a sharp breath, and lets it out with a huff.

Their sex life was over as soon as it began, she says.

"We've decided not to [have sex again] because even without pregnancy, and only having sex once, the repercussions were so strong and both of us felt really, *really* guilty, and it had a bad emotional effect on both of us," she says. "We don't want to go through it again."

Katrina feels that her boyfriend betrayed her, since he promised they wouldn't have sex, and then they did. She also feels that she has betrayed herself. But she's also broken up about something else entirely: she has betrayed God and her entire faith community.

"I willingly engaged in something that for so long I had stood against," she says:

> I gave [my boyfriend] my first kiss, too. I was going to save my first kiss until I was married. I was one of *those* people. It's made me feel guilty and made me feel like I wasn't able to live up to even my own expectations, so I felt kind of, I don't know, dirty and unholy. Like I couldn't reconnect with God because I had separated myself from him with this big sin.

Katrina is not yet ready to go back to church. "I still feel really bad about it when I think about it," she says. But like Cara, she has decided to go through her faith to deal with her sin, rather than around it:

> I try to think about it in light of what is important to me: that God can make me pure again. I can't regain my physical virginity, but he can help me out of this little rut that I've gotten myself into or help me not do it again. And I think even though a person's lost something, like lost something *physically*, if you allow God to purify you again and accept his forgiveness for it then you can still enjoy intimacy with your husband later on as if you were a virgin. Like, it will still be really special to you.

She has also begun confessing to her friends.

"I told my friends about it, and they just constantly kept reminding me that he was forgiving and that he knows everything," Katrina says, making the connection again between "it" (sex) and "he" (Jesus). "He knew that I was going to have sex and that he chose to die on the cross for me anyway and that he loves me anyway. Having that constant reminder really helps, I guess, the healing process because for a while I felt like there was this big barrier between me and God."

The healing process isn't over yet. She faces a long road ahead to purity. It will be difficult, she knows, but she's hopeful. And she is determined to redeem herself.

GAY AND CHRISTIAN? STEVEN PARSONS

When I ask Steven Parsons my standard question about sexual orientation, he hesitates.

"Um," he says with a sigh, looking everywhere but at me.

As I wait for his answer, I take the measure of this young man, a senior at the same evangelical university as Katrina. He is tall and built, with bleached blond hair and blue eyes. He wears a soccer jersey, shorts, and cleats, as if he's about to go play a game right after our interview. As he contemplates my question, fear seems to overtake him.

"Um, heterosexual," he finally answers. There is little conviction in his voice.

I have asked every student to identify her or his sexual orientation toward the beginning of each interview. The question comes in the midst of a battery of additional basic information: undergraduate year, age, major, ethnic background, current religious affiliation (if any), and whether they live on or off campus. Most students have fired off one-word answers. I always explain before I turn on the digital recorder and begin the interview that these initial questions are for gathering basic background data and that they will have plenty of time later in the interview to discuss these matters in depth. I almost never gave in to the temptation to press a student about an answer at this early point in our conversation. Details could come later.

With Steven, I make an exception.

Steven has already given the other demographic data. He is 22, a double major in chemistry and Chinese, living off campus, and white. He is also a Christian, but when he offers "Christian" as his religious affiliation, he quickly adds, "as liberal as possible." I wonder why Steven feels the need to underscore his liberalism, but for the moment I am more interested in pressing him about his indecision on the sexual orientation question.

"Why did you hesitate?" I begin, but Steven knows where I am going and interrupts before I can finish.

"But, well, I'm heterosexual, but I have, I don't think, like," he stammers. "I don't really think I'm homosexual, but I've had some homosexual experiences, but I don't know what to say because, well, anyway, I think I'm heterosexual."

Thus begins what for me was the most difficult interview I conducted. When our conversation turns to relationships, dating, and sex, I stop trying to interject with questions. I mainly listen to Steven talk. I listen because he is *desperate* to talk about his sexuality. Steven has found it impossible to talk openly about sex among friends, family, or faculty. But I am an outsider sworn to keep his anonymity, so Steven feels it is safe to talk to me. Once I open the door to talk about sex, he rushes through.

At first, Steven's answers focus on dating and eventually marrying the perfect Christian girl. But he is hemming and hawing, trying to spit out what he believes are the sorts of answers expected from a good Christian guy like him. But keeps tripping over the fact that he resists dating altogether.

"No. No, I'm not," Steven stutters, when I ask if he is currently involved in any kind of romantic or sexual relationship. "I'm kind of behind in that area," he admits:

> I mean, I've liked girls before and, um, no, no, I mean, well, also it depends on the relationship. . . . In a lot of ways, I don't ever want to be in a relationship. . . . I'd like to get married to my best friend and love her and, and, um, be a good husband, but um, um . . . I've always found, like, I've never been big on casual dating. I'm not against it now, but it'd just be really strange. But, I mean, well, honestly, I'm very inexperienced and that's actually caused me some problems. . . . I don't know how to communicate to girls if I like them. . . . I mean, I'm not perfect. People have to accept that. But, anyway, I've never been in what I would call a good relationship. I've never really had a girlfriend.

When I press Steven about his sexual experience, he admits that he's never kissed a girl and that he finds the idea of sex, even within marriage, to be "disgusting" and "gross."

"I really don't have a positive view of sex and marriage . . . like, almost, you know, if you love your wife, you'd never have sex with her," he says. "It always grossed me out. I didn't like knowing that my parents wanted to do that. . . . Sex is kind of, I mean, if you think about it, [it's] disgusting . . . so I don't value, you know, all the pastors here being like, 'The best sex is in marriage.' And [I'm] like, '*Gross*, I don't want that.'"

When I ask Steven to discuss whether he's ever had any sexual feelings for or experiences with anyone, his attention immediately turns to men, and the words start tumbling out.

"Well, ever since middle school, I thought about having homo-sexual sex, but I, um, I wouldn't," he assures me. He takes a breath before launching into another long soliloquy:

> I always thought it was bad. But I mean, like, the sexual experience[s] I've had are masturbating with people, but that was only a couple [of] times. And I definitely, I mean, I would *never* want to do that again. I think it was wrong, and I felt it was wrong. I think it, the problem, is in my head. . . . But I'm obviously normal as a human being. I mean, I have sexual desires . . . but the homosexual thing, I think, that, um, I don't know. I don't think I'm biologically homosexual. I think it's something that maybe, I don't know what caused it when I was in middle school, but it's just something I messed with. And, um, maybe it's related to my experience [of] trying to ignore my sexuality for most of my life.

Steven is intensely ambivalent about sex and about his sexual ori-entation. He expresses tremendous guilt about the times he has en-gaged in sexual activity by masturbating "with people" (by which he means in front of other boys), but wonders whether perhaps what he did with them wasn't really sexual—that maybe it didn't "count."

"Well, I mean, this is weird, but one time when I did it, like, I never felt that guilty for it," he says, shaking his head as if this mystifies him. "The other times I always felt really guilty. The better I knew the person, the less I felt guilty. Maybe it's because I feel like, since I know him so well, it's not so much I did something with another person. It's just hard to feel so guilty. I admit, I think that I'm messed up."

Steven continues on, one minute repeating that he would like to get married to a girl someday, that he looks forward to this future, and the next returning to the notion that he is really "messed up" sexually. Eventually Steven says that aside from his best friend, I am the first person he has ever told about his feelings for men and his sexual ex-periences with them.

Steven is tortured by his struggle with sex and with his sexual identity. He tells me that "he felt like committing suicide for a week" after his first sexual encounter with another boy, adding, "I couldn't believe I had done that."

Here is a young man who, in all ways but one, is a typical evangelical college student. Had our conversation steered clear of sex talk, I would have pegged him as just that. Steven's parents are missionaries, and during high school he lived in Latin America, where his family still resides and where he goes on breaks. He loves the missionary life. "It was the most profound experience," he says, and until the last couple of years, he has always imagined following this path himself. Steven's family attended services every Sunday while he was growing up, and Steven reminisces about how he was "always good at reading the Bible" and served as "a role model all through grade school and high school" when it came to living the Christian life.

Once Steven left home for college, his idyllic Christian life began to fall apart. Everything he had once taken for granted about church, faith, and God shifted. Like Katrina, Steven now counts himself among the "spiritual but not religious." And, like Katrina, he got there by experimenting with sex. "I've had a lot of, um, challenges to my faith. Like, I don't see God like I used to," Steven says with sadness.

> I used to see God in everything, and now I just see chance. . . . Like I used to always think, "Oh God's telling me this," and "I'm praying to God." And then I thought, "Why am I praying to God if, like, God never talks to me?" [But] I'm not completely satisfied—I mean, convinced that my religion is wrong—because I have lots of friends, and they have these, you know, miracle stories that I can't really deny . . . [and] they're always looking for God, so maybe if you look for miracles, you'll see them. But mostly, just for me personally . . . I'm always reading the Bible, but now when I read the Bible, and I can't understand what it's saying or I find contradictions . . . [and] I still don't see, like, the biblical God being in charge of the world right now like I would expect. And I'm hoping and I'm assuming that there's just something *I* don't understand. That's why I'm going to college here. I'm assuming there's some problem with the logic *I'm* using.

Steven now "disagree[s] with the pastor a lot," and he worries that science and Christianity are incompatible. And because he "doesn't live as if [he] believe[s]" in Christianity anymore, he is reluctant to go to church. When he *does* go to church, he tells me, "I feel like I'm dead." I ask Steven how religious he is now compared with before college. "I think if you define religion as having scheduled activities and community spirituality," he says, hesitating again, and this time hanging his head, "I would be almost *zero*."

When I ask if Steven discusses these shifts in his faith life with his parents, he responds with an emphatic no. They wouldn't "respond well," he says. Steven does talk with college friends about what it means to be a Christian and what the Bible says about this or that, but he does not reveal the depth of his spiritual crisis.

Plainly, Steven believes that homosexual behavior is incompatible with being a good Christian—and he wants to be a good Christian—so his confusion about his sexuality is complicating his struggle with faith. But not everyone I interviewed feels this way.

Christina Marsden, the out lesbian, who gathered supportive faculty and students to help her form a club for sexual minorities (and people questioning their sexuality) on her campus, also identified as "spiritual but not religious." But Christina still maintains a strong connection to her faith and a desire to better understand how to be a good Christian as she identifies as lesbian. She is determined to make sense of her situation *within* her community as opposed to going it alone.

Then there is Molly Bainbridge, the woman who is both deeply Christian, a member of Heretics Anonymous, and who identified as bisexual—though she is still pretty confused about what that really means in practice. Molly believes it is important to be open, comfortable, and affirming about being a "sexual being." Yet she isn't out about her bisexuality.

"I'm not out here because quite frankly I'd rather people see me as just Molly instead of as bisexual Molly," she says emphatically. She's confident that her friends, "especially in theater," would be "incredibly open" if she decided to tell them:

> It's not something that I feel compelled to tell people because it's something I'm still not sure about. . . . In some ways, I am attracted to women; in some ways, I'm attracted to men. And it's kind of all soupy and amorphous. I'm pretty sure I'm more attracted to men because it happens more often, but I don't know because I've never had an experience with a woman.

Molly has felt her share of guilt and separation from God when dating guys, and she believes that, like most of her Christian friends, she will marry a man eventually. Nonetheless, she is confident that *all* relationships—romantic or otherwise, with men or with women—bring a person closer to God in at least some small way. "I think when you get closer to other people, I think you get closer to God too," she tells me. "I don't mean to say that a way to get closer to God is by making out with your boyfriend, but things that bind you closer to other people start to transfer over—other people are how I see God, so it's all connected."

As for the dating advice she has received from pastors and in youth groups, she doesn't think much about it because she doesn't date much, though she does note, after a moment of thought and a squint, pushing her glasses higher on her nose: "It was *always* about members of the opposite sex."

Molly and other gay, lesbian, and bisexual students at evangelical colleges found it impossible to talk about their religious identities without also talking about their sexual identities. They may wish they could simply separate, even divorce, sex from religion as easily as do their peers, straight or otherwise, at the spiritual colleges—but they can't. Like virtually every other evangelical student I interviewed, these students' sex lives and religious identities are inextricably intertwined—but in a way that is more fraught and even more frightening to them than for their heterosexual peers.

SEXUALLY ACTIVE, SPIRITUALLY THRIVING: BROOK LILLITH

Brook Lillith is tall and willowy, a graceful young woman with black hair that reaches all the way to her waist, a melodious voice and a ready laugh. She is covered in silver jewelry: bracelets, rings, and a necklace with all sorts of colorful stones. When I ask her about them, she explains that she is Native American and that the jewelry is traditional.

In terms of her religious faith, Brook has come into her own during her time at college. Although most of her evangelical peers have stuck to the same worship style that they had in high school, Brook is an experimenter who is thrilled and astounded by the varieties of Christianity to which she has been exposed in college. Every chance she gets, Brook tries out a new church with a friend, just to see what it's like. She has something of a home church, but she also goes to Pentecostal churches because, she says, she likes to see "people getting a little bit more riled up in worship." Brook has gone to Catholic services, with their "much more subdued reciting and stand-up, sit-down routines," and feels comfortable there, too.

Brook is exuberant about her faith.

"When I was growing up, I didn't really need my faith. It was kind of just how my family lived," says Brook, who now is 21. But she's not interested in talking about growing up Christian—the typical weekly services, youth group, and Bible study. She wants to discuss *her* Christianity in the here and now. It's a challenge, she tells me, to be "stripped of all the familiar things I had taken comfort in. . . . I needed my own tradition, apart from what my parents told me and my grandparents did," and she has found that in college. "So, if you want to talk about my spiritual life," she continues:

I'd say 80% of it has been in [college]. Only in the last four years have I lived such experiences that have made me adjust and have a faith that I can say is really me and what I believe and what I accept and what I value and what I want to live by. The last four years have just been huge in shaping my spiritual personality.

To Brook, college has not been about preparing for a career or finding a husband. It has been about learning to be a good Christian—her own sort of Christian. For Brook, that means putting God first in whatever line of work you find yourself—ahead of money and even ahead of nation.

"Whatever you are doing, wherever you are, [you are] working for God and not for worldly pursuits and not for yourself," Brook says with passion. "Even if you are a doctor or a physical therapist or a history teacher, you are doing those things with your faith at the front end of things and *not* because you want to make a lot of money and *not* because you want to make a difference in this country." According to Brook, faculty members at her school are not there only to teach in their particular areas of expertise. Faculty members "most value" their "students being able to experience God in a meaningful way and to incorporate whatever they are learning here, in the classrooms or in the dorms, into Christian work."

Like many of her evangelical peers, Brook has traveled all over the world on mission trips. She has been to Africa, Asia, and South America during her summers and on a semester abroad. At school, she hangs out with the international crowd. She loves getting to know people who grew up in other countries and in different cultures.

Brook and her friends are inseparable, and they regularly hold "accountability circles," gatherings in which they talk about their faith, pray together, and encourage each other in their respective Christian walks. Sometimes, they drink and dance, too. Brook is one of only a couple of evangelical students who acknowledges partying occasionally, and she doesn't seem to see this as an admission. Unlike her peers, she doesn't worry about whether it is "sinful" to drink now and then. Brook and her friends also seem untouched by the "senior scramble" to find a husband. Though she is a senior, she isn't vexed about being single. In fact, she laughs about all the scrambling on campus.

Brook met her current boyfriend—he's from Nigeria—through the international crowd. They had sex after dating for three months. For a student at an evangelical school, Brook is fairly experienced sexually.

She's had oral sex and vaginal sex and been sexually active with three different boys, all during college, while her faith has been soaring. Her first sexual partner was a boyfriend of a year and a half. They had oral sex only, and even that made them "feel bad," she says. "We'd say we want to be more pure in our relationship."

Brook has hooked up a couple of times, too. Once, she just kissed the guy, and another time she had sex. She said hooking up made her feel "cheap," but she chalks it up as a learning experience and seems past worrying about it now. Brook's current relationship didn't start on typical evangelical college terms, either. Their relationship quickly got intense both emotionally and physically, in part because they had known each other a long time before getting together. They hadn't had the typical talk to determine the relationship, either. She felt they didn't need one; their commitment to each other was understood.

Brook has had ups and downs in her sex life, but her current relationship is very fulfilling on many levels, including sexually, which is why it's hard to stop having sex. "The guy that I'm with now I'm so in love with, it's something that you want to express, so that's made it difficult" to *not* have sex anymore, something she and her boyfriend are contemplating.

> I had planned on staying a virgin until I was married, before I had ever had a boyfriend. Once I was in a relationship, I felt like "Oh, I want to express myself sexually to this person and I'm OK with that," and so my view changed. . . . I didn't plan for the relationship that I'm in now to involve sex and it has. I feel like the relationship is healthier if we don't have sex just because we can focus on other things, and I feel like I can be a lot stronger spiritually and in my faith if I'm not having sex with him.

Brook and her boyfriend are both very religious, but religion is not something that has been a central part of their relationship so far. The first and only time they have gone to church together was the day before our interview. Brook is aware that, given the sexual ethic on campus, she "wouldn't be thought of as very pure." And she does feel a certain "spiritual distance" from God due to her sexual activity, but she exhibits little of the anxiety demonstrated by Katrina Tan. Brook is the only evangelical student I interviewed who is both sexually active and spiritually thriving at the same time. Moreover, she is the only such student who spoke of sex as sacred not simply within marriage but inside a *committed, loving* relationship.

"I think God created sex, for it's a great expression of love," she explains.

I think it's something that God did mean for people who are committed to each other and who do love each other. And when that is pure, it's a very spiritual or sacred thing. . . . I think that my religion and faith are saying the right things about sex. I think it's unhealthy that you engage in sex before you are with the person that you are going to be with for the rest of your life—but I don't think people are very open about why that is.

Brook wishes someone had told her when she was growing up that sex is great when it is within a loving relationship and that it makes a person feel wonderful—not cheap at all. But she learned all this through experience instead. Although Brook feels some anxiety about the sexual dimension of her current relationship—enough that she contemplates reining it in—what is important about her story is that her decision to remain sexually active has not put the brakes on her ardent pursuit of a good Christian life. On the contrary, Brook's spiritual life is, she says, at an all-time high.

NINE

Dividing Sex from the Soul

Why Religion Doesn't Matter
When It Comes to Sex

I think people should understand that sex happens, basically.

—student at a Catholic college

WHY CATHOLIC TEACHINGS ABOUT SEX
ARE SO MYSTERIOUS

Unlike evangelical students, whose concerns about sex are inextricably connected to their religious tradition and spiritual identity, most students at the spiritual colleges keep sex and religion separate. Religion is a concern, yes, but it is often a superficial one. Students are confused about how to relate sex and the soul—in their campus communities religion is a private affair and in their religious communities (if they still have one) sex is a private affair. So religious views about sex go unexamined. When prompted, some students can call upon a very limited repertoire of religious knowledge regarding sex. Religious teachings about sex may even tug at them vaguely in the form of guilt. But the pressures and stress related to sex that many students face have little or nothing to do with religious identity and everything to do with hookup culture.

Even Maria Angelo, the poster girl for the ideal first time, who is in love with and committed to her boyfriend and has mutually pleasurable sex with him, feels uncomfortable sharing her faith in the context of their relationship. Her own beliefs are different from her boyfriend's, she explains. She is Catholic, and he is an atheist. Among evangelical students, this sort of mixing in a relationship is rare, and for many it is a deal-breaker if a potential boyfriend or girlfriend turns out not to be a Christian or not an evangelical Christian. But Maria and her boyfriend didn't even discuss faith commitments until well into their relationship, after they started having sex.

"Well, he didn't tell me for a while, but he doesn't believe in God, and it's very weird for me," Maria says. She hopes he's changing his mind about God, but she doesn't pressure him; it's a personal decision he needs to make, she says. It isn't her place to intrude. Sometimes he teases her about her religious beliefs, but she tries not to take it personally. "He'll, like, make fun of me, kidding, like saying, 'You are such a Jesus freak, you go to church all the time.' I know he is just kidding. He definitely has his set beliefs and I have my set beliefs, and they don't always come together." Maria also knows that, because she is Catholic and unmarried, she's not supposed to be having sex, but she isn't sure *how* she knows this. "It was almost just a known thing," she says, as if prohibitions about premarital sex are a form of innate knowledge. Maria doesn't really know what young Catholics are supposed to do about dating, however, though she does remember "watching videos in high school religion class—they would say you can go on dates, you can have a boyfriend, but you can't do anything below the waist. That was the rule they taught us," she recalls.

Another young woman, an Episcopalian from Maria's Catholic college, tells me that she isn't sure why she feels this way, but she is pretty sure that Episcopalians are more accepting about sex than Catholics. No one taught her this explicitly, or even taught her anything about sex from an Episcopalian perspective, but she is confident that if "you consider yourself a *real Catholic* then [sex is] not acceptable."

When I press her to think about where she got this view, she can't quite put her finger on it. "I know I must have gotten it from somewhere," she says, trying hard to remember. "I think it came out of my youth group in some sense," she says, pausing again. Sex as a topic in general "was sort of brushed over," she adds, so all talk about religion in relation to sex is pretty fuzzy for her.

"I think a lot of it is osmosis," says one young woman at this same Catholic college, laughing loudly about how Catholic teachings about sex were glossed over when she was growing up. Her decision to have sex with a boyfriend had more to do with curiosity than anything else, and maybe a little rebellion. She just "wanted to do [her] own thing," and she was in love with her boyfriend and never found any real "reason not to do it." Sex is "spiritual," she explains, if it's about love and connection, because it involves "bringing two bodies and spirits together." But once you bring Catholicism into the picture, sex suddenly becomes about rules and shame. "Even in marriage you are not even supposed to have sex except for reproduction purposes," she says, rolling her eyes, as she explains how *she* understands (or doesn't really) Catholic teachings about sex, as if this is the most ridiculous idea she's ever heard.

Both Catholic and mainline Protestant students tended to perk up when our discussions turned to what their religious or spiritual traditions teach about sex, love, and romance, though not in the way one might imagine. In interview after interview, students laughed out loud when asked what their faith tradition might have to say about these matters. They laughed at the idea that their faith had anything to say about sex—especially to gays—other than not to have it. They laughed because they see religious views about sexuality (at least what they know of them, which is typically not very much) as outdated and irrelevant. And they laughed because they were confused about the prospect of their faith having anything useful to say about these things.

When I asked Catholics in particular what their church says about dating and romance, many told me that the Catholic teaching is that sex is for the purposes of having children only. "My perception is that sex is something reserved strictly for procreation and that would be basically about it," says a young man, scornful about how impractical this teaching is for unmarried young adults who are hooking up, having sex, and in some cases involved in long-term, loving relationships.

Of everyone, the Catholics laughed the most, or if they didn't laugh, they looked at me quizzically when I inquired what they learned from their faith tradition about sex and dating. Common responses included the following:

- The Catholic Church's strict prohibitions on sex and birth control are outdated, archaic.
- Saving sex for marriage and procreation only are unrealistic expectations.

- There is no practical relevance for the Catholic Church's teachings about sex even if you are married, but if you are unmarried, these teachings are particularly irrelevant.

Some students had no response at all when I asked whether they were taught anything about dating and romance in the context of their faith, or even about sex. They simply volleyed the question back to me, curious about the possibility that the Catholic Church might actually have something to say about these matters but having no idea what it could be.

THE COMMUNICATION GAP BETWEEN CATHOLIC YOUTH AND CATHOLIC TEACHING

Not one student with a Catholic background mentioned a single Vatican document, such as the 1968 *Humanae Vitae*[1] encyclical by Pope Paul VI on birth control, or the more recent *Familiaris Consortio*[2] encyclical about marriage and family from Pope John Paul II. Students were equally unfamiliar with Thomas Aquinas's classic theological reflections on sex in his *Summa Theologica*,[3] or even so-called popular books such as *The Good News about Sex and Marriage* by Christopher West, a conservative Catholic who travels the country giving lectures about Catholic sexual morality.[4]

One Catholic analogue to the evangelical sex manual, *God's Plan for You: Life, Love, Marriage, and Sex (The Theology of the Body for Young People)*[5] by David Hajduk, is written expressly for a young adult audience, but it avoids the topic of dating altogether. There is a lengthy discussion, however, of sexual sin and the joys of married sex under very particular circumstances. A "Did U Know?" sidebar conveys the following information: "Biologically, sexual intercourse (coitus) refers to the joining of the male and female sexual organs. It implies sexual difference. That's why it is technically impossible for homosexuals to have sexual intercourse."[6] Although evangelical college students have quite a battle ahead of them *prior* to marriage, they do occasionally discuss the wild sex lives they expect to have (and are promised they *will* have) once they make it to the altar. Catholics, on the other hand, must circumscribe the types of sex they have. In *God's Plan for You*, any orgasm that occurs outside of intercourse is sinful:

> Masturbation has no place in God's plan for our sexuality.... [S]exual acts that prepare the spouses' bodies for intercourse and are intended

to sexually stimulate them—commonly called foreplay—cannot be separated from sexual union. Spouses who engage in such acts apart from or in place of sexual union use one another exclusively for individual sexual pleasure and purposely choose not to become "one body." They intentionally make the gift of sex a "partial gift," in effect saying, "You can have 'all' of me, except my fertility." ... *Marital sex is willingly fruitful.* In order to be marital sex it must be *willingly fruitful.* That is, the spouses must always remain open to becoming parents and never do anything that *directly and intentionally causes* any sexual union to be infertile. This would include sexual acts that are brought to climax apart from sexual union.[7]

In other words, no orgasms outside of intercourse. Men must never "spill their seed" outside a woman's body. And, women, no orgasms just for fun because this dishonors God and your duty to procreate—at least as Hajduk interprets Catholic sexual teaching.

Theologian Luke Timothy Johnson regards Catholicism's official teachings about sex as "severe and consistent," and praises them as prophetic insofar as they run against the grain of what he regards as an oversexed contemporary America. The problem for Johnson is not the teachings themselves, but the way the Catholic Church has failed to communicate them to ordinary Catholics: "The 'reception' of Catholic sexual teaching by Catholics themselves—both clergy and lay—is an essential ingredient of that teaching. Only to the degree that moral teaching is expressed by the attitudes and actions of Catholics themselves can it challenge anyone."[8] Johnson recognizes that the Catholic who not only knows but strictly follows these sexual teachings is part of an endangered species and calls on church leaders to invite married Catholics and all women to better discern how to communicate this ethic. But, like most Catholic theologians, he does not address the unmarried.

This neglect is typical. Somehow, the messiness of sex between the onset of puberty and the moment of marriage gets overlooked whenever Catholics talk about sex. The most promising, cutting-edge intellectual work in Catholic sexual ethics—the kind that doesn't avoid the toughest issues and which I believe has the potential to reach young adults—is found among the writing of three prominent scholars. The first is Lisa Sowle Cahill, who has written widely on feminist sexual ethics, publishing many articles and books (especially in the 1990s) that are widely read in academic circles including *Sex, Gender, and Christian Ethics.*[9] But the second two, James Keenan, whose articles "Can

We Talk? Theological Ethics and Sexuality" and "Virtue Ethics and Sexual Ethics," present an alternative, virtue ethics approach to Catholic sexuality, and Margaret Farley, whose magnum opus *Just Love: A Framework for Christian Sexual Ethics* reframes sexual ethics through the lens of justice, have shown an interest in reaching out to Catholic youth about sex.[10] Farley even includes a section (albeit a very brief one) about young adults.[11] Who will bring this scholarship directly to Catholic youth and in a popular accessible form remains to be seen.

There *is* evidence that some Catholic youth do care what their tradition teaches about sex. In *The New Faithful: Why Young Adults Are Embracing Christian Orthodoxy*, Colleen Carroll shares evidence that young people both enthralled by and committed to Catholic teachings about sex and celibacy do exist.[12] And in the chapter on Catholic teens in *Soul Searching*, Christian Smith speaks of finding "girls exhilarated by the idea that they might actually take charge of their romantic relationships and may not have to barter their bodies simply to get boys' attention," and guys who "seemed compelled [at a Catholic youth conference] by the evidently novel idea of living lives of romantic and sexual purity, integrity, and self-discipline."[13] Yet, in the very next paragraph, Smith explains how these are the exceptions among young Catholics.

I have occasionally met young people who practice "Catholic orthodoxy" when it comes to sex, but I didn't interview a single college student who fit this description. The average Catholic student I interviewed was either clueless about Catholicism's teachings about sex or didn't care. Whatever Catholic sexual ethics these students have acquired, they acquired by osmosis. "Somewhere along the line I got the notion that premarital sex is bad," one young Catholic woman tells me. "I don't know if that was from my parents or church. I think you can, I think you can have a pretty powerful make-out session just like kissing and holding each other close," but that's as far as it goes.

"So the Catholic church is OK with kissing?" I press her.

"Yes," she confirms. "But everything else is *not* OK."

FLYING BLIND: THE SPIRITUAL BUT NOT RELIGIOUS

Alyssa Ryan grew up Catholic but now considers herself "spiritual but not religious." When it comes to figuring out what to do about sex, dating, and romance, she is pretty much on her own. Now that she is finally out of her parents' house, she has stopped going to church, which also means she has stopped being religious since, according to Alyssa, being religious means going to church *and* loving it. She's not really into "church stuff" anymore, she tells me, though her parents think she still is because she goes to mass when she is home. She doesn't find God in church. She doesn't know why. She does find God when she's hiking, though, or sitting by herself in silence, or painting, or listening to music.

Talkative, friendly, and polite, Alyssa chats enthusiastically about religion and any other topic I raise. She says she has been "reassessing her priorities" throughout her first year of college, and when I ask which ones, she tells me she's reevaluating "basically everything in her life"—religion, family, career, what matters and what doesn't. Relationships, too, of course. Alyssa says she feels "incredible pressure" to hook up. It's the number one window into the social scene, she says, adding that she envies juniors and seniors who "get to be more grounded" because they have already gotten through this particular social hazing process.

Hooking up is part of a broader process of sexual experimentation, which in Alyssa's view is part and parcel of the Catholic college experience. "We're all grouped together in one big atmosphere where there are no rules and no parents and no nothing," she explains. "So, I mean, there are school rules, but no one telling you, 'You can't do that. You've got to get home now.' You know what I'm saying? It seems like you're free."

Among the things that Alyssa felt free to do was to hook up with a boy she met a few weeks ago at a party. They were drinking. They hooked up (but they didn't have sex; she's a virgin). This is not her ideal entrée into a relationship or whatever it is that she and he are doing. Alyssa is not sure what to call it, but it's definitely "spiritual," she tells me.

"It's very complicated," she says, bubbling over with excitement about this budding something or other:

> We just have a connection. I don't even know how to describe it, but it felt right and natural to like him, and he likes me, and I just never found a guy like that. I was feeling lost about everything, and he was feeling the same way, but we didn't know it at the time. Something clicked. I don't even know how to describe it. I just felt like we met for a reason. There's a reason we met.

She echoes herself, as if she is just now realizing how significant this new "connection" is. "And it's weird that he can, like, read me, and

I can read him, and we're, like, opposites, but we're the same. It's like, I've been looking for a counterpart to myself and it's him, and he said the same of me. I don't know what we are right now," she adds, "but it's not going out or a relationship."

Things in this nonrelationship have gotten pretty intense—both emotionally and physically—quickly, but the connection is not about the physical side of things, she says. "I know he's not purposely trying to say nice things to me just to do sex stuff. . . . It's not about physical attraction. It's more that we're knowing each other for ourselves first, not for physical things. . . . It's something bigger than I can explain. I think I would call it something spiritual."

This spiritual something is new for Alyssa. In other relationships, she reports, she's never truly been appreciated by the other person. Alyssa is not yet ready for sex, however. It might be in the cards for them, but she's not sure. She doesn't want to "ruin" the relationship and "destroy something" that is going well—a fear expressed by many women I interviewed, that having sex can ruin things, at least from their point of view. Somewhere inside, Alyssa has misgivings about being sexually active, but she is not sure why. According to Alyssa, you have sex "when you find someone you truly, truly love and they feel exactly the same way." Sometimes, she wonders why she's still a virgin, and she chalks up some of her hesitancy "probably to some of my upbringing."

Catholicism has nothing to do with why Alyssa is waiting, however, at least not in her eyes. "If the church is like, 'Don't have sex,' I mean, just because the church says don't have sex isn't gonna stop me," she says. Alyssa thinks the decision to have sex or not is all about personal preference. As for what else the Catholic Church has to say about sex, Alyssa isn't quite sure: "I think all [the church] accept[s] is kissing, if I'm not mistaken. Yeah, I think they just accept kissing. That's it."

When I ask what she learned from Catholicism about dating, her answer is succinct: "If you're gay, you can't." End of story.

But Alyssa has cobbled together her own understanding of what spirituality may have to with her current romantic situation. In the case of the new guy in her life, this means attaching words like "spiritual" to their "connection" and convincing herself—not exactly that *God* brought them together, but that they "met for a reason." They were both "lost" before they "found" each other, she says, using classic religious language to describe their coming together, though Alyssa doesn't seem aware of this.

Turning from Catholicism to a more amorphous sense of spirituality is helping Alyssa begin to frame and put into words—if not quite to navigate and understand—a romantic relationship that she finds very significant yet confusing, a relationship that already exceeds the boundaries of what she thinks Catholicism allows in terms of sexual activity. Like so many other young adults I interviewed, Alyssa is unknowingly experiencing a wedge being driven between herself and her religion in large part because her religion seems to have nothing relevant to say about dating and romance.

So Alyssa, too, is left to make it up as she goes along.

DIFFERENCES BETWEEN CATHOLICS AND MAINLINE PROTESTANTS AT THE SPIRITUAL COLLEGES

Catholics are not the only college students confused about what their religious tradition has to say about sex. Sandra Popovitch is a first-year student at a Catholic college who self-identifies as Presbyterian and says she's "both spiritual and religious." Her story shows a difference between growing up Catholic and growing up mainline Protestant when it comes to what you are taught (or not) about dating and sex.

Sandra had an extensive church education on dating and sex, including the kinds of in-depth conversations common among evangelical students. In her youth group, Sandra was given a variety of books to read about guarding her purity and dating, which she and her friends and their youth group leaders then discussed. She was taught to save herself for marriage and to date other Christians. She learned what the Bible says about sexual behaviors (the Catholics I interviewed *never* mentioned the Bible) and took an abstinence pledge when she was in middle school.

Sandra has kept this pledge. Sort of. She's never had "*sex* sex," as she describes it—she plans to be a virgin until she gets married. But she has performed oral sex—something she really regrets—on three partners.

"I know that sounds hypocritical, . . . but I was thinking that it wasn't as big of a deal," she says about claiming she's still a virgin despite engaging in fellatio. "But it's not like I can take it back now. I think it was stupid."

Sandra says it's hard not to end up in these situations when you are part of the party culture and everyone around you is hooking up and being so casual about sex. Besides, "now people are getting married at, like, 25 or 26 so now you have to wait that much longer before" having sex, assuming you want to play by the no-sex-until-marriage rules. Sandra and her first boyfriend, the first guy on whom she performed oral sex, shared their faith and certain values—not drinking, swearing, or partying—which she says had a positive effect on their relationship, even though they "went further" sexually than they had planned. Sandra even holds out hope that "maybe he's the one" she'll marry some day. But she hooked up with the last couple of guys "more out of pressure by friends," and she "did not enjoy that." Still, Sandra is confident that she has God's forgiveness for these activities because she's genuinely sorry for them, although she finds it really hard to stop the behavior once you have tried it.

"I'm not proud of it," she says, but she has spoken about it inside her church community. "When I told my [youth group] leader she did not see me any differently," Sandra reports. "I mean, everyone knows that it's hard to be a teenager, and it happens to everyone. She was just really glad I didn't have intercourse, like, go all the way too."

To help Sandra think about what she wants out of a dating relationship, the youth group leader had her make a list of "everything she wanted her husband to have." Hers has 15 things on it. Sandra's not sure if her first boyfriend, the one she still thinks about, fits the bill—he might—or if her husband will turn out to be someone else, though she trusts that she will find somebody with these 15 qualities. "If you want all those things, then God has someone for you," she says. "You just have to wait, and eventually you'll find them."

The difficulty of living up to religious values about sex while attending a spiritual college was evident among those students I interviewed who were committed to their faith. At evangelical colleges, students of faith feel pressure from their peers *not* to have sex. At the spiritual colleges, students feel pressure to have *more* sex.

Chris Chang, a student at a nonreligious private university, tells me how it is difficult both to make time for his faith in a community that doesn't prioritize or even think much about religion and to hold fast to values about sex that counter the predominant culture on campus. Chris is doing his best, but he sometimes feels as if he and his girlfriend are up against the world. A 20-year-old junior, Chris dresses and talks the part of an aspiring Wall Street banker. Like other business students I meet, his manner is impeccable and formal, and his answers professional and reserved. His cool demeanor is belied by a glimmer of emotion when I ask about his sexual history. He's had sex before, but he's not proud of it. Chris says:

> It was a high school relationship in which I felt that both my partner and I were very young and naïve at the time. . . . Things fell into place

where we experimented sexually, and it became something that I felt diminished our relationship. Eventually, we separated because our perceptions of each other changed because of the sexual activity. It was a decision motivated by lust and attraction.

Chris's high school girlfriend wasn't just anybody: she was the leader of the church youth group Chris attended *and* the minister's daughter. She was also his reason for attending services and youth activities in the first place. Chris's family isn't religious at all and didn't raise him in any one tradition, though during our interview he identifies himself as Presbyterian. He didn't start participating in church activities until his junior year of high school, when he started dating this woman. Though this high school relationship ended badly and his church involvement faltered as a result, since arriving at his university, Chris has attended services every Sunday. At college, as in high school, he has found a girlfriend whose faith commitments remind him how important faith is within his own life—she is helping him to stay on track. Chris is determined not to make the same mistake twice: this time, he's not having sex with this girlfriend until they are married. Period. He doesn't want to "harm" this girlfriend like he did the other, or harm himself in the process.

The way that Chris connects waiting for sex to religious well-being is rare at private schools. When it comes to this kind of chastity vow, Chris and his girlfriend have each other for support, but that's about all.

LIVING A DOUBLE LIFE, PART CHRISTIAN, PART SECULAR: KYLIE DAVID

At the spiritual colleges, not all religiously committed students are at odds with their peers when it comes to religion. And not all are at odds with the dominant campus atmosphere when it comes to sex, either. One student I met moved rather seamlessly between her identity as an evangelical Christian and her identity as a full-fledged participant in the student culture of her nonreligious private university.

Kylie David finds refuge in her school's chapter of InterVarsity Christian Fellowship.[14] Kylie grew up Lutheran, but she never really took to this tradition. She describes herself as a Christian of the non-denominational variety. Now 19, this smart, friendly sophomore didn't want to attend a religiously affiliated school because the church she grew up in was "really conservative," and she wanted to experience diversity. During her first year of college, she met some people from InterVarsity and they helped her change her mind about religion. But not about sex.

Shortly after arriving at college, Kylie says she became more "open-minded in [her] opinions about religion"—exploring various religious traditions through religious studies courses, talking to people of different faiths, and settling on one that felt right to her. She became more sexually active, too. Kylie keeps these two dimensions of her college experience separate from one another. It's just easier that way, she thinks.

On the InterVarsity side of things, Kylie has found a wonderful subculture that feeds her spiritual hunger and introduces her to like-minded Christians who are also fun to hang out with. She is part of a Bible study group that gets together once a week, and she goes to general chapter meetings every Monday and Friday. InterVarsity meets her need to talk about faith and religion with friends—something that isn't easy to find at her school. "I love talking to people about my current faith walk and all the questions that I have," she writes in her journal. "I get a lot of pleasure about learning what others think. I love that it is such a big part of my life right now." Being a part of Inter-Varsity also keeps Kylie out of the party scene, because of the Friday night meetings. It doesn't keep her from having sex.

Kylie has had sex with a handful of people—the first time with a high school boyfriend of three years. He pressured her and pressured her, and finally she gave in, deciding she "just didn't agree with having to wait until marriage." She doesn't regret it, though, because she loved him, and they still have feelings for each other. "I am happy that my first time could be with someone that I had been with for a long time and [who] was a big part of my life," she says.

The rest of Kylie's encounters have been during college. One was a one-night stand—a hookup with a random guy she met in one of the residence halls. The next day, she felt awful about it. "I regretted it, I guess, because I didn't want to get a reputation," Kylie says.

Kylie has been dating her current boyfriend for over a year. When I ask if she met him through InterVarsity, she says, "He is a Christian, but he is not very religious." After they started dating, he went with her to church a few times and even joined her at InterVarsity meetings once or twice, but that stopped after a while. She doesn't mind that religion isn't something they share. Sex, however, is "a big part" of their relationship and a positive part too. It brings them emotionally closer, though Kylie can't say that she has ever experienced sex as in any way sacred or spiritual.

Being sexually active sets Kylie apart from her InterVarsity friends, so she maintains a "don't-tell policy" with them when it comes to sex. "They know that we are dating," she says. "I think many people wish that I would be dating a [more active] Christian . . . but I don't really have a problem not having it be that way. I certainly don't talk about the sexual aspect of my relationship with those people." She doesn't do so because she knows they will disapprove.

"A lot of my friends who are in InterVarsity recognize that the first time they are going to have sex is going to be on the day of their marriage," she explains. "They see [sex] as spiritual because it [is] this agreement that they have with God and with this other person that they are going to be sharing themselves with." Kylie doesn't share this view, though, and when it comes to the relationship between sex and Christianity, Kylie is a bit rebellious. "I started to question a lot of the teachings from my church specifically about sexual impurity including sex before marriage and homosexuality," she writes in her journal.

> [Sex] feels like another way to express my love and affection. It seemed odd that we would do all other intimate acts besides the actual act of intercourse because of a line in the Bible. I decided that it was acceptable to express affection with the one I was with, and if that included sex, then that was alright.

Unlike so many of the other committed Christian students I interview, Kylie doesn't believe that having sex hurts her relationship with God. God and Kylie get along just fine, sex or no, perhaps because Kylie has decided to view religion and sex as separate spheres—to bracket religious teachings from her sexual life. Kylie thinks that her InterVarsity friends would have a really tough time navigating their faith life if they started having sex "because of their very strong beliefs about it." It's not that they don't struggle about sex at all, though:

> I initially thought that people didn't have any desires, but then I started to realize they actually did. . . . I mean, I don't think people struggle so much with having sex, because I feel it's very ingrained that they shouldn't do that, but with boundaries of kissing and then oral sex and touching, I think people struggle with what is acceptable in that spectrum.

Kylie is yet another student who is unable to disclose her sexual self to her religious community, this time, an InterVarsity group which is unable to talk openly about sex. Kylie picks and chooses very carefully what she tells her friends at InterVarsity about her life. She and her boyfriend may share everything else and see each other regularly, but Kylie is careful to separate her boyfriend from her religious community. It is as if she is living a double life. It seems that, even within evangelical subcultures at the spiritual colleges, secrecy and duplicity about sex are common.

CONCLUSIONS AND PRACTICAL IMPLICATIONS

I don't believe in God, but I feel like it [sex] can have an effect on your spiritual or religious life.... Like, you're torn between the social pressures of having sex and... the [religious] pressure to not have sex. I feel like it can... sever anyone's connection to a religion because they don't know which way to go. They don't know which is the lesser of the two evils.

—student at a nonreligious private university

TEN

Seeking a Sexy Spirituality
for Students on Campus

WASH ME WHITER THAN THE SNOW

It's a beautiful afternoon. The sun is shining in a cloudless sky and the air smells of spring, with green buds poking through what was wintry ground just weeks ago. As I walk across the evangelical college campus to attend Thursday afternoon chapel, it seems as if half the student population is walking there, too. I see Cara Walker with a friend. Cal Saunders and a young woman who must be his girlfriend are chatting as they move with the flow of everyone around them. Bodies are streaming into the church from all directions, some students alone, some in pairs and groups. Chatting. Laughing. Smiling at me, the newcomer, if they happen to catch my eye.

I am relieved to be outside after spending days in the interview room. It's my last afternoon here, and I'm looking forward to this weekly event that so many students suggested I attend. This would be a really good one, they assured me. Lauren Winner is the guest speaker, and she'll be talking about *Real Sex*, one of her most popular books.

Music greets us as we walk in the door. Two young men are on the stage, singing their hearts out, playing guitars. As we file into the pews, the singing grows stronger as more students join in. The lyrics scroll across a huge screen by the stage. I look around me—some students are swaying, some have their eyes closed, taken by the melody. Most smile and raise their voices until the entire room is filled with song. That's when I begin to pay attention to the words:

> I am evil, born in sin;
> Thou desirest truth within.
> Thou alone my Savior art,
> Teach thy wisdom to my heart;
> Make me pure, thy grace bestow,
> Wash me whiter than the snow.

I am evil. Make me pure. Wash me whiter than the snow. I am startled by these lyrics, even though by now I probably shouldn't be, even though I know they are inspired by one of the Psalms, 51:7. As I read along, taking in many more lines about sin and purity, I wonder if the musical selection was chosen intentionally to coincide with my presence on campus and the lecture Lauren Winner is about to give. Is this a not-so-subtle call to purity in the face of all this sex talk? Or is such a song typical of weekly chapel meetings, a reminder of what the average evangelical college student faces on a regular basis?

All week, I've heard students express angst about sex, about even talking about sex, about being honest about their sexual pasts, about the extraordinary pressures everyone feels to be "whiter than the snow," about the fear that someone, everyone, might find out about any blemishes or impurities, about the suspicions that others harbor sexual secrets too. In this light, the song seems a perfect choice. It is part and parcel of the culture about which students have just spent days telling me—and not only its words, but also the gusto with which the students around me are belting them out.

A few minutes later, Winner begins speaking, taking everyone far, far away from purity talk. The students listen with rapt attention. She loosens the vise a bit, challenging her audience to ask why so many Christians understand sexual sin as the worst of all sins, and underscoring the point that, despite what they usually hear, women are sexual beings too, and not all men are sexual predators.

Looking back, I see this chapel experience as indicative of the evangelical colleges I visited, their students' attitudes about sex and the soul, and the complex and powerful campus culture they have created. One minute, they are singing a beautiful melody whose words argue that they are by nature, evil and sinful, and they must purify themselves for Christ, and the next they are hearing a frank talk that challenges this view. All this while sitting in the college chapel amid their peers, plus half the faculty, members of the administration, and the university's president.

This community does not shy away from contradiction, from encountering the messiness of their faith in light of human sexuality. This sort of explicit, on-campus, school-sponsored effort to marry sex and the soul, any such effort in fact, would rarely happen at a spiritual college. I can't help but wonder whether the above scenario, however imperfect, is healthier for students struggling with questions about faith and sex than the alternative, which is not to engage a community holistically on such subjects, or even at all.

As I have noted throughout, the great divide in American higher education is not between religious and secular schools, but between evangelical colleges and everyone else. When it comes to sex and religion, Catholic schools are little different from public and private ones. Many parents surely imagine that sending their children to a Catholic school implies that they will be educated within a Catholic community. But unless the college of choice is an institution well known for its orthodoxy, this is likely not the case. What matters most to either faith maturation or spiritual seeking at college is not so much whether an institution has a religious affiliation but whether it has a religious campus culture—one that is meaningfully integrated into campus life and therefore feels and acts like a powerful presence. Catholic colleges should have this edge, and some of their students do benefit from the ways a Catholic affiliation can influence the college experience. But for the most part, these schools are Catholic only nominally, relegating religion to the margins of the campus experience.

What fosters hookup culture at the spiritual colleges is not student culture alone. Hookup culture is aided and abetted by all sorts of additional factors: administrators turning a blind eye, parents who don't know and perhaps don't want to know what their kids are really doing, the ongoing marginalization and trivialization of feminism by younger women and men, and a society that still treats men as if they are gods and women as objects for male sexual pleasure and enjoyment.

All of this raises the question: How far should a university go in addressing students on romance and sex? Does it have any such responsibility at all? Surely, administrators and student affairs professionals at spiritual colleges would not want to go to the extremes of their peers at evangelical colleges, where visitation rules are strictly enforced and sex is often a punishable offense. But some organized effort to shape student attitudes about romance and sex, religion and spirituality, is necessary if students are to be liberated from navigating the shortcomings and pitfalls of hookup culture alone, and empowered to nurture their seeds of spiritual and religious desire in community.

UNFINISHED STORIES

During my campus visits, I was offered a small but intimate window into students' lives. I saw students smile, heard their laughter, watched as a tear rolled down a face. Now that I'm away from them, I can't help but wonder how these students have moved forward with their lives, their struggles, their relationships, their spiritual interests—the kind of things I wonder about my own former students, whether I taught them for one semester or for years.

Has Amy Stone found her soulmate? Or is she still worrying that virginity marks her, leaving her vulnerable to dishonorable suitors and alone in her doubts?

Where have the spiritual meanderings taken Max Bradlee? Has he settled on one path or cobbled together a unique spiritual concoction befitting his big life questions?

What about Jessica Marin? Is she still switching her promise ring from the left hand to the right in the hope that a boy will notice her?

Has Steven Parsons made peace with his sexual identity? Will he ever?

Have these students and others found the community resources they need at their colleges to work through their struggles? Or are they still struggling on their own?

Privacy made this study's interview process work: students found a space to share some of their deepest feelings about faith, sex, romance, and the mysteries of putting these things together—all behind closed doors. No one else was present—no faculty, no parents, not even friends. Students could walk in, say whatever had been bottled up inside them to a perfect stranger, and then walk back out into their regular lives as if nothing had happened. I wonder how many times this short interview provided the only moments during their college years when students could give voice to these questions, experiences, opinions, and hopes, the only moments when they did something other than simply ponder these things in their hearts.

When it comes to sex, the campus resources available to students—whether religious, spiritual, or otherwise—seem, for the most part, to be ineffective. The cultures, attitudes, and practices related to sex and sexuality at both spiritual and evangelical colleges are extreme: on one end is a free-for-all hookup scene and at the other a narrow, strictly monitored purity standard that forces many students to deny their sexuality altogether. While most evangelicals can't get enough traction when it comes to sexual freedom, virtually everyone else can't get a foothold on sexual restraint.

True, we are all sexual beings, but we are not *only* sexual beings. With regard to sex and religion, far too many college students feel as if they are faced with an either/or proposition. The prevailing religious message about sex among students is either to guard purity with one's life or to see sex as irrelevant to one's spiritual practices and religious commitments. Young adults are either set up for war (in the case of evangelicals) or for alienation (in the case of everyone else). Many college students seem to encounter religion and sex as if they are two powerful and jealous gods. When they interact, as they do among evangelicals, it is a battle to the death. Either religion wins, and sex withers away (until marriage, theoretically), or sex wins, and faith founders. The alternative, evident among students at Catholic, nonreligious private, and public schools, is for these two gods to remain isolated from one another, warriors in entirely separate realms. Both options leave students in the lurch, consumed in many cases with anxiety about sex and, in some, about the state of their souls.

For the most part, students at evangelical and spiritual colleges have strikingly different college experiences. But their experiences are alike in four ways:

1. They are highly invested in their religious and/or spiritual identities.
2. They experience sexual desire and long to act on that desire.
3. Romance and experiencing a fulfilling romantic relationship are priorities.
4. They don't know how to reconcile 1–3.

Ideally, the first three characteristics would work together to help students develop meaningful, fulfilling romantic attachments enhanced by maturing religious and/or spiritual identities. Self-confidence in and self-knowledge about their sexual desires and romantic attachments would be both influenced and nurtured by their spirituality and religious commitments. All members of a college community would work together to address and even transform a campus culture that tends to devalue sex, romance, and relationships at the spiritual colleges, or one that often trades on fear and denial at the evangelical colleges. Sex and romance would be seen as domains allied to religious and spiritual growth rather than as enemies at war for students' souls. Sex and romance, religion and spirituality would be given collegewide recognition as serious subjects for intellectual and personal reflection, not only within student life and/or campus ministry, but also among faculty, administrators, and staff.

Students at both evangelical or spiritual colleges also share common struggles that further complicate the task of addressing their dilemmas about sex and the soul:

- *1. They are anxious about sex.* Almost all students experience a degree of shame, regret, or angst with regard to sex, though for different reasons.
- *2. They identify romance as asexual.* Almost all students separate sexual activity from their notions of the romantic ideal.
- *3. They don't know where to turn for advice, or if they can turn to anyone.* Students at evangelical colleges lack mentors when it comes to sex, and students at spiritual colleges lack mentors for spiritual formation.
- *4. Reconciling sex and the soul is not only extremely difficult for them, it's rare.*

The difficulty of reconciling sex and the soul is acute at evangelical and spiritual colleges alike. At evangelical colleges, reconciliation amounts to maintaining a heroic and unrealistic level of sexual restraint and even denial. At the spiritual colleges, it often ends in divorce. How *will* these institutions address this difficulty? What stands in the way of a better campus culture when it comes to sex and the soul? Where do the seeds of change lie?[1] What can evangelical colleges teach other schools, and where do they fall short? What lessons do spiritual colleges offer, and in what areas do they require improvement? Which students offer models for reconciling sexuality and spirituality? Most important of all: Why do colleges tolerate a situation in which students are left alone in facing these problems?

PORTRAIT OF A SPIRITUAL COLLEGE

Students at spiritual colleges may register at the top of the charts when it comes to spiritual hunger, and some of them identify with a particular religious tradition and even attend services somewhat regularly. But most don't feel compelled to commit themselves to any particular spiritual or religious path or guided way of living—at least, not whole-heartedly and not if it requires them to share their faith and beliefs communally. They live as if there is a wall between the classroom and the residence hall; between students and faculty, staff, and adminis-trators; between spiritual life and real life. They develop their own rules free of supervision. Many students who do hold deep affiliations with social, religious, and ethical frameworks often respond to the dissonance they see around them by learning to keep whatever com-mitments they have private.

Religious resources are available through campus ministry and parachurch organizations, but only a few students take advantage of them, and most relevant classes teach religion using methods that re-quire students to check the personal (and the spiritual) at the door. The dominant but implicit attitude on campus, not just among students but also perceived among faculty and administrators, is that spirituality and religion are private—not matters for public consumption. As a result, spiritual seeking is difficult and lonely. Student discussions about reli-gion and spirituality even behind closed doors during interviews tend to be quite simplistic; students' capacity to discuss religion and spirituality intelligently, critically, and comfortably seems stunted and unusually immature for college-age people. For many, "practicing faith" is like going to a seminar—it's something you do once a week, and then you stop thinking about it.

When it comes to sex, students are seldom influenced by faith or by any identifiable moral framework—at least not one they can name or that appears to hold any power over them. Student social life is instead legislated by a powerful peer minority that values hooking up, having sex, and getting drunk. The message about sex is simply that it's a normal part of the college experience, that it's casual, and that ro-mantic relationships are formed through having sex, often with part-ners one hardly knows. The hookup has replaced the first date despite the fact that most students—women and men alike—privately wish the peer attitude about sex was less casual and that more committed rela-tionships, romance, and meaningful sexual experiences were available. The hookup culture, though pervasive, does not appeal to the average student.

Theme parties—the most recent manifestation of hookup culture—are emerging as popular opportunities on many campuses for women to dress sexy, feel sexy, and express or experiment with sexual role playing. Yet at the same time these parties degrade women as sluts and whores (ho's). Parties with sexually explicit themes place the man in the dominant role and the women in the submissive one, giving men on campus an opportunity to indulge in lived fantasies once common only in the pornography industry.

Students at spiritual colleges may have all the sexual freedom in the world, but it is not giving them much reward. In this environment, religious teachings about sexuality (if students are aware of them) seem outdated, impossible to uphold, and sometimes literally laughable. It's no wonder that most students learn to divorce their faiths from their romantic and sexual lives.

Nonetheless, students at spiritual colleges also talk about sex and the soul in ways that challenge the dominant culture. In private, students are willing to critique the downside of hookup culture and admit their desires for committed and fulfilling romantic and sexual relationships. This means that student life on campus is only a small step away from transformation—the beginnings of change lie in the willingness of students to openly discuss what they really desire in romance and sex and, in so doing, to break down the false belief that hookup culture is normal and what everybody likes and wants.

With regard to religious and spiritual identity, students offer a more complex spiritual portrait on paper, where they seem comfortable expressing their religious and spiritual interests. This signals that there *is* a space where they feel safe to talk extensively about faith. For a few students, identifying as spiritual as opposed to religious empowers them to connect "the spiritual" to sex, since they see it as a freer, more forgiving framework—however vague—in which they can reflect on their sexual values and experiences and affirm both as meaningful.

Can community members at the spiritual colleges take the perceived freedom offered on their campuses—tolerance for all sorts of behaviors and beliefs so widely touted by peers, faculty, administration (and especially admissions officers)—and use it toward their own empowerment, reining in the sexual excesses that make their students uncomfortable and ashamed while pushing their communities to listen more holistically to the voices of the approximately 80% of students who care about religion and spirituality? The possibility is there, but I fear that campus support for helping students tackle a culture of sexual excess is meager because of public image risks for the college. Moreover, because silence and complacency about sex and religion have typically been the norm, the task of drawing private faith into the proverbial public square of the campus seems to make everyone anxious.

PORTRAIT OF AN EVANGELICAL COLLEGE

Most people assume a lot about what college students know about sex and about how much sexual experience they have. Most students at evangelical schools, unlike their counterparts at other school types, cannot boast of their sexual maturity, nor do they aspire to, since acquiring it goes against everything they have been taught—even if their bodies cry out otherwise.

The idealization of sexual purity is powerful at evangelical colleges, and it exacts demands on students that can be severe, debilitating, and often unrealistic. The pressures to marry are extreme for women, and college success is often determined by a ring, not a diploma. Because of the strong hold of purity culture, many students learn to practice sexual secrecy, professing chastity in public while keeping their honest feelings and often their actual experiences hidden. Students are aware that officials at evangelical colleges see it as their duty to monitor male-female romantic relationships and to strictly enforce campus rules about visitation in the residence halls. This has some positive benefit for students, most notably by shifting some of the burden of maintaining sexual propriety and boundaries onto adults. However, these colleges often combine monitoring with legislation about sexual activity on campus (including, in some instances, requiring students to sign agreements that, under penalty of expulsion, they will not have sex during their college years). Such monitoring can create an unfortunate communications breakdown—a campus atmosphere akin to a high school environment that fails to recognize and trust that students are already powerfully bound by the sexual tenets of their faith tradition, particularly in the area of restrictions on premarital sex. As a result of this oversight, many students feel compelled to hide their sexual practices not only from friends but also from all adults with whom they come into contact, including clergy; this stops them from seeking adult advice about sex and helps to create a culture of fear regarding sexual activity and identity on campus.

Religion and sex are inseparable for evangelical students, but often the connection is negatively charged. Becoming sexually active outside marriage can lead to social and spiritual ruin and can jeopardize one's desirability as a spouse, especially for a woman. The one transgression powerful enough to reconfigure and in some cases obliterate a student's faith is sexual sin. Lying or stealing might make a student feel sheepish for a while, but having sex, even once, can jeopardize everything forever.

On the other hand, evangelical college students not only show intense interest in their faith tradition and spirituality, they also attend schools where education and spiritual formation go hand in hand, and religious mentorship is widely available, especially from fellow students. As a result, most students experience a seamless religious transition from home to college. Though the student body is not diverse in terms of religious tradition, evangelical colleges are diverse in many other ways—ethnically, economically, geographically, and with respect to student attitudes and experiences within the Christian tradition. Student conversations about their religious tradition and spiritual identity are, as a rule, enthusiastic, knowledgeable, intelligent, and critical. Students can talk about their faith and are adept at discussing how their beliefs influence their politics or professional aspirations.

Unlike students at the spiritual colleges, evangelical students *are* offered models for sexual morality that fit with their ideas about romance and their religious commitments—however imperfect and rigid these models. Even though these resources are drawn from the realm of Christian purity culture—and therefore are restricted to what is often a severe, narrow understanding of sex and sexuality—students, faculty, clergy, and staff try to use these resources to foster opportunities for students to think about integrating romance and religion as part of the college experience, including within the curriculum. Even if these efforts fall short of the needs that students will reveal only behind closed doors or on paper, such options as born-again virginity offer students a way to productively deal with sexual regret, repair their relationships with God, reclaim their spiritual purity, and even gain spiritual authority among their peers.

How can officials at these colleges shift away from the status quo of monitoring and legislation toward something approaching a culture of trust? One where students can sort through, honestly and thoroughly, the many messages they get about sex from both their tradition and mainstream culture in the same way they do with other subjects relevant to their religious identity? Can evangelical colleges create an atmosphere that encourages students to navigate their sexuality by calling upon the spiritual resources already so widely available to them on just about every issue *but* sex?

Some students are cobbling together answers to this dilemma—or at least trying to. Most of them do so on their own, without the help of friends, clergy, parents, or faculty, and most see this pursuit as entirely separate from their experiences in the classroom. None of these answers is perfect, but they deserve a hearing beyond the confines of these particular students' lives. The students seem to fall into three categories, which I'll refer to as (1) heroic virgins, (2) sexually active seekers, and (3) born-again virgins.

Heroic Virgins

These students are mainly evangelicals and are the most religiously traditional. Publicly, these students accept without question the narrow path handed them by their faith. Against all odds—and often through extreme sublimation and denial of their desires—they avoid anything that would blemish their sexual purity, and they are deeply proud of this accomplishment. "Heroic virgins" endorse an ethic of constant vigilance, and guarding their own purity is directly in line with the teachings they receive from campus ministers, faculty members, administrators, peers, parents, and the popular Christian sex and dating literature. These are the students who are winning the evangelical war on sex. For now.

The relationship with God and the spiritual identity of these heroic virgins typically depend on whether they remain on this path until marriage. This factor makes these reconcilers the most fragile of the three groups. If they trip up (and tripping up is easy), they are vulnerable to a crisis of faith. As a result, being a member of this group is often temporary at best during college, and the potential fall is steep and costly.

Sexually Active Seekers

The "spiritual but not religious" students are typically sexually active and, when pressed, a few will associate certain sexual experiences as spiritual. But because their spirituality is amorphous and ill defined, it does little to guide their sexual decision making. Calling a sexual experience "spiritual" happens after the fact, and it's a one-sided assessment: rarely does the couple who engaged in the sexual activity sit down and determine together that a sexual experience had a special, sacred character. More likely, one of the two will decide on her or his own that the encounter was spiritual and, upon reflection, may also assume that this feeling is too intimate to share even with the sexual partner, never mind with friends.

On the positive side, labeling a sexual experience spiritual helps these students to frame sexual experiences in a meaningful way. Exactly what these sexual experiences mean in spiritual terms is difficult for students to explain. Like Alyssa Ryan, many students in this group feel some ambivalence about their sex lives. Given their meager spiritual and religious resources and conversation partners, it is difficult for them to find ways to flourish both sexually and spiritually.

It is easy to criticize these students for being satisfied with a fluffy faith and a relativistic sex ethic. But I also see hope in this group. These are the students who are tired of the hookup culture on their campuses. At the very least, they've identified the need for sexual activity to be more meaningful. They've begun to look to the spiritual as a potential resource to make meaning of sexuality despite their immersion in a culture of sexual excess. If these students are able both to acknowledge to themselves *and* to articulate to others—no small feat—that they long for meaningful sex, not random encounters, then positive change is possible. Spirituality and religion could play an important role in this change, empowering students in the name of God or the Buddha or perhaps simply the ideal of spiritual sex to say no to unhealthy peer pressure and unhealthy behavior, perhaps even to hookup culture itself. Religion and spirituality might help chart a path out of hookup culture.

Born-Again Virgins

Many people dismiss the concept of born-again virginity as ridiculous. But there is something admirable about young people like Cara Walker who act to turn their backs on behaviors that have hurt them. Restoring virginity may be a physical impossibility, to use the language these students have been taught. But returning to a place where they are challenged to reflect on what they want and don't want from sex, romance, and relationships, asking for forgiveness not only from God but also from their religious communities, is a positive option, especially when the alternative is losing faith and self-esteem, and especially if this option empowers them to say no to behaviors that have brought them shame and pain. Rather than trying to hide a piece of their past, cowering in fear of social and spiritual ruin, young women like Cara who vow to reclaim their virginity are constructing an effective framework for working through their past and incorporating it into their present. In Cara's case, this incorporation includes transforming the born-again virgin into someone with special authority among her peers.

Unfortunately, the above student methods of reconciling sex and the soul are stopgap measures, temporary bandages under which lie still-festering wounds. In many cases, a student's faith and religious identity hang on a level of sexual restraint that is for most young people unrealistic. In the long run, being a heroic virgin, a born-again virgin, or a sexually active seeker does not provide the adequate support, the tolerant community, or the nuanced conversations required for sexual and spiritual health. These methods are largely short-term fixes for a few. They do not provide long-term satisfaction for very many.

Not helping matters at spiritual colleges is the fact that, short of policies about sexual assault, few efforts are made to address sex and sexuality on a personal level either inside or outside the classroom. Theoretically, Catholic schools promote abstinence before marriage, but this official religious teaching has almost no practical relevance or meaningful traction among the student body (nor do any other official Catholic teachings about sex). Some nonreligious schools sponsor LGBT programs that provide mentors, community, and other resources and activities geared toward, though not exclusive to, sexual minorities. But these groups operate in much the same way as parachurch campus organizations—they create a subculture that is meaningful to students who take advantage of them but have little to no influence on the college curriculum or wider campus sexual ethic.

Students may indeed feel uncomfortable about where "sexual freedom" has led them, but they learn to keep this disquiet to themselves, much as the evangelical students are afraid to say that they want (or even need) more sexual freedom. In either case, the result is greater silence in a community badly in need of greater communication. Many students dump their religion during college. Many others have no religion to dump: they were reared in families in which religion was absent or was significant only in nominal ways. Yet most of these same young adults don't have, don't look for, and aren't urged to seek any viable alternative frameworks of meaning through which they might navigate the difficult decisions that college brings, especially with regard to sexuality.

But these are secondary causes. All these considerations point to deeper causes, systemic problems on college campuses that force students into unrealistic paradigms and makeshift fixes.

WHAT HAPPENS WHEN THE PERSONAL
DOESN'T PASS ACADEMIC MUSTER

One day during the semester that I taught my dating class at St. Michael's College, I was in the faculty lounge getting coffee. A professor I'd never met introduced himself and asked what I was teaching.

"So you're the professor who's teaching *dating*," he interrupted me, unable to mask his skepticism. The tone of his voice turned condescending. "What do you do in there? Gossip about boys?"

I am aware that it is unorthodox for a college to add a "dating class" to its course catalogue and that a professor who happens upon such an offering might, at first, be startled, even quizzical, as to its content and purpose. But one might also imagine that a colleague would move beyond his initial puzzlement to, at the very least, a basic curiosity— perhaps even to the respectful demeanor of a professor addressing a colleague about her area of expertise.

This professor's insulting comments and dismissive attitude embody what many academics believe about inviting the personal into the classroom and reveal common biases about what some see as "feminine subjects" such as relationships and spirituality—areas of inquiry that, when not ignored altogether, are usually relegated to gender studies or women's studies courses, considered the domain of psychology (a discipline often dominated by women majors), or occasionally taught (often by female faculty) in selected literature classes. Like theme parties that have college boys dressing as professors and college women showing up as schoolgirls, academia is still a man's world. It has its own version of the purity ideal which prizes the objective over the subjective, distanced observation over personal reflections, and traditional male values over traditional feminine ones. To this day, many faculty members teach students that the personal pronoun "I" is verboten in papers and on tests because inserting oneself into a discussion of research diminishes its value. The overarching message: the personal is not rigorous enough to warrant a place in the curriculum, space on the syllabus, time in the classroom, or room on the page.

People wonder why even the best colleges in the country harbor *Animal House* behavior, but the reason is simple. There's a thick wall between the classroom and everything else. Brilliant students may hone sophisticated reasoning abilities in their courses, but they don't seem inclined to take those abilities with them once class ends. They either don't know how or haven't been offered the tools to apply what they learn to their personal lives. Although many evangelical students wax poetic about mentoring by faculty, administrators, and staff, these professionals' counterparts at spiritual colleges offer students knowledge but not the passion to act on it. It was rare for a student at a spiritual college to speak of a member of the faculty or administration as a mentor to whom he could turn for *anything* not on the syllabus, never mind a talk about sex and spirituality. Few students felt that their coursework should be challenging (much less changing) their behavior in arenas beyond the classroom.[2]

Why do so many colleges tacitly support this culture by refusing to question it? Who is responsible for determining and enforcing the view that addressing subject areas via the personal is not a rigorous method of intellectual inquiry? How does academia's own set of purity standards affect a college student's ability to mature, change, and grow intellectually, relationally, and spiritually? To become a contributing member of society? What does this dismissal of the personal to the realm of the private convey to students about what counts as serious scholarship?

Finally, why is it so rare for colleges and universities to offer courses that explore dating, sex, and romantic relationships—their intricate and complex histories and attendant psychologies, their effect on how we understand gender roles and sexual orientation, and how those relationships affect religious and spiritual identity?

My former colleague at St. Michael's College may have sneered at such a course offering, but given the centrality that sex and romance, religion and spirituality have within our individual and social lives, it is important to give serious thought to the deeper reasons for this glaring omission in higher education, including identifying what is behind the fear of and resistance to these subjects. Plainly, sex and the soul matter intensely to the overwhelming majority of human beings, no less during the college years and regardless of sexual orientation and religious/spiritual background, and so it has been for millennia. Why do colleges and universities resist tackling these topics directly and explicitly inside the classroom?

At the spiritual colleges, one answer to these questions is that religion and sex are private matters. Yet this approach results in a campus conversation about sex that is often vulgar and uncritical, and almost entirely uninformed by faith. Spiritual colleges foster communities of young people who not only see religious and sexual identity as private, but are typically incapable of confidently, comfortably, and respectfully communicating their desires and beliefs on these issues, even if they feel desperate to do so. What happens when what a college sees as "religious tolerance" really amounts to "embarrassed silence"? When sex is degraded, and young women along with it? Why shouldn't we expect students, faculty, administrators, and clergy on campus to engage these subjects with as much intellectual rigor as they do any other?

At evangelical colleges, the opposite is true. Sex and religion are so public, so inseparable, and so overdetermined by religious and communal rules, boundaries, and standards that students have no personal space in which they can assess where they stand on the relationship between the two. Nor can they easily find, access, and evaluate opinions that respect their religious commitments while also challenging the evangelical "party line" on sexuality. Students who question the purity culture or who want to become or already are sexually active live in fear of being ostracized by their communities and in some cases literally expelled. What happens when the power of purity culture sends students into hiding? When sex and sexuality are degraded and suppressed outside of marriage and heterosexual orientation? When a single sexual act can jeopardize students' relationships with God, their faith commitments, and their education?

Colleges that insist on enforcing a wide divide between academic life and student life, between what happens during the day in classrooms and what goes on after dark in the residence halls, are, at least in effect if not in intent, denying their students that "education of the whole person" so many institutions like to boast that they offer. Much academic work, however esoteric, has practical relevance to the way we live our lives. Why restrict students from asking, alongside their professors, how relevant this intellectual material is to their lives?

SEEKING A SEXY SPIRITUALITY FOR THE COLLEGE STUDENT'S SOUL

I believe that together both categories of colleges—the spiritual and the evangelical—possess the seeds for transforming the relationship between sex and the soul on American college campuses. But what each contributes is distinct.

What evangelical colleges uniquely offer is an example of how a compelling core culture can be life affirming. After hundreds of hours of interviews, and hundreds more poring over journal pages and online survey data, I have come to believe that young people lose something important when they collectively turn away from religious and spiritual traditions. Yet what they lose is not necessarily particular to a specific tradition. What they lose are four basic benefits that most religions and spiritual disciplines offer:

- *Boundaries*: the notion that there are limits, protocols, and gradations of what is and is not permissible sexually.
- *Sense of right and wrong*: the idea that there are certain ways a person should expect to be treated and not be treated; that a person has a *right* to say no to sex; that it is possible to *wrong* another person sexually—and that these ideals are backed up on not only a personal level, but also on communal and even divine levels.
- *Framework for discernment*: rituals, activities, and processes to which one can turn in making decisions regarding sexuality and the pursuit of romantic relationships. Ways to ask, "What should I do?"
- *Forgiveness and redemption*: the sense that if one "makes mistakes" or "stumbles" or does something regrettable, there *is* a tangible—if not a well-traveled—path available to work through these struggles to a place of self-forgiveness and redemption, communal forgiveness and redemption, and even divine forgiveness and redemption.

Spiritual colleges also have something important to contribute. They foster an ethic of sexual freedom that, if offered along with these values, confers two important benefits that religious communities and traditions typically do not:

- *The possibility of yes*: the assurance that when limitations are extreme, seem unjustified, or are out of touch and irrelevant, a person has the right to cross a boundary and say yes to a forbidden experience or relationship. This might be interpreted as a kind of civil disobedience when it comes to sex, or even regarded as space for challenging the dominant ethical framework.
- *Tolerance of sexual diversity*: the right of all persons, regardless of sexual orientation, to pursue a loving, sexual, romantic relationship.

The diversity of the ways in which young people identify sexually is recognized at spiritual colleges, much less so at evangelical ones. But college students cannot be reduced to their sexuality, either. What matters to sexual and romantic satisfaction and maturation seems to be a moderate combination of the following: *some* freedom, but not unrestricted freedom; *some* tolerance, but not an "anything goes" ethic; and lots of honesty and openness—but not the kind that leads to a casual attitude that devalues sex and romance.[3] Unfortunately, when left unchecked, the dominant hookup culture denies these very needs and makes religious and spiritual desire seem incongruous at best.

Religious traditions and spiritual disciplines may indeed be diverse and difficult to navigate at private and public schools (especially on a personal level), and even at Catholic schools, but this does not mean these communities should discourage their public expression. If communities of higher education would openly acknowledge and cultivate the high levels of interest in religion and spirituality on all types of campuses, students could be empowered to move their faith from the margins to the center of campus life, to see religious faith as a strength rather than an embarrassment, and to view their faith as an avenue for critiquing both the culture of sexual excess (at spiritual colleges) and the culture of excessive sexual restraint (at evangelical colleges).

If all members of a campus community take responsibility to foster a culture of tolerance and forgiveness, and recognize the reality, the power, and the goodness of emergent sexual and spiritual desire among young adults, students will instead begin to see how they might foster a healthy balance between the two. It is incumbent upon faculty, administration, and clergy to encourage college students to ground themselves *somewhere*, to put all this religious and spiritual desire into practice, to tap into its undeniable energies, because religion and spirituality have something important to offer. More than any other resources, they can help students to recognize who they are and to pursue who they want to become—not just as bodies or minds or souls, but as whole people.

A Practical Guide to Sex and the Soul

Three Musts for Your College To-Do List: What to Say to Your Child, Student, Parishioner, Friend

America is obsessed with higher education—especially winning the admissions battle (if you are a parent or applicant) or the rankings war (if you work at a college or university).

Parents, counselors, and applicants are preoccupied with "getting in." In the hunt for the right college, many parents read countless articles, books, and *U.S. News & World Report*; consult with a friend who already has two kids in the Ivies; and drill their kids with SAT words as they cart them to extracurricular activities. Whether they realize it or not, when it comes to college admissions, their children are products to be bought and sold, and a lot of energy and resources go into teaching kids how to sell themselves. Colleges and universities are public relations juggernauts, competing for the "best product" possible with ultra-glossy admissions packets, residence halls that look like hotels, culinary options resembling hip neighborhood restaurants, and even presidents who blog daily.

So parents are in a frenzy over trying to get their kids admitted, and college administrators are in a frenzy over admitting the kids they want to enroll. In this process, is anyone asking the right questions about the college experience itself? Is anyone helping teens to think about what really matters and what they really want once they arrive at campus? What happens when these young women and men actually *go* to college?

Sure, lots of time and resources are devoted to helping college students choose their major, usually with an eye on job prospects. Parents offer counsel, students "try on" different subjects, and faculty and staff are available to advise (often in ways that go against the grain of parental pressure for "practical," pre-professional options). Some applicants will even consider the religious life of an institution—though, aside from evangelicals, most will do so only in a cursory way, or much of this concern will come from parents and not from the student or a mentor. The vast majority of parents focus on education and the prestige of the institution, and some probably think about athletics, too.

Almost no one gives serious thought to whether one college or the other will be more suitable for finding love and romance, or even which institution is best suited for seeking an adequate spiritual path. I also doubt that faculty and staff—even those in student affairs—spend much time (if any) addressing how their expertise or sponsored programs provide students with opportunities to reflect deeply on love, romance, and sex; what it means to find fulfillment in these at college; and how a student's religious affiliation or spiritual interests might intersect with or pose an obstacle in this domain. If these issues are considered at all, they are likely not discussed openly, especially not between parents and children. When it comes to college, since when has finding romantic fulfillment or the right religion been high on the list of pros and cons?

Well, it's time to add to that to-do list.

Religion and spirituality need to be priorities in college-related discussions, and so do love, sex, and romantic relationships, *if* we want students to be adequately prepared for college, and to have a rewarding experience when they get there. Poor guidance, alienation, and regretful experiences in these areas can make or break a student's college experience. It's a mistake to ignore them—even if they may seem unorthodox topics for pre-college discussion.

An institution can have all the prestige in the world, offer the best education and an impressive swath of majors, and even have a great basketball team—but what if this same place has your daughter dressing up as a "secretary ho" on a Friday night? Fosters a classroom culture that stays safely removed from the larger campus life? Harbors a peer ethic that leads students to believe that finding a boyfriend or a girlfriend at college is like "playing the lottery," as one of the students in my dating class put it? (You have to hook up with 99 people before you hit the jackpot and find someone who will stick around.) Or leaves its students to develop a split between sex and the soul, or even dump one for the other, because what else are they going to do? Those values with which they grew up or thought they had don't seem to fit with the social scene all around them, and the resources for navigating this minefield aren't readily available.

Here, I offer what I believe are the three most important tasks for parents, peers, faculty, administrators, and clergy responsible for helping students find their way through their college years.

TASK 1: THE COLLEGE ADMISSIONS TOUR

Eyes Wide Open: The Questions You Never Thought You'd Ask but Should

The battle to win applicants is fierce. Top-tier colleges compete with each other, and smaller ones are fighting to move up the ranks. Everyone is petrified of bad press—especially with respect to sex (think: Duke). This fear often leads well-meaning college administrators to brush important conversations under the rug. Many colleges also know that religion is one of the most important issues on the global political stage. But they've yet to figure out how to deal with religion in a way that doesn't make people feel uncomfortable, or they worry about First Amendment issues, and it just seems easier to let the religion department (if they have one) and maybe some small campus groups handle this subject.

This is where parents and applicants—*you*—have the power to change things.

Guard against the awe factor when you embark on that idyllic summer college tour. Ivy-covered buildings and vast, green quads are no doubt beautiful; city schools can be impressive; and student tour guides are often sweet-natured, funny, and convincing. But sometimes that good-looking tour guide is the same guy who just held a CEOs and Office Ho's party the weekend before, and that stunning, sun-drenched campus is a place where people trip over half-naked students passed out on the grass in the wee hours of the morning.

It's in this admissions process that parents and applicants have the most influence. Yes, many schools have an ever-shrinking percentage of acceptances each year, but during application time, they are pitching to *you*.

Hold the college accountable and ask the really tough questions. It's the college's job to answer. If an admissions officer or tour guide says "I don't know," ask her to follow up with the answers, and make sure she does. Colleges and universities need to become more forthcoming about the struggles they face with regard to student sex and religion on campus—but they will likely hold back on tough issues unless *you* push them.

The price of college is shocking. Make sure you know what you are paying for.

Here are 15 questions you should ask on a college tour: 10 about sex and 5 for the soul—though each influences the other. Many of these will make a tour guide or admissions officer blanch or render them silent, but don't let this dissuade you from asking or pushing them to answer. I also suggest asking for statistics or examples in certain instances. For many of these questions, colleges will not keep track of these specific issues, or if they do, they will "categorize" them as something other than what they really are as a way of protecting themselves against potential scandal.

Top Ten Questions to Ask about Sex (and Love and Romance)

1. *Are theme parties ever held on campus? If so, how often do they follow the "pimps and ho's" model, or the "girls wear as little as possible" format? Do you have any statistics?* Campuses where these parties are popular or where they are becoming popular are places where women students are regularly degraded (though many young women think that they can be "empowered" by attending them), where men are further socialized into seeing women as sex objects and expect them to act accordingly, and where women's dress is legislated by a peer social culture, and not their own style and desires.

2. *How is dating perceived? Do people date here? If so, what do people typically do on dates?* This is the issue that will help you to determine whether the first date has been replaced by the hookup. If the answer to "what people do on dates" is meet up at a party, a club, or after a party or a club, warning bells should go off.

Press the issue by asking how often two people go out to dinner and "just talk for hours," about which students fantasize so much. Beware of answers that refer to the "college marriage"— which is not the preliminary sort of dating about which I am referring, and is more akin to the kind of intense, 24/7 exclusive relationship that (often) evolves from a serial hookup. If you are looking at evangelical colleges, shift the question a bit, and ask how strongly dating is tied to marriage and whether students feel comfortable dating without the pressures to determine the relationship with an engagement ring.

3. *How many courses here prioritize sex, love, dating, and/or romantic relationships? Which departments sponsor these? Can we get a list?* Students crave resources and discussions about these topics— and not just among themselves. Having taught a course on dating myself, and spoken with colleagues who have integrated themes on romance into their classes or sponsored courses exclusively devoted to these subjects—I can assure you that they are far from fluffy in their rigor and import. They provide students with a wide range of resources—philosophical, historical, literary, religious—to help them struggle with and debate relevant questions, and a space to discuss them within classroom walls. These courses could not be more relevant to the average student's college experience. Especially at Catholic schools, the answer will be "yes, we have a marriage and family course"—but don't be fooled: this is not an adequate answer. Remember that—unless you are looking at evangelical colleges where a large population is expecting to be engaged and even married by graduation—marriage and family are about as far removed from the hookup culture as you can get. These topics are only tangentially related to what the majority of students need to discuss, and "marriage and family" courses often leave students twisting material about marriage into something relevant to their real experiences of sex, dating, and romance—if they try to make the information fit their situation at all.

4. *How many student activities and/or discussions have been sponsored in the last year regarding sex, love, and romance? Who sponsors these— and from which organizations and academic departments?* Most spiritual colleges (though not always the Catholic ones) sponsor first-year student programs about using condoms and about date rape. Although these conversations are very important (and you should make sure the colleges you are considering regularly hold

this kind of programming), press beyond this particular "sex talk." Students also need higher-level, intellectual conversations, too, but usually don't find them available. Find out how many faculty give outside-the-classroom talks on these subjects—perhaps even in the residence halls. Ask how often campus ministry and religious organizations give talks on these subjects. Inquire whether students themselves sponsor related discussions.

5. *How do students who get reputations handle social ruin? Is it possible to make a comeback? If so, how?* It's easy to get a reputation as a slut or a "ho" on campus—especially if you are a woman. Men sometimes get reputations as "players," but this label is more of a badge of honor than anything else. In deciding between small liberal arts colleges in tiny towns and big-city schools, an important factor to consider is that a lot of students I interviewed who attended large institutions commented that one of the serendipitous things about going to a huge school is that if you "mess up" and get a reputation in one social circle, the university is large enough that you can quite literally start over socially. Though this may not be an ideal situation—to have to start over in the first place—students at the smaller liberal arts colleges often expressed remorse about how fast word traveled, and people's reputations were ruined overnight in ways they couldn't shake for the rest of their college experience.

6. *How many students do you know with reputations? How did they get them? How are they treated by others as a result? What has the school done to handle this problem?* Just remember the ho train, the yes girls, and even the dirty girls—and then imagine your child handling all the responsibilities of college with that kind of label hanging over her head. The ways that students gossip about one another and the negative stereotyping of women on campus can tell you a lot about the students at a given institution.

7. *Can you describe the traditional hazing rituals geared at first-year students on this campus? What has the college done to address this behavior?* It may seem a college cliché that senior guys prey on first-year girls who look up to them, but it's not a joke. People do make bets, take photos, and conceive of all sorts of other hazing rites that often involve lots of alcohol. First-year students are especially vulnerable to assault and, in the era of MySpace and Facebook, they are also vulnerable to having photographs they may not even remember posing for posted on the Web.

8. *What organizations on campus support the gay, lesbian, bisexual, and transgender student populations?* Public and nonreligious private colleges and universities often have excellent resources for sexual minorities and sponsor a variety of related programs on campus—both educational and social. Tolerance of sexual diversity is often a highly charged issue at Catholic and evangelical colleges, however. You can tell a lot about schools just by finding out if they sponsor these organizations as well as programs like Safe Zone (which trains faculty and staff on campus to foster "safe" spaces on campus for students struggling with their sexual identity). Also, ask how sexual minorities are perceived and treated by their heterosexual peers. Find out about the dating scene for LGBT students—is there one? This acceptance of diversity and creation of safety for sexual minorities is good for *all* students, even the heterosexual ones.

9. *What organizations on campus support abstinence?* Though evangelical college students may not need a support group or organization specifically devoted to chastity, I have come to believe they are important for some students. Abstinence organizations—including the Anscombe societies at Princeton and MIT, or True Love Revolution at Harvard—show signs of resistance to hookup culture and promote sexual diversity in their own way. The existence of such groups on campus means that there is space and a supporting community for students to explore love, romance, dating, sex, and often their faith in relation to these—a place they can go that operates outside of hookup culture.

10. *In the last four years, how often have students been caught hiring strippers for parties? Do you have any statistics?* Many people will shrug this off with a "boys will be boys" mentality—but I urge that you don't. Stripper parties—how often they are held and how the administration handles them if they find out (often they try to adjudicate this behavior under the guise of a rather benign policy violation)—are often a barometer of how men are supposed to view women on campus, and how women are valued—or *not*. A related follow-up question could be: *Has anyone ever been caught with a stripper pole installed in on-campus housing?* Though I did not at any point document this as a reality in my travels, I heard many rumors from students about how "the new thing" is for guys to build stripper poles in their apartments and then use them to haze first-year girls

(especially) by getting them drunk, convincing them to strip, and taking pictures of the event. This sends chills up my spine—and I hope it does yours as well. It may be just a rumor—but it doesn't hurt to ask.

Top Five Questions to Ask about the Soul

1. *How many campus ministry or religion-related organization activities were sponsored about dating, love, romance, and/or sex in the last year? Do you have statistics? Do you have programs/flyers from these events?* It's safe to assume that at most colleges, evangelical and otherwise, events geared toward thinking about sex in light of faith and spirituality are relatively rare, if they happen at all. If they do occur—which is a start—they are often suffocated by concerns about orthodoxy. This, in turn, often prevents truly honest, and therefore helpful, relevant conversation with students. If there are no programs to speak of, ask why. This should be a warning signal. If the school *has* sponsored activities, ask for materials that will reveal the content and attitude of the events.

2. *What sort of pastoral counseling/spiritual mentorship and/or advising is available to students?* Since the majority of college students—regardless of institution type—cite interests in religion and spirituality, it's important that colleges provide adults to help them in their exploration of and practice of faith on campus. Don't settle for the answer "We are publicly funded" as a way of explaining why a college "can't" deal with this kind of mentoring—*all* universities need to figure out how to attend their students' needs, even if those needs are spiritual in nature. (Read Sharon Daloz Parks's *Big Questions, Worthy Dreams: Mentoring Young Adults in Their Search for Meaning, Purpose, and Faith* for more on this issue.) Students get lots of advice on choosing classes and a major—so who is doing the advising when it comes to choosing the right spiritual path?

3. *Are students comfortable talking about their religious/spiritual beliefs with others—beyond abstract philosophical debate? In what ways are these discussions explicitly encouraged on campus? Can you provide specific examples?* At the spiritual colleges, many students talked about how faith on a personal level is something you just don't talk about with friends or even faculty: they are often left

searching alone. Yet colleges also boast of religious diversity on campus, and sometimes a religious affiliation is what makes a college unique: ask for evidence that shows how this "plus" adds to student life. At evangelical colleges, you will want to make sure that the school is creating space for doubt and dissent from orthodoxy, as well as helping students to find companions—both student and faculty—on this particular journey.

4. *How many courses make religion and/or spirituality a priority—beyond the religious studies/theology department?* Some of the students I interviewed who were actively seeking were doing so by taking courses sponsored by a religion or theology department—and that's where their conversation ended. Though these departments or affiliated programs are excellent and obvious resources for students, if colleges are delegating all talk and education regarding religion and faith to one department, they too are compartmentalizing and isolating these topics from the rest of the campus. Religion and spirituality are relevant to so many disciplines—and today more than ever are central to the wider world. What are other departments and programs doing to meet this interest? And how is the evangelical college that you're considering, which is likely integrating faith into a diversity of student majors, handling religious literacy when it comes to other religions?

5. *How many faculty/administrators/staff make themselves available to give religion/spirituality-related talks, participate in religion/spirituality-related activities, or avail themselves of religion/spirituality-related retreats—apart from those already established in the religious studies or theology department and those who run religion-related organizations? Can you give specific examples?* For students to build a bridge from the classroom to the rest of life, it's important for faculty to show how their subjects affect their lives in practice, and for students to see faculty and administrators taking stands on issues they care about. Many students are afraid to profess their belief in any one particular ideology, set of values, or even a faith tradition; they need adult models on campus.

I hope that reading the stories and comments of the college students in this book will help to change the way parents and children investigate colleges and spark some transparency among admissions officials—or, at the very least, inspire some campus conversations about the extent to which all of these issues affect the student body.

Sex education in America is a quagmire of divisiveness. With regard to public schools, it pits the Left against the Right, secularists against the religious, and there is a tug-of-war over abstinence education. Most religious communities either take a militant approach to purity or ignore the conversation altogether. (In my experience, Catholics love the "ignorance is bliss" approach.) And although plenty of parents take the sex talk in stride, begin early, and are thorough, many other parents tremble at this part of their job. In a culture where thongs are marketed to 10-year-old girls, and Hollywood starlets who are idolized by those same little girls pose nearly naked on the covers of magazines, adequate sex education becomes even more complicated.

Take such a child out of the home, give him or her a room in a college residence hall, and just imagine the possibilities.

You may think you've already done your job with the sex talk if you are a parent, or if you are a student, you are sure that those awkward sex talks are a thing of the past. Not so. To go off to college—or to send your child off—without an adult conversation about sex in higher education is irresponsible. The task of sex education doesn't end at puberty and high school. If anything, sex education during the middle school and early high school years will seem like a piece of cake when compared to the conversation that should happen prior to and during college. The purpose of the college sex talk conversation is to ensure that sex, love, and romance, not just education, are adequately discussed and reflected upon before move-in day; this conversation should carry on throughout the college experience—and the extent of this conversation shouldn't be "make sure you have condoms."

How to Use the "Top Ten Questions to Ask about Sex" (above)
 If you are a parent: use this list as a guide to identify the relevant issues to discuss and maintain a truly open dialogue with your child both before and during college.
 If you work at a college: use this list to inquire whether these activities or problems exist there and to identify ways to respond to these issues.
 If you are clergy: use this list to educate yourself about the realities that college students face so that you can help them tackle these issues from the perspective of your faith tradition.

A few caveats:

For those applying to or enrolled at spiritual colleges: It's not that there isn't good sex going on at America's colleges and universities—there *are* students having pleasurable, fulfilling sexual experiences of all varieties, and there *are* students having these within committed, fulfilling relationships. However, the wider perception among students appears to be that to find good sex and fulfillment, students must first immerse themselves in hookup culture and have at least a little—if not a lot—of bad, unfulfilling, uncommitted sex in the process.

One of the most important things to help college students understand is that, if they believe they are the only dissenters from hookup culture, they should think again. Chances are, the person next to them (and next to that person), whether a man or a woman, doesn't like hookup culture either. Parents and colleges need to empower students to challenge that powerful minority who controls the peer sex ethic by emphasizing that they are not only *not* alone, they have strength in numbers.

For those applying to or enrolled at evangelical colleges: At evangelical colleges, there is plenty of dating, much less sex, and hookup culture is virtually nonexistent. Yet at these schools, the typical student complaint is that there is too much silence and taboo about sex. These students aren't seeking something resembling hookup culture, but they certainly want the freedom to talk about sex openly and, in some cases, to acknowledge that yes, they've had sex, and it wasn't a tragedy; aside from the intense guilt they feel, it was actually good sex.

Evangelical students need encouragement to speak freely about their sexual desires and histories in order to deal with them in a healthy way and affirm the reality that they experience sexual desire—and that this desire is exciting! Within evangelical youth culture, born-again virginity is one option to navigate past sexual experiences in light of faith, but it shouldn't be the only one. Fostering open, honest communication about sex is the first step toward expanding the possibilities. Handing someone a promise ring or speaking endlessly about chastity are woefully insufficient for tackling the kind of sex talk these students need and desperately want to have.

TASK 3: THE RELIGION AND SPIRITUALITY COLLEGE TALK

Chances are—even if you didn't bring your children up to be all that religious, and even if you did, but it didn't seem to take very well—they are probably curious about it and ready to learn more about their own faith and/or explore different traditions, as well as experiment a bit with practice. Whether or not they gain the courage to do all of the above and whether or not they are able to mature in the faith you already passed on to them (if indeed you did pass one on) may depend on your willingness to be proactive about religion and spirituality.

How to Use the "Top Five Questions to Ask about the Soul" (above)
   If you are a parent: use this list as a guide to have a religion/ spirituality talk with your kids just as you would the sex talk.
   If you work at a college: use this list to evaluate how religion and spirituality are engaged (or not) at your institution, and to identify ways to respond to this particular student interest at your school. Colleges expend a lot of resources to advise students: Why not figure out how to extend this to religion?
   If you are clergy: use this list to identify how to reach out to both college students and those who work in higher education, helping them to find appropriate forums and activities that foster spiritual seeking and religious practice on campus.

One caveat for students and parents looking exclusively at evangelical colleges:

If you come from what I've called a typical evangelical family, then it's likely that your children are already invested in their faith tradition—though they may be looking forward to space for doubt during college, since many of the evangelical students I interviewed were grateful for this opportunity. If your children want a solid Christian education within a passionate Christian community, an evangelical Protestant college is the way to go. But they may have other ideas. Make sure you inquire: Do they want to attend a school with *religious* diversity in particular? Do they want to experience life outside their faith tradition for a change? Are there non-Christian colleges that interest them and that also boast a strong Christian subculture (e.g., a well-established InterVarsity group) where they can find a sympathetic religious community and maintain their faith while at college?

Some Practical Advice on Broaching the Topic

If I were faced with talking to my children or students about religion and spirituality, and I was uncertain myself about this subject, and had no idea how they were feeling either—I might try the following steps to engage them:

STEP 1: OPEN UP THE CHANNELS OF COMMUNICATION

Remember, just because you never prayed at home or talked about religion outside of weekly services or simply brought your children up agnostic doesn't mean it's OK to skip this topic. Begin by asking if they ever think about the faith with which they grew up (or if they think about faith at all), or if they are curious about other spiritual disciplines or religious traditions.

If you are nervous or if your children are already away at school, you may want to broach this subject in e-mail or instant messenger first. Students seem more forthcoming in writing about faith anyway. Then you can bring it up in face-to-face conversation once the topic is open for discussion.

STEP 2: ASK LOTS OF FOLLOW-UP QUESTIONS

If it turns out that yes, your children are interested in religion and spirituality, or even frustrated with them, then follow up by inquiring what sparked this interest. Have they felt religion has been "forced" on them growing up? And if so, how would they describe their curiosity about religion and/or spirituality now? Are they trying to find their own way into your tradition, or are they looking for another one that suits them better?

STEP 3: TAKE ACTION

If they have yet to enroll in college: Would they like to go to a school where exploring religion and spirituality is a priority on campus? Help them look for evidence of religious diversity and spiritual questing among students: through student activities; through the availability of different faith-based groups and campus chaplains of different faith traditions; by inquiring whether there are classes for nonmajors in the religious studies or theology department.

If they are already at college: Are they interested in exploring these questions through a minor or even a major? Or joining a campus organization related to their spiritual interests? Help them to find ways to explore faith and spirituality in community and not just on their own. This kind of exploration can be a rewarding social experience, too.

(Take note: the methods for broaching a topic in steps 1–3 can also be applied to sex talk.)

Last, there are some simpler, lower-stakes issues that can affect faith once students leave home. For any parent, professor, minister, or friend interested in promoting a young person's transition into college with his or her faith intact, here are some issues that students report are coming between them and religious practice:

1. Being "too busy" to find time to go to services in the midst of the typically overpacked college student's schedule. In other words, while managing the many new social and academic responsibilities and opportunities, weekly worship tends to be one of the first activities cut—even on a predominantly evangelical campus (apart from required chapel attendance).

2. Being unable to find a worship community and/or service that feels like it fits and in which the student finds her- or himself comfortable—and doing so in a timely manner.

3. Attending a large university or college where he or she is in the religious minority, and it is difficult to find a community of like-minded peers.

4. Having to go it alone when it comes to services because few other students worship.

Everyone Wants to Talk about Hooking Up

New Reflections after Nearly a Decade of Conversation

A HOOKUP VS. A CULTURE OF HOOKING UP

Since this book was first published I have visited and lectured at over a hundred colleges and universities across the United States to discuss its findings with students, professors, and administrators. I've learned a lot from these conversations, but most of all I've learned how potent a topic hooking up has become within higher education, particularly at Catholic, private-secular, and public institutions. Far more than spirituality and religion, what people want to discuss (often even at evangelical colleges) is hooking up: What is it? Who does it? How often? Why? Students long to know their peers' attitudes about hooking up as well as the attitudes of students at other colleges. Many want to know what's perpetuating hookup culture and whether students are alone in their desire for romance and dating. The people who work on campus want to figure out how to effectively respond to a phenomenon that has grown to dominate the college experience. But what does it really mean to say that hookup culture dominates the college experience? Does everybody hook up? Is it really the only form of sexual intimacy on campus?

Yes and no.

Most students at Catholic, private-secular, and public residential institutions will hook up at least once during their college years—residential being key, since commuter schools are quite different (hooking up exists there, too, just not quite so intensely, and campus culture is often less cohesive). Students typically use three criteria to define hooking up: it involves some form of sexual intimacy (anything from kissing to intercourse), it's brief (maybe even just a few minutes), and no one gets attached (neither person is supposed to care about the experience or their partner afterward). Many students will engage in this practice directly by hooking up—some will hook up regularly, some only a few times. A lot of students on campus will participate indirectly by collecting and spreading gossip, or by lying to each other about having hooked up in order to fit in. Some students will participate by denouncing hooking up, and others will sneak off quietly to get away from this aspect of the party scene. But it's safe to say that *all* students at the average Catholic, private-secular, and public institution will contend with hookup culture in some way, shape, or form (even if it's by dissenting). It is the umbrella culture on campus today and it is the centerpiece of the social scene. The hookup is the first stop, the expected mode of initial sexual intimacy on campus. Dating remains an aspiration, something many people want, but that no one really does anymore. Long-term romantic relationships abound, and you can find plenty of couples who are deeply committed to each other, but most of these couples got there via the hookup (which is only problematic if they feel it's problematic, which many of them do). Students will often say that the great thing about having a significant other is that it gets you off the exhausting hookup treadmill. Then again, they will also say that this can also be the worst thing about it because it makes you socially nonexistent, and people will pressure you to get out of the relationship so you can dive back into the "real fun" of the hookup scene.

The thing that surprised me most when I first began this research was how many students—both men and women—were really angry about hookup culture. They felt that it robbed them of choices around sexuality and the potential to take other roads toward romance and relationships. Yet they also felt they had to go along with it because there was no alternative. I was shocked at how unhappy men were, since everyone assumes that men are living it up within hookup culture. Many years later, the above is still true; and though I'd say that both men and women have become even more resigned to hookup culture, their ability to shrug it off is growing stronger.

Based on my visits to campuses, it still seems true that evangelical institutions don't have hookup culture—at least not in the same form experienced at other kinds of schools. There may indeed be rampant kissing at certain Christian colleges, which administrators, faculty, and staff worry might be the tip of the iceberg. Yet whether this can be called "hookup culture" as it applies at the Catholic, private-secular, and public institutions discussed in this book is an open question. Evangelical Christian colleges face other challenges with respect to their formal policies around sexuality, to which I will return.

Perhaps the most important thing people need to understand about hookup culture more generally is this: there is a difference between a single hookup, a "hookup in theory," and a *culture* of hooking up. The difference is vast and essential to any real understanding of hookup culture today. The "hookup in theory" is that fun, exciting, pleasurable, and liberating sexual experience that students are told is the pinnacle of the college experience, the one that is supposed to make them feel a thrill and look back on their university years with a nod and a wink about how crazy and wonderful it all was. The "hookup in theory" is the one that college students are given the hard sell about, the one that will mark them as laid back and fun-loving. But the "hookup in theory" really is theoretical, a fantasy of what's *supposed* to happen, yet nearly disappears when a culture of hooking up takes hold on campus. Though the vast majority of college students I've spoken with over the years defend their right to experience the "hookup in theory," they'll also tell you that within a culture of hooking up, that fantasy hookup seems nearly nonexistent. It's common for students to be both in favor of the "hookup in theory" and against hookup culture. This seems to be the most common position among both college men and women today.

My goal going forward is to enumerate some of the biggest issues and concerns that have arisen across my conversations on college campuses—to further discuss the findings that have really gotten to students and those who teach and care for them on campus. My hope is to propose new, practical ideas and sources for reflection on how we might respond to hookup culture on campus. I will discuss the (very different) issues that arise around policies regarding sexual activity at evangelical colleges in a separate section.

Critics of hookup culture, myself included, are often thought to be prudish moralizers, antisex and antifeminist, who want to force young women to sign abstinence pledges and go to purity balls. And, undoubtedly, some critics do come from that perspective. But I approach this problem as a feminist, and the best, most sex-positive feminist I can be is one who critiques hookup culture.

The difference between a hookup in theory and hookup culture is essential to this critique. At its most basic level, feminism is about voice, choice, and liberation from oppressive circumstances. It is about empowerment to speak truth, to explore options, and to forge one's own path even if it diverges from that of everyone else around you. It is about creativity and flourishing.

Hookup culture squelches all that. It is antifeminist through and through. Within hookup culture, the hookup is not an exciting, liberating sexual encounter that introduces its participants to the freedom of unfettered sexuality and pleasure. Instead, young adults learn that they have no choice but to accept—whether they like it or not—that the hookup is the norm for sexual intimacy. They learn that they must be casual about sex—even if they don't feel that way. They learn that sex is something that you can "trade" for social acceptance; that sex is something to *get done* much like the dishes; and that pleasure is low on the list of concerns, if it's there at all.

To do and to want things other than a casual hookup is to feel shame—a shame that can be tamped down with large amounts of alcohol. Within hookup culture, a young adult does not look out and see a wide range of options for sexual experience and expression. She sees one option and feels obliged to prove she's okay with that one option because to do otherwise would invite ridicule. To speak up and out against hookup culture is to risk social ostracism.

When I critique a culture of hooking up, I am critiquing the *narrowing* of choice, the *silencing* of voice, the sense that there *is no freedom* around matters of sexuality. I am against coercion and shame around sex, including when it's shame about *not* having had enough sex. I am defending the right to see a range of possible options for sexual intimacy and romantic relationships (one of which includes hookup in theory), because only when people see many paths ahead can they truly seek liberation and be empowered. And if, for certain individuals, being empowered means not having sex or having less sex, then we should allow them to make that choice. I believe that most people, feminists especially, want all young adults to feel safe and confident about their sexuality, to know to their cores that they have the right to decide what they want and do not want to do with respect to sex, as well as what they want and do not want to have done to them. I believe they have the right to experiment around sexuality—which can mean many different things. And I believe that within hookup culture they lose sight of those freedoms, those rights, the possibility of experimentation, and the sense that they can opt out of being sexually active altogether if they choose—if it doesn't fit who they are, what they believe in, or what they are ready to experience at the moment.

I am often asked whether I am against hookups altogether. What I usually say is that I'm not against the individual hookup, in theory, though I am against a culture of hooking up. Hookup culture tends to be coercive—people feel trapped by it, like they have no other option but to participate in ways direct or indirect, and are often disempowered within it. So yes, I'm against any culture like this. I wouldn't be a good feminist if I weren't. As far as individual hookups go, it is not my place to judge students' behavior, unless that behavior provokes suffering, confusion, or alienation on their part or the part of another. When both partners are truly content with their hookups, then I'm not against it.

I also believe that those feminists who defend hooking up as a practice have confused the hookup in theory with a culture of hooking up. They believe they are defending that theoretical hookup—exciting, norm-challenging, and pleasure-teaching. But finding a young adult who has experienced one of those wonderful hookups is incredibly difficult. The hookup in theory is rare in reality. Instead, we find a culture that devalues and oppresses both women and men, one that feminists should fight against.

HOOKUP CULTURE IS A JUSTICE ISSUE (AND WHY APATHY IS A FORM OF SUFFERING)

Within hookup culture, students learn that one must devalue one's partner in order to engage in a successful hookup: diminishing a partner's worth and avoiding communication allows everyone to walk away unscathed. Students learn to see their partners not as people, but as a means to an end, thereby discounting the agency and happiness of their partner in the process. While one participant may indeed be "fine" with his or her hookup experience, there is always more than one person involved. When I ask students who say their hookups are "fine" if they know whether their hookup partner was also fine during the encounter, they often have no idea. For a hookup to truly be fine, both partners need to be okay with it. If a student can't answer this question, then the hookup experience is problematic on many levels, especially with regard to the possibility of sexual assault.

This makes hookup culture a justice issue.

Many young adults care a great deal about social justice. Talk of human dignity and human rights is on the tips of many students' tongues. Yet we've become very good at exporting such concerns off campus, away from the communities and cultures our colleges and universities foster, one of which is hookup culture. During lectures I often raise the subject of social justice and ask the audience how many of them care about human dignity—every single hand in the room will go up. Then, when I ask—*So where is the human dignity at the parties you go to on the weekends?* and *Where is the dignity in the way you've learned to think of your hookup partners?*

Encouraging, empowering, and even requiring college students to focus on social justice on their own campuses, and within their residence halls, their social lives, and their interactions with each other is one of the most powerful and effective responses to hookup culture that institutions of higher education can employ. This is especially true at Catholic schools, which have a rich social justice tradition to draw on, and where large percentages of the student population are often engaged in social justice work. Many students are so passionate about changing the world, it is only sensible that we ask them to be just as passionate about their peers and their partners.

Which brings me to apathy. Apathy is both a source and a cause of suffering.

When I did my initial fieldwork, 23% of students who answered an online survey question about how they felt after a hookup responded with ambivalence; "whatever" was the most common answer. It didn't make them happy or sad—they didn't really feel anything at all. They didn't worry about the bodily intimacy they'd shared with another person and, what's more, they seemed numb to it. The hookup was just sort of *there*, and afterward they gave it a shrug.

I've come to think of this "whatever" group as the most "successful" of all participants in hookup culture—successful in fulfilling the social contract of the hookup. As mentioned above, one of the essential features of the hookup is not getting attached (neither person is supposed to care about the experience or their partner afterward). If the hookup experience is *too* good or you're *too* into it, then your ability to not get attached is threatened. Therefore, students who regard their hookups with a shrug seem to be the ones who get closest to "success" within hookup culture. They are able to use their bodies to engage with other people as though using their own bodies and the bodies of others doesn't matter much. Being able to shrug afterward is what keeps the hookup casual.

The longer hookup culture dominates the campus social scene, the better students are getting at not caring about their partners—and even not caring about sex. Students are learning to *not* care as though it's a skill all young adults must acquire as they mature. They know it's a learned skill, and they work hard to develop a callousness about sex and their partners in a culture that requires it. I have even spoken to students who've told me that somewhere along the way—they're not sure exactly where, how, or from whom—they've internalized the notion that to fall in love during college is a sign of weakness, a failure to show independence, and even an impediment to future success.

For anyone who cares deeply about young adults and college students, it's depressing to hear how numb they've become to their own bodies and the bodies of others. If young adults are going to engage in sexual intimacy, I would prefer them to *want* it, to experience desire, pleasure, and excitement, to have the overall experience be positive, and to perhaps even feel a bit of a thrill about the partner they've chosen. I want them to respect and revere the capacity of bodies to experience and give pleasure, and to understand the ways in which we can be hurt and hurt others by using and abusing our bodies. I would like young adults to have expectations for themselves and their partners, and not feel the need to tamp down all expectations for the sake of walking away unscathed. The skill of callousness is a skill no one should have to learn.

To teach oneself (and encourage others) to feel ambivalent about sex is to deny oneself one of the most wonderful sources of pleasure and human connection that we have. Apathy is a form of suffering because it denies the respect that all bodies deserve; it denies the validity of emotion, connection, and attachment with respect to sex. Apathy is a cause of suffering because it denies our partners all of these things as well. By doing so, we are denying an important aspect of our humanity.

One last thing: in light of hookup culture, I believe that empowering young adults to ask about their rights in relation to sex (their rights to have it, to draw boundaries around what they will or will not do, the notion that they have rights at all), as well as contemplate the meaning and purpose of sex in their own lives (what sex is to them, what they want from it, what good sex might look like) as well as in the lives of their partners, is a matter of social justice, one that we need to help students unpack. It never even occurs to many students that they have *any* rights around sex, or that it would be a good idea for them to reflect on the meaning and purpose of sex. Denial of one's own dignity and that of another, the lack of respect for one's own body and the bodies of others, apathy around sex and one's partner, outright callousness around oneself and one's partners, are all, ultimately, issues that will challenge a person's social justice commitments. One of the best ways to challenge hookup culture is to foster a campus culture that empowers students to explore their rights and the meaning and purpose of sex.

THE GOOD NEWS ABOUT PEOPLE RUNNING CAMPUSES (AND WHY SEX IS NEITHER A LIBERAL NOR A CONSERVATIVE ISSUE)

In the years since this book was first published, I've been pleasantly surprised by the outpouring of interest from departments of student affairs and their openness to discussing hookup culture on campus as well as how to respond to it in their programming. I also quickly learned that plenty of people on Catholic and evangelical colleges across the United States are open and eager to talk with their students about sex, romance, dating, hooking up, purity, and everything in between, and that professionals and administrators in student affairs and campus ministry at all types of institutions are searching for resources to start conversations with their students about hooking up. The vast majority of people in higher education want to forthrightly address their students' concerns. It's also true that there will always be people at universities who worry more about the board, the bishop, the alums with deep pockets, and their own personal religious agendas, than about the needs of students on their campuses. And while at Catholic colleges professionals in student affairs certainly want to know how to walk the line of addressing hookup culture in a way that doesn't jeopardize the Catholic commitment of the college or their jobs—a walk that can be tricky depending on administration and the local bishop—this hasn't dissuaded people from addressing sex and hookup culture. At evangelical schools, people are not afraid to talk about sex either and know that it's important to do so because it's important to their students.

Something else I've learned since the release of *Sex and the Soul* is that most people make assumptions about the politics of those people who are willing to talk about hookup culture and sex on campus. Everyone thinks that only liberals will talk about sex and only conservatives will critique hookup culture. People often ask if I get both liberal and conservative hecklers at my lectures, the assumption being that just about everybody is uncomfortable and unwilling in some way to have conversations about hookup culture on campus.

In my experience, it's impossible to predict who is open to any of the above conversations by their politics. Some of the most politically conservative people (both religiously devout and otherwise) are the most liberal in their willingness to have conversations about sexuality with their students—regardless of where those discussions lead. It's true that there are politically conservative, religiously devout people who would like to deny that their campus needs a conversation about hookup culture. And there are liberals who rant and rave about anyone who seems to critique hard-won sexual freedoms, without taking a good look at how hookup culture denies those freedoms.

However, the vast majority of faculty, staff, and administration put the health and well-being of their students first, no matter the subject, and regardless of their personal politics. This is good news for students and good news for parents. It should make current students, prospective students, and their parents feel reassured.

While attending the average Catholic, private-secular, and public institution today may indeed mean contending with the pervasiveness of hookup culture (and, at evangelical colleges, contending with what can be, at times, an oppressive and isolating culture of purity), students have access to a wide range of people who are devoted to caring for their safety and who wholeheartedly want their college experience to be the very best it can be.

What can these well-intentioned people do to help? That's where we'll turn next.

LEARNING TO SLOW DOWN, TAKE A STEP BACK, AND REST
(AND WHAT RELIGIONS OFFER US IN THIS REGARD)

All of us, not just young adults, have trouble slowing down these days. New technologies have sped up our lives and turned them into a version of the 24/7 news cycle. Facebook and other types of social media existed when I first embarked on this research, yet its role in our lives has changed dramatically since then, taking up far more time and attention. Young adults growing up in the age of the smartphone believe they are expected to be "on" and available at all times. Then there is the culture of success at college and the enormous pressure students feel to demonstrate their accomplishments in quantifiable ways. Students drive themselves to exhaustion in an effort to get through their to-do lists, though they often can't tell you why they're doing the things on that list or how each item got to be there in the first place. Their fear of failing to get through everything before they graduate is profound.

This spring I taught a course on memoir and my students got into a number of discussions about their inability to sit still. They explained how difficult it was for them to deal with the influx of complicated, sometimes challenging thoughts and emotions that would emerge in this stillness, and how they were unprepared to deal with them, process them, or, quite literally, sit and simply let them come. They spoke of avoiding periods of stillness at all costs, and how the frenzy of college life coupled with the presence of so much new technology is facilitating this avoidance. They acknowledged that this might indeed be a counterproductive, problematic state to maintain, yet avoidance seems easier than having to confront those difficult thoughts and emotions, especially when the society around them is pushing them onward, forward, and upward at all times. My students also discussed how, during college, it is a point of pride to get virtually no sleep because of how hard you work and how much you get done. The more exhausted, frenzied, stressed out, and overscheduled they are, the more they must be heading toward success.

At what cost is all of this go, go, going and do, do, doing? And what effect does it have on hookup culture?

Hookup culture thrives when people don't stop and think, when young adults haven't developed the skill of being able to sit still, and when all of their going and doing happens at a frenzied pace. Students talk of being *swept up* in the tide of the party scene and all the drinking that goes on after those long hours of working and not sleeping. They also talk of "finding themselves" having sex or "suddenly" having sex with someone as though amid all the crazy partying they didn't notice where their evening was headed. The constant pressure to be on, 24/7, and available for comments, texts, and various other communications, plus updating their profiles in order to tell everyone about all that they are doing, plays right into the continued dominance of hookup culture.

Being able to sit still, being able to stop and think, is its own challenge to hookup culture. For the vast majority of students, the moment they stop and think—the moment they really take a step back—and assess what they truly want from sex, romance, dating, and the partner with whom they engage in these activities, they quickly realize that hooking up is not the best way to find all of those things. As far as sexual intimacy goes, hookups are pretty lame and unfulfilling. Generally, good, fulfilling, truly liberating sexual intimacy requires the capacity to communicate with a partner about what feels good, is good, what a person wants and would like to try, what works and what doesn't. It requires a certain amount of comfort with that partner in order to communicate all of the above, and it requires the explicit consent and reciprocal interest and participation of that partner. The hookup rarely offers any of these things. In fact, it works against them since intimacy rests on communication, a certain level of comfort with one's partner, and, generally, enough time for pleasure and enjoyment and experimentation to take place (and a hookup is supposed to be a brief, one-time occurrence). What's more, the typical context of the hookup: the crazy drunken party, the frenzied fun after the frenzied college work week, also contributes to the diminishing of sexual intimacy and satisfaction.

When students slow down, take a step back, and start asking them-selves questions about what they want—not just from sex and hooking up, but from life, work, play, relationships, family—they often realize that what they are doing is not going to get them there. One reason why the thoughts and emotions that emerge during periods of stillness are so uncomfortable is because in those moments students begin to realize they don't know why they are doing what they are doing, whether their activities and life choices matter to them in a larger sense, or if they've allowed personal happiness to factor into their life pursuits.

Challenging hookup culture on campus can seem an overwhelming task, yet some of the best methods for challenging it are indirect. Providing students with structured opportunities for slowing down, rest, and stillness is one of those methods, and its benefits reach far beyond hookup culture. Any structured opportunity or incentive to unplug from technology and leave that smartphone behind for a while can help students learn these skills, and encouraging students inside the classroom to question the college culture of success and the fren-zied way we go about living our lives is another step in the right direction. Open the door to conversation and critical thinking about this subject and students will jump at the opportunity to reflect, analyze, and discuss these very things.

For schools with religious affiliations and for those who work in campus ministry or run worship-centered organizations and communities at secular schools, this is one area where the rituals and practices of a religious tradition can work to the benefit of students overall and challenge hookup culture in the process. Opportunities to go on retreats, to seek spiritual direction, to practice mindfulness, contemplation, or attend worship, and any other structured time that facilitates slowing down and developing the ability to avoid being overwhelmed by the many distractions and pressures students face, has never been more important. Engaging in these rituals and spiritual practices is potentially more life-changing for students than engaging in their plugged-in world.

Staff and administrators at religiously affiliated institutions tend to believe they are in the worst position to confront hookup culture because of their religious affiliations. But religiously affiliated institutions are often *better* prepared than secular schools for opening up new dialogues about sex, sexuality, and hookup culture, *because* of the additional resources and spiritual practices they provide on campus. The reason we struggle with conversations about sex and religion is a simple failure to be creative. We too often fail to employ the full wealth of resources a religious tradition offers. Particularly at Catholic universities, people assume they must stick to the big Catholic "don'ts" about sex, neglecting to use the many other rituals and spiritual practices of that same tradition to open up conversations and critical thinking about sex and sexuality, as well as using the tradition to help teach students how to stop and think in a technological world where stopping and thinking is often discouraged.

SETTING ASIDE THE WORRY ABOUT "LEARNING OUTCOMES"

In my experience leading professional development sessions with student affairs, I hear a lot about "learning outcomes." What sort of learning outcomes does a program have? What sort of learning outcomes will the students get if they come to a particular event? People worry about what sort of learning outcomes I can provide as well, so they can report back to their higher ups exactly what people have gotten out of my visit. Concern for learning outcomes—being able to enumerate them very explicitly—is a way of justifying a program's existence to the people who control the funding. It's sometimes a way of justifying a staff member's existence—a formal, ongoing explanation as to why a particular employee is necessary and their salary worth paying. Everyone's concern about being able to outline (ahead of time) and report (after the fact) exactly why a program was conceived and what results it achieved is understandable.

But.

When we worry about the learning outcomes of every program, including the programs that happen in the residence halls on weekends and at night when students are supposedly taking a break, we reinforce a culture of high expectations, success, stress, and the notion that *all* activities must have a takeaway. If a student doesn't "learn" something from the program—if someone can't point and say, *this is what I got out of the experience*—then we begin to think that the activity is worthless. This teaches all of us that the aftermath, the takeaway, the capacity to say *I did this* and *this is what I got from it* is the most important thing of all. We begin to worry so much about what we can say after the fact, that we stop being present during the fact itself.

Many young adults today aren't quite sure what they count as fun anymore. Many of them have no idea why they do the things they do, aside from being able to put them on their résumés to prove to someone later that, indeed, they did X, Y, and Z. I worry that our focus on learning outcomes reinforces this. Many schools no longer support programs for students just because it might be fun or because students need a break. Instead, we program so that we can *teach* students something and prove to someone else that "learning" happened, often accompanied by a big stack of evaluations. We rarely encourage our students to do something simply because they enjoy it, or explore something simply because it might be interesting, and not because it might get them somewhere or something in the future.

This culture of learning outcomes and evaluations is related to the perpetuation of hookup culture in several ways. First, it reinforces college students' inability to slow down, or even understand the value of slowing down. Second, it reinforces students' sense that everything they do must be done for the sake of something else, not for its own sake. Third, it reinforces a rather unforgiving culture of success, where students internalize the notion that activities and interests are only worthwhile if they propel them farther up the ladder of success.

When you apply our larger cultural concern about "outcomes" to hookup culture, you begin to understand why so many students fail to see that sexual intimacy can be enjoyed for its own sake, enjoyed because it's fun and pleasurable and emotionally fulfilling. Instead they focus on hooking up as yet another task to accomplish so they can say they did it, and so it moves them farther up the social ladder. It becomes easier to see the logic in why a hookup partner so easily becomes a means to an end for many students, instead of someone to whom they must give their full attention and respect. In a culture dominated by concern for "outcomes," sex becomes an instrument, a way to fit in and achieve social status, another line on a student's college social résumé—one that helps them justify to friends and peers that yes, indeed, they have a lot to show for their college careers.

CONSIDERING NEW WAYS TO PROGRAM AROUND SEXUAL ASSAULT

The last couple of academic years have seen an enormous number of sexual assault scandals on college campuses—Northeastern, Florida State, and Columbia University among them. The scandal is not only about specific accusations or even the prevalence of sexual assault on these campuses—and *all* campuses—but about how universities handle (or don't) claims of sexual assault by students, and the fact that so many who are assaulted are victimized a second time by the process (or lack of one). The Obama administration has made sexual assault on campus a priority, and for the first time since Title IX was established in 1972, the White House has chosen to highlight how it is meant to protect students from sexual misconduct. The attention is forcing colleges and universities to reckon with how many assaults go unreported (altogether and certainly to the police) and how many go unprosecuted because the resources for assault victims are poor or even nonexistent, or because the process has been botched by unprepared (or unwilling) administration and staff.

That President Obama, Vice President Biden, and members of Congress such as Senator Kirsten E. Gillibrand of New York have chosen to shine a light on sexual assault has led to cheers by many of us who spend our lives talking about this issue. But it also has colleges and universities scrambling to respond and wildly unprepared to do so. Questions abound about how to handle victims and alleged perpetrators, how to involve (or not) the police, and how and when to educate students around sexual assault. At religiously affiliated colleges these questions can be even more complicated, especially if the institution is heavily invested in proving to itself and the public that sex doesn't happen on *its* campus.

When I visit colleges and universities and talk about sexual assault, I operate on the assumption that *all* institutions offer at least the typical required sex education program for all first-year students—and have been surprised to find out that some colleges don't even do this. Those colleges are almost always religiously affiliated. To state the obvious: the most dangerous and reckless path a university can take is to assume—or to decide for the sake of public perception—that sexual assault is not an issue on its campus because its students are committed to their faith tradition, which teaches no sex until marriage. Even at colleges where statistics show that few students are sexually active (as at evangelical colleges), college students are vulnerable to sexual assault. That *all* universities and colleges, including religiously affiliated institutions, need to address this topic should be self-evident.

How and when to educate students about sexual assault is one of the biggest concerns for colleges today, and over the last several years a program focused on bystander intervention has emerged, largely sparked by the efforts of Jane Stapleton at the University of New Hampshire. It is now catching on at institutions across the country, and it shows extraordinary promise. It educates students about how (and why) to help a fellow student who seems to be in a risky, vulnerable situation, before an assault can take place. But the average sex education and sexual assault programming for first-year students is abysmal. Typically, large groups (hundreds or even thousands) of students are herded into a giant auditorium for a required program (translation: they are forced to go), where resident assistants and student affairs staff, but no one else, are present. At this point students are subjected to someone talking at them for an hour about sex, STI's, and sexual assault, often in a "comedic" style. This invites discomfort, insecurity, and anxiety and often results in students making light of the whole ordeal. Needless to say, this is not the kind of reaction universities (or anyone for that matter) should want an educational program on sexual assault to provoke. Yet finding alternatives to this kind of programming isn't easy either.

Some universities have adopted human resources–like, online programs (albeit with colorful photos) where students are required to scroll through a tutorial on sexual assault and answer a series of questions that prove they paid attention at the end. Yet these programs provide zero opportunity for conversation and give students a sense that getting through the course is akin to a business transaction, with universities more concerned with covering themselves legally than doing the hard work of finding programming that really works. What's more, they send the message that sexual assault is not a matter for public discussion.

As someone who has been talking about sex to college students on campus for over a decade, I've learned a lot about the best types of forums for this discussion—and the worst. The best forums are relatively small groups (ideally 50–200 students), in relatively intimate settings (a brightly lit room where everyone is packed together and the speaker is standing close to the audience—not far up and away on a remote stage), where attendance is voluntary, and where the audience includes students, obviously, but also plenty of faculty, administration, and staff interspersed among them. If a college offers a program about sex for all members of a community—because it is, indeed, a communal topic—the students should look around the room and see their professors among the other staff and administrators. This sends the message that the subject at hand is not just a student issue, but one that the whole community cares about. What's more, they see potential allies to whom they might go if they need to talk. Small, intimate, intergenerational settings for discussions around sex, hooking up, dating, sexual assault, and STI's work best because this is a conversation that students are incredibly insecure about—and large, student-only gatherings exacerbate their anxieties. When you cut the numbers, when you downsize the room, when you have faculty, staff, and administrators listening intently because they feel this talk is important to them, too, and when you make attendance voluntary—you dismantle a good deal of the unease among students. When students see professors around the room they behave differently and take the topic more seriously.

The least productive forum for conversations around sex is in a large group setting (300+), in a gigantic auditorium where the speaker stands apart from students up on a stage, when the students are forced to go, and worse still, if all students attending are first-years and they've just stepped on campus. Students are already so nervous about what lies ahead for them, putting five hundred or even a thousand of them in an auditorium to talk about sex for an hour is pointless. Universities and colleges do this because they fear liability for *not* having done it, and because they know that sexual assault is a possibility from the very moment a student arrives on campus, because the partying starts immediately. They require the program because, of course, *all* students need to know about sex and sexual assault, not just those who would attend a program like this of their own volition.

Is there a middle ground?

I think so. I propose that we rethink how we open the discussion about sexual assault on campus. The simplest, easiest way to truly change the dynamic—and still require all first-year students to attend—involves the following:

1. Offering a series of dates to attend the program, even if those dates all occur during the first two weeks on campus.
2. Drastically reducing the number of attendees (ideally to around 50 per session, or even less on smaller campuses).
3. Making sure that faculty, administrators, and staff are present at each session, or ideally, leading the session.
4. Making sure that upperclassmen are present at each session.
5. Making sure the room is small (if it happens in a classroom, this indicates to students that this is a classroom-worthy topic).
6. Cutting out the comedy and amping up the rigor—students (in small group settings where professors are present) are not only capable of engaging in but want opportunities for real, critical discussion of these issues. If we take the subject seriously, students will too.
7. Making sure each session is opened by a faculty or staff member who can help frame why everyone is present and making everyone comfortable in the process. If the person standing up front is comfortable with the subject matter, it will reduce students' anxiety.

Are these suggestions costly? Yes. Are they time-intensive? Yes. Do they require a lot of work? Yes. Do they require a high level of dedication by at least a critical mass of faculty, staff, and administrators? Absolutely. (And I say this having worked for six years in student affairs, knowing how difficult it is during August and September.) But if we are talking about *truly* educating our students about sexual assault—and ideally preventing it—isn't this a worthy investment? And to be purely business-minded about it: right now the federal government is threatening to pull federal funding from universities that do not effectively educate about and respond to sexual assault on campus. Relatively speaking, isn't it more cost-effective to invest in high-quality and thorough sexual assault programming than to lose federal funding and immerse the campus in a high-profile scandal?

I would think that the answer is yes.

While the attention from the White House, Congress, and the media is promising, I've been disappointed to see how little the role hookup culture has played in the discussion. Hookup culture teaches young adults that communication creates intimacy and attachment, therefore not communicating at all with one's partner is best (which is also often where alcohol comes in to help). This has obvious repercussions for sexual assault, yet our discussions around consent have yet to take into account hookup culture's effect on the growing *inability* to talk about sexual intimacy. Hookup culture teaches people that the best way to approach sexual intimacy is to learn how to act like their partner is an inanimate sex toy. It objectifies and dehumanizes. So does sexual assault. I'm not suggesting that hookups are assaults, but I am suggesting that during a hookup it is often the case that consent is murky at best.

In hookup culture, young adults learn that communication can create attachment, so it's best to communicate very little or not at all. Students are often wildly ambivalent about their hookups, and both men and women will use alcohol as a way to distance themselves from their own agency in the encounter. We need to ask ourselves: How can we best educate young adults about the nature of consent, when they are at the same time immersed in a culture where the social contract of the hookup teaches them that communication is problematic? When they are living in a culture that teaches them that the best attitude to have about sex is an ambivalent one—about sex in general, and also about their partners? Consenting to sex, and ensuring that one's partner does the same, requires a level of care for one's partner and investment in the encounter that hookup culture works against. Consent may not seem like a difficult concept to understand or even to teach, but within hookup culture it's far more complicated than many of us would like to believe. Unless we grapple with the nature of hookup culture, our conversations about consent will be missing an essential piece.

Finally, some of the best preventative programming we can do on campus never mentions sexual assault. A common mid-year prevention program I've seen advertised on campuses is "Can I kiss you?" When I first saw a flyer for one of these events, I thought to myself: what a great program, since a complaint I often hear from students is how—without alcohol—nobody would ever make out. Then I learned the program was actually about consent and sexual assault—a worthwhile topic, obviously. But if *all* our programming about sex ends up being about sexual assault (or STI's), then we are reinforcing problematic notions about sex. We are teaching our communities that sex is *always* potentially dangerous and *always* potentially violent.

A program called "Can I kiss you?" that is not about sexual assault, and instead about how to ask out, take out, and maybe even kiss someone to whom you are attracted—all skills that most young adults today are lacking (at least while sober)—would probably be a hit with students, and would do a great deal to teach healthy sexual behavior and develop healthy understandings of consent. Students often discuss how they don't date—even though they'd like to—because they don't know how. They don't have the basic communication skills to talk to people to whom they are attracted. By hooking up, they avoid risking the potential embarrassment that comes with trying something new. They avoid the possibility of failure. Teaching students to walk up to someone while they are sober, during the day, to say, "Hey, would you like to go for coffee?" would help foster healthier ideas about sex, and that can only help reduce sexual assault on campus. Consent is grounded in our ability to communicate, and *any* programming that we do that helps develop basic communication skills related to relationships is ultimately a program that helps teach the nature of consent.

CCCU COLLEGES: POLICIES ON SEX AND CONFRONTING LGBTQ ISSUES ON CAMPUS

I have made many trips to institutions that belong to the Coalition of Christian Colleges and Universities (CCCU). These communities have an impressive ability to foster intergenerational conversations among faculty, administrators, staff, and students, as well as to support the flourishing of students' faith lives. It is not uncommon that students on campus know the families of the faculty and staff, and even babysit for the college president's children. The effort and care that go into supporting students' lives beyond the classroom is unique among college environments. Like student affairs professionals at Catholic, private-secular, and public colleges, CCCU colleges make an extraordinary effort to reach out to their students around the topic of sex and provide those students as many resources as they can.

There are two sticking points I often run into on such campuses, however. Both points are related, and they have to do with policies stating that a student can be adjudicated or even expelled if it comes to the institution's attention that the student has had sex, or if the student is gay. Yet, when the subject of these policies comes up among faculty, administrators, and staff, people nearly always state (and passionately so) how they would *never* actually expel a student for having sex or for coming out, and that they want *all* students to feel comfortable and safe coming to them to talk about sex and sexual identity. A couple of years ago, when I gave a keynote for the annual conference of CCCU presidents, I heard more of the same from the presidents themselves. Despite these policies, just about everyone on campus wants students to feel safe coming to talk to them about sex and sexual identity.

The problem, of course, is getting students to feel truly safe when everyone knows these policies—and therefore the risk of punishment and expulsion—exist. During visits to CCCU schools, I am often given the opportunity to have a students-only conversation, which is also typically the moment when students will say things like, "Everybody *claims* we won't get into trouble if we talk to them about sex, but how are we *really* supposed to be sure, if they can still decide to kick us out for telling them things?" And someone will always bring up an example: "Three years ago they expelled this kid for coming out and not ending a relationship he was in with another guy, so how do people expect us to believe it's really safe to talk about this stuff?"

In general, students feel that if the policies exist, and they can point to at least one example when the school did in fact act on these policies, then they can't *really* trust faculty, administrators, and staff on campus—a circumstance that hampers those wonderful intergenerational conversations I mentioned above. If a student hasn't yet been sexually active, they can participate in a discussion safely, but if a student has become sexually active then that door to honest conversation closes. The same goes for coming out and being in a gay or lesbian relationship—students can probably get away with admitting they are gay, but beyond this, they believe that they are risking the loss of their place at their college.

The argument I often get when I raise this concern with faculty, staff, and administrators at a CCCU school is that because it's a Christian college, these policies must exist. Without such policies, it wouldn't be a Christian college. My response is always the same: both when I did the initial research for my study and today when I visit CCCU schools, I find a robust, peer-supported culture that is pro-chastity, pro-purity, and focused on trying to live up to traditional Christian values around premarital sex (the topic of sexual identity is another story—I'll come back to it in a moment). CCCU schools do not literally need a policy that threatens expulsion to convince their students that waiting for sex until they are married is part of the Christian tradition. Most students enter these institutions already believing they must live up to this expectation, and even students who have become sexually active during college often hope to get back to living up to the teaching about premarital sex. A policy that threatens adjudication and even expulsion for sexual activity does not a Christian college make. The Christian attitudes of the students themselves is the stuff of that Christian identity—not something that many Catholic colleges can boast, but one that nearly all CCCU schools can. Whether or not CCCU schools will learn to trust in their students and strike such rules remains to be seen, but truly safe and honest intergenerational conversation will only be possible—at least from the students' perspective—if this policy ceases to exist.

The topic of sexual identity is more complex. There is a growing generational divide. Students at CCCU schools—even if they are unsure what, exactly, their position is on homosexuality—want opportunities to safely discuss the topic, if not also to come out and be in an openly romantic relationship with another gay, lesbian, or bisexual student on campus without threat of punishment or expulsion. Overall, this generation of Christian young adults seems headed toward a more open position on LGBTQ issues, and students are aware this makes many of their elders uncomfortable. Faculty, administrators, and staff on campus know that their students are clamoring for more conversation about this subject and some of them are rising to the occasion, but many of them are a bit paralyzed about what to do. I can say that just about everybody *wants* to find a way into a conversation about LGBTQ issues, and I've already begun to see this happening on campus. Whether or not these schools will find a way to address their policies about homosexuality, however, remains to be seen.

5 Simple Ideas for Responding to Hookup Culture on Campus

For Faculty, Administrators, Campus Ministry, and Student Affairs Staff

So, if you work on a college campus, what can you do to help foster a better campus culture and help students develop healthier attitudes about sex? Here are five simple ideas:

1. Make a list of people on campus who feel comfortable talking to students about sex, romance, dating, and everything in between—a *formal* list. This will require various groups on campus (student affairs, as well as campus ministry, athletics, the health center, faculty, etc.) to take the time to meet and talk about who from within those groups should be on that list. This sort of conversation isn't for everyone—talking about sex is often as difficult for adults as it is for young adults—but *someone* on campus needs to be willing to have the conversation with students. It is important for everyone to know who, specifically, is willing and able to do it.

2. If the only programming about sex that you offer is about sexual assault, you're doing something wrong. Offer a "Can I Kiss

You?" program that is about just that—kissing, as in, how in the world can you kiss that person who interests you *outside* of a hookup, when you are *not* trashed at a party. Students lack basic communication skills around dating, romance, and the like (never mind sex) and need to learn those skills somewhere. If we link *all* programming to sex and then to sexual assault, then we reinforce to students that everything leads to sex and that everything leading to sex is potentially dangerous. Offering more innocent programming (how to ask someone out, a tour of the top ten most romantic places to kiss on campus) says to students that there is more to sex than sexual assault. Intimacy and romance are good things.

3. If you are a member of the faculty, open up the conversation in your classroom to students' personal reflections on love, dating, romance, sex, gender roles, sexual orientation (and everything in between) anywhere that it seems natural from your already assigned readings—even if you only do it once during the semester. If the discussion for a day involves a novel, a play, poetry, philosophy, theology, psychology (the list could go on) that talks of love, relationships, heartbreak, infatuation (again, the list could go on), simply ask the students a direct question about the topic about which they are reading in relation to their own personal experiences. Students are hungry to do rigorous critical reflection on all of these topics within the classroom. They will be happy if you empower them to do so in your course.

4. If you work at a school with a religious affiliation, or if you work in a campus ministry–related group or program on a secular campus, dedicate a certain portion of your spiritual direction sessions or a weekend retreat to talking about sex, dating, romance, and hooking up. Simply offering the possibility of thinking about these things in a religious context opens the door to considering the relationship between religion and sex. Plus, it gives students an opportunity to engage in that all-important act of slowing down.

5. Offer a Dating 101 program. Remember that students are unbelievably nervous about dating—even though they'd really like to date, they lack the skills and experience to do so, which reinforces hookup culture. They are worried about being rejected and making fools of themselves in front of their peers. On the flipside, faculty, student affairs and campus ministry staff, and administrators often don't have to worry about these issues.

Offering a fun, lighthearted panel on the how-to's of dating, asking someone out, dealing with rejection, and recovering from heartbreak is a program that is guaranteed to fill to capacity with students eager to talk about the perils of dating as well as to hear the war stories and how-to advice of their favorite professors and staff.

Appendix

On Methodology

A "COMMUNAL" APPROACH TO STUDY DEVELOPMENT

The study on which this book is based, Sexuality and Spirituality in American College Life, was inspired by the 21 students in my dating course and the newspaper they wrote as a final project. Six of these same students participated in the development and interpretation of the interview process as research assistants over the 2005–2006 academic year. One additional student, a psychology major I knew from other courses, was invited to be the seventh research assistant. Though I was the primary investigator of this study, oversaw and conducted the project from start to finish (including the school visits), and worked with two psychologists, Dr. Jeffrey Adams and Dr. Molly Millwood, to develop and interpret the data from the online survey, the 7 undergraduate RAs were an important part of the success of this project.

As a scholar trained in feminist research and pedagogical methods, an educator with extensive experience in hands-on, participatory learning, and a former student affairs professional strongly invested in breaking down the (false) sense that the classroom and overall student life are divided on campus, I believe that research involving young adult participants and communities should aspire to (a) include young adults as investigators and advisers when possible and (b) have a transformative impact on the community from which the project emerges and, ultimately, the wider community to which the research is relevant. My teaching philosophy includes the belief that students are themselves unique and diverse resources within the classroom. Though I may be the primary instructor and facilitator in the room, students also have teaching roles that are important to everyone in the class, including myself, and each brings a certain amount of authority to our subject. As a result, from the very beginning, as I conceived this study and sought funding to conduct it, including undergraduate researchers from the original dating class was a priority. I solicited interest from those students who would be returning as seniors and planned for their participation in the original grant proposal. I considered it a matter of ethics to invite student participation from this particular class since they were part of this project's conception, and also because it doesn't seem right and doesn't make sense (to me) to develop a study about college students without inviting a group of college students to advise on the project.

The subsequent participation of seven student researchers (all women) in conducting this study allowed one dimension of this project to employ an altered version of the participatory action research (PAR) method.[1] Generally, this is a method of research in which "the distinction between the researcher and the researched is challenged as participants are afforded the opportunity to take an active role in addressing issues affecting themselves, their families, their communities." In addition to using "fairly traditional methods of social scientific inquiry such as . . . questionnaires and interviews," PAR also uses a variety of nontraditional methods, including group discussions, seminars, and storytelling.[2] The seven student RAs were not technically *participants* in this study, either in being interviewed or taking the online survey. In this case, "the distinction challenged" was between a professor as researcher and a student as participant.

The RAs were instrumental in five different steps necessary to conducting this study: (1) the background and secondary literature research; (2) developing the in-person, on-campus interview questions; (3) developing the online survey; (4) transcribing interviews; and (5) providing both written and oral interpretive feedback based on the particular set of interviews from a range of institutions assigned to them. Apart from reviewing the online survey for content and being part of the student test group that took a preliminary version of the online survey and later advised on the clarity of the questions and the length of time necessary for completing the survey, the bulk of the RA work was invested in the interview side of the study. Research assistants' participation in the interview process included one-on-one meetings with me about interview topics and questions; participating in a weekly seminar during the spring of 2006 that included group discussions about study development, progress, and debriefing of my school visits, and online chats while I was away at school visits; individual research and transcription work; plus a final paper and audio-taped one-on-one conversation with me about what they learned from the experience and their judgments about the interview data to which they were given access.

I conducted all 111 interviews myself. None of the RAs made campus visits or had personal interactions with the students who were interviewed.

Participatory action research has three main guidelines, and together, we experienced all three—again, in an altered form—as researchers. First, PAR seeks to address an oppressed or exploited population. In this case, the student RAs had identified the hookup culture on campus as problematic, especially for women, and were interested not only in transforming it on their campus but also in finding out whether their peers at other institutions felt similarly. Also, they experienced the Catholic identity of their college as largely irrelevant and lacking influence in transforming hookup culture. Their participation in this study as RAs allowed them to "address" their peers about these issues. Second, PAR investigates the causes of the problem and seeks to enact social change. In many ways, the dating class as a whole and these RAs as part of the class had already begun to enact social change on their campus through the newspaper, and their participation in this study was motivated by their interest in raising awareness at other campuses about the struggles in relation to sex and religion (if, indeed, there were struggles elsewhere) that they experienced on their campus. The publication of this book seeks to help bring about social change on college campuses. Finally, PAR involves personal transformation as a result of participation in the study. As within the classroom, where I believe that, ideally, both professor and student are transformed by the learning environment they create together, one of the most important pieces of this study (for me) was the reciprocal learning and transformation of all of us together as a result of investing ourselves in this project.[3]

THE TEACHER, THE FEMINIST, THE LISTENER
IN THE ROOM: INTERVIEW METHODOLOGY

There are many different approaches to qualitative research, and I spent a good deal of my preliminary work reviewing the methodologies of other interview-heavy studies of teens and young adults and taking advice from the wealth of essays on feminist methodologies for qualitative research in Deborah L. Tolman and Mary Brydon-Miller's *From Subjects to Subjectivities: A Handbook of Interpretive and Participatory Methods*, especially Mark B. Tappan's essay, "Interpretive Psychology: Stories, Circles, and Understanding Lived Experience."[4] Tappan's discussion of the interpretive-hermeneutic approach to psychological research was helpful in grounding my own approach to the qualitative part of this study, and the way that I prioritize the qualitative over the quantitative—a priority usually reversed by social scientists, who prize the quantitative, often to the extent that qualitative data are simply not collected because they are not considered "objective" enough. Though I am not a psychologist, my academic formation in feminist theory and religious studies includes a heavy emphasis in hermeneutics and the idea that *everything is interpretation* at some level. We, ourselves, are interpretations, "texts," "stories"—and we live our lives within many different interpretive frameworks, many of which we are not consciously aware of.[5]

This methodological starting point had four significant practical implications for the interview aspect of this process.

First, I regarded the student interviews as the primary and most important sources collected in this study. Although quantitative research provides important statistical data about particular groups of students and a particular college or college type, it is only through providing an open-ended space for participant storytelling that one can begin to understand a student's unique experience and to piece together a "master narrative" about an area of interest—in this case, about sex and religion.

Second, the interviews I conducted were semi-structured and, in many ways, resembled my approach to teaching in the classroom. Though I brought up a general series of topics and questions with each student, I left room in the process for him or her to direct the conversation in new directions and for me to ask questions targeted to that particular student's story. Rarely, this led to interview sessions that did not hit on all of the topics I typically raised with the majority of students. In some instances, this approach led me to add questions to subsequent interviews, since several participants raised interesting issues that were not addressed on the basic questionnaire.

Third, the interview process itself was an interpretive act. The student participant brought preconceived notions about the experience, presented one version of himself or herself—a story—about a variety of topics, all the while "performing" the interview in front of me, the interviewer, who brought her own biases and experiences to the process.

Fourth and finally, I was left to interpret which student stories would be highlighted for the purposes of discussing sex and the soul, to interpret the most important overall themes across all the interviews, and to engage in this process with the particular concern of *gender* in mind. Though the interviews could have been further filtered (in addition to religion and sex)—through the primary lens of race, for example, or economic status—because of my background in feminist theory, a concern for gender has generally been the reigning angle through which I "read" the data and the information imparted in the interviews.

PARTICIPATING INSTITUTIONS: SELECTION AND ADMINISTRATION

My initial concern was finding a range of participating institutions that fit my four main categories: evangelical, Catholic, nonreligious private, and public. I began my search by approaching personal acquaintances and colleagues at a number of schools and by requesting introductions to potential campus contacts from other colleagues. These campus contacts ranged from faculty to campus ministry to student affairs administrators.

Each campus contact had the responsibility of getting the study approved through the proper channels on the campus (whether "official" approval was required varied from school to school). Each contact was also presented with the approval documentation for the study from the Internal Review Board (IRB, for studies using human subjects) at St. Michael's College. In addition, campus contacts were expected to distribute the online study via e-mail, help arrange my campus visit by setting up space for the in-person interview process, distribute payment to participants, and handle any other logistical details that arose.

Finding nonreligious colleges and universities to participate was easy. The decision to promise institutional anonymity was, in part, to protect the privacy wishes of the religious colleges. In my search for participant schools, the most difficult task was securing willing religiously affiliated colleges. And though I found many contacts who pushed the study through the highest levels of approval at their institutions, from the formal IRB boards to the provost and president, there were two colleges where the faculty, students, and the IRB boards approved the schools' participation in the study, but the provost and/or president forbade their involvement.

ONLINE SURVEY PARTICIPANTS: SELECTION AND ADMINISTRATION

The online survey was developed in conjunction with two psychologists, Jeffrey Adams and Molly Millwood, both of whom were hired through study funds expressly for this purpose. I worked with Dr. Adams primarily on the questions and survey instruments related to faith, religion, and spirituality, and with Dr. Millwood on the study elements related to sex and relationships.

At the three smaller colleges (with populations under 5,000)—both evangelical Protestant schools and one of the Catholic schools—the survey invitation was e-mailed to the entire student body via the campus listserv. At the remaining four schools, students were invited via e-mail listservs of large, general education, required courses and, at one school, via the listserv for a residential hall of approximately 1,400 students. In addition to being given information about the study, the survey, and confidentiality, the invitation to participate was sweetened by offering a random drawing for three "prizes," one of $100 and two of $25 in cash at each participating school.

More than 2,500 students across the seven schools took at least some part or all of the online survey. Once students clicked on the link embedded in their school's survey invitation e-mail, they were required to give consent to their participation before they were able to move to any other part of the survey. All students were promised anonymity. Students were free to skip questions that they did not want to answer or to simply answer part of the survey. As a result, the number of student answers for each topic fluctuates, depending on how many students chose to answer the relevant question(s).

The students who answered the questions at the end of the survey about basic demographic data broke down as follows:

Gender: 67% female, 33% male

Religious preference: Roman Catholic 20%, evangelical Protestant 32%, mainline Protestant 19%, no religious affiliation 14%

Number of states represented among participants: 45

White/Caucasian participants: 86%

Lesbian, gay, bisexual participants: 5.1%

First-year students: 28.4%, sophomores: 22.5%, juniors: 23.4%, seniors: 25.8%

There is one important limitation to note about the online survey process. Because students were allowed to skip questions and complete only part of the survey, and because most of the basic demographic information regarding gender, ethnic background, sexual orientation, and so on, was solicited at the end of the survey (religious affiliation does not apply here, since it was solicited early on), it is difficult to ascertain with accuracy the true demographic breakdown of the participants—especially with regard to ethnicity and sexual orientation. There were a large number of students who started the survey and did not finish it. If I were to readminister the survey, I would ask for all of the demographic information up front.

As a last note, this book does not by any means exhaust either the qualitative or quantitative data, and will not be the only product that will result from this national study. In fact, very little of the quantitative data is released here. Most of these findings will be published in other forms, especially in journal articles, several of which will be written in conjunction with the online survey developers, Jeffrey Adams and Molly Millwood.

INTERVIEW PARTICIPANTS: SELECTION
AND ADMINISTRATION

The only factor affecting participant selection at each campus was the goal to achieve gender balance. Otherwise, students were selected at random from a pool of volunteers who identified their interest in an in-person interview via the online survey. At the very end of the online survey was a request to leave their contact information if they wished to continue their participation in the study.

To arrange the interviews, prior to my campus visit I e-mailed detailed information about the interview process and a list of possible interview slots to the selected group of students and requested that each respond with all possible available times. I generally e-mailed 24 to 26 students, with the hope of at least 15 responses from students willing to follow through on their initial interest. I actually interviewed anywhere from 13 to 19 students at each institution. At the four religiously affiliated campuses, student no-shows were rare. At two of these schools, every student who signed up for an interview slot showed up. At the private and public universities, student no-shows were more of a problem.

Interviews were conducted in a private setting on campus—either an office or small seminar room—arranged by the onsite campus contact. Interviews ranged from 40 minutes to 75 minutes, and they were taped with a digital audio device. Before I started recording, each student was again given basic information about the study and interview process, was told that they could skip any question they did not want to answer (almost no one exercised this option), was given time to read an "informed consent" statement they needed to sign before we could start the interview, and was taken step by step through this form, which described participant information, confidentiality, and the required steps before payment (which required participants to complete all or part of an online journal over the course of about 10 days following the interview, after which their $25 check would be released to them by the onsite campus contact). Each participant was also given the opportunity to ask any questions they might have both before the formal interview started and after the interview ended, when the recording device was turned off.

The standard series of interview topics included the following:

1. *General questions about their college experience.* This section included questions about how students selected their college— whether students had considered any religiously affiliated colleges or considered the religious affiliation of their colleges in the process, the positives and negatives of their experience so far, the major influences on student life at their college, and general priorities and values exhibited by both peers and the faculty and administration.
2. *Religious background.* This section included questions about religious upbringing; current religious activities and participation (if any); participation in campus ministry; religious affiliations and activities of friends (if any); perception of how religion, spirituality, and faith-related issues are prioritized (or not) at

their college and in what forums (if any); how the students would label themselves (religious, spiritual, or otherwise) and how they define these terms; and whether/how students share these affiliations and practices with friends and the wider community.

3. *General questions about campus social life.* This section included a basic description of campus social life. What do people do to have fun? It also asked about parties in general, theme parties, drinking (of both the person being interviewed and others), how people dress when they go out, gender differences (if any) in relation to the social experience, areas where peer pressure (if any) is experienced.

4. *Dating and hooking up: Perceptions of others.* This section included basic questions about the dating scene; how gender affects attitudes about dating (if at all); definition of hooking up; perception of whether people hook up or not; how and why hooking up occurs (if at all); what people hope for from hooking up (if it is common); whether gender affects the intent and interpretation of hooking up; how people feel after a hookup; whether, how, and why people get reputations; and whether gender affects who gets reputations.

5. *Sex and virginity: Perception of others.* This section included questions about peer attitudes about sex on campus and about the definition of "what counts" as sex. Is sex a popular conversation topic? Is love? Marriage? What are the attitudes of peers about virginity? What is the gender influence (if any) on being a virgin? How is "virginity" defined? What is the participant's perception of whether/why people ever lie about sexual history (either their experience or their inexperience).

6. *Dating, hooking up, and sex: Personal experience.* This section included questions about whether the participants had ever hooked up, their feelings about the experience before/after (if relevant), level of sexual experience, and when they first became sexually active (this could be anything from kissing to sexual intercourse, depending on the student). Students were asked the parameters for becoming sexually intimate, who (if anyone) they talk to for advice about sex, whether sex is a possible spiritual/sacred experience, and their feelings about their own sexual history. Were they dating anyone at the time of the interview, and, if so, how did the relationship start and how long had it gone on? Had they been sexually active with this

person, and what is their evaluation of sex within this relationship?

7. *Religion and sex.* This section asked the students about their (current or childhood) religion's attitudes about sex in general and premarital sex. What are the teachings about sex specifically? What are their personal opinions about these teachings, and how were teachings communicated (if at all)? What were their sources of information? They were asked whether they had taken abstinence pledges, what kinds of sexual activity/intimacy (if any) are permissible within their particular religious tradition, whether they think engaging in sexual activity affects spiritual life/relationship with God, their religion's attitude/ teachings (if any) about dating, specific guidance about dating from within their religious tradition (books, sermons, etc.) or clergy (if any), and whether they think dating affects spiritual/ religious life.

All of the students referenced in this book have been given pseudonyms, and certain identifying features have sometimes been changed to protect their identities. Their comments and stories are told as accurately as possible, with some commentary edited for readability.

Notes

Introduction

1. All of the names and certain identifying features of the students referenced in this book have been changed to protect the identities of the participants. Their comments and stories are told as accurately as possible, with some commentary edited for purposes of readability.

2. Amy's description of her style of dress comes from her journal entry. Almost all of the students interviewed (107 out of 111) for this study completed a written questionnaire—a "journal"—from which some of Amy's testimony is taken.

3. It was common across all students in the study for them to say that they have more of a chance of landing a relationship when they are seniors because that is when people are ready to "settle down."

4. This news may be a surprise to some given the recent spate of books that rail against religion and belief. See, for example, Sam Harris, *The End of Faith* (New York: Norton, 2004) and *Letter to a Christian Nation* (New York: Knopf, 2006); Richard Dawkins, *The God Delusion* (Boston: Houghton Mifflin, 2006); and Christopher Hitchens, *God Is Not Great: How Religion Poisons Everything* (New York: Twelve, 2007). See Stephen Prothero, *Religious Literacy* (San Francisco, CA: HarperSanFrancisco, 2007), as a counterargument to these atheist manifestos. The popularity of these books in the United States attests to religion's enduring power.

5. Alan Finder, "Matters of Faith Find a New Prominence on Campus," *New York Times* (May 2, 2007), http://select.nytimes.com/search/restricted/article?res=F10810FF3B5A0C718CDDAC0894DF404482, accessed 5/19/2007. For additional thorough assessments of teens, young adults, and faith, see, for example,

Tom Beaudoin's *Virtual Faith: The Irreverent Spiritual Quest of Generation X* (San Francisco, CA: Jossey-Bass, 1998); and Lynn Schofield Clark's *From Angels to Aliens: Teenagers, the Media, and the Supernatural* (New York: Oxford University Press, 2003).

6. Two major studies' findings released during the spring of 2005 show that interest in religion and/or spirituality is at an all-time high among teens and college students. In his National Study of Youth and Religion, sociologist Christian Smith inquired into the religious and spiritual lives of America's teenagers, paying particular attention to the "spiritual but not religious" proclivities of youth. Initiated in 2001, the study is an ongoing research project aimed at understanding the spiritual and religious lives of 13- to 17-year-old Americans. The project has completed its first large-scale quantitative phase of telephone surveys and a second phase of in-depth interviews from a narrower sample. Though the third and final phase is not yet off the ground, the data collected thus far have been published in Christian Smith's *Soul Searching: The Religious and Spiritual Lives of American Teenagers* (New York: Oxford University Press, 2005); and Mark D. Regnerus's *Forbidden Fruit: Sex and Religion in the Lives of American Teenagers* (New York: Oxford University Press, 2007). For a thorough history of the concept "spiritual but not religious," see, for example, Robert C. Fuller, *Spiritual, but Not Religious: Understanding Unchurched America* (New York: Oxford University Press, 2005). For a thorough analysis of the development of individualistic, personal spirituality in America, see, for example, Robert Wuthnow, *After Heaven: Spirituality in America since the 1950's* (Berkeley: University of California Press, 2000); Wade Clark Roof, *Spiritual Marketplace: Baby Boomers and the Remaking of American Religion* (Princeton, NJ: Princeton University Press, 1999); and Leigh Schmidt, *Restless Souls: The Making of American Spirituality* (San Francisco, CA: HarperSan-Francisco, 2006).

The second study to which I refer was conducted by the Higher Education Research Institute at UCLA and surveyed 112,000 college students on similar subjects. Both of these projects found that affiliation with religion and/or spirituality is alive and well among young people in America, to the tune of approximately 82%. The research institute began the Spirituality in Higher Education project in 2003 with funding from the John Templeton Foundation in order to examine the intersections among spirituality, religion, and college experience. In the project's first phase, the College Students' Beliefs and Values survey was administered to more than 112,000 entering college freshmen. The survey is designed to produce data on the spiritual and religious makeup of the respondents and their college expectations. While phase two, the longitudinal follow-up, began in the spring of 2007, the initial results of the survey appear in a report and various other publications, such as Alyssa N. Bryant, "Exploring Religious Pluralism in Higher Education: Non-majority Religious Perspectives among Entering First-Year College Students," *Religion & Education*, vol. 33, no. 1 (2006): 1–25.

In *Soul Searching*, Christian Smith reports that 82.2% of respondents to his study claimed some form of "religious affiliation" (31). The final report of the UCLA institute's survey data shows that 17% of those respondents chose "none" as a "religious preference," and the remaining 83% chose a specific religious group (17).

7. Smith, *Soul Searching*, 34.

8. See the Associated Press's article, "Surveys: Young Adults Search Spirituality," *Beliefnet.com* (2005), http://www.beliefnet.com/story/164/story_16493_1.html, for the 35% statistic about students who identified as "spiritual but not religious." See also the final report of data from the Higher Education Research Institute's survey of beliefs and values, which states the following:

> While today's entering college freshmen clearly expect their institutions to play an instrumental role in preparing them for employment (94%) and graduate or advanced education (81%), they also have high expectations that college will help them develop emotionally and spiritually. About two-thirds consider it "essential" or "very important" that their college enhance their self-understanding (69%), prepare them for responsible citizenship (67%), develop their personal values (67%), and provide for their emotional development (63%). Moreover, nearly half (48%) say that it is "essential" or "very important" that college[s] encourage their personal expression of spirituality. (6)

9. Note: these percentages refer to students who have engaged in oral, vaginal, and/or anal sex at the Catholic, nonreligious private, and public schools that participated in my study.

In 1995, the Centers for Disease Control's (CDC) National College Health Risk Behavior survey (*Morbidity and Mortality Weekly Report* (MMWR) Centers for Disease Control (CDC) Surveillance Summaries 1997; 46 [SS-6]: 1–56;) found that the percentage of college students 18–24 years old who had ever had sexual intercourse broke down as follows: females, 81%; males, 77.8%; total, 79.5%. The percentage of students who had engaged in intercourse within three months of participating in the study broke down as follows: females, 66.8%; males, 56.8%; total, 62.1%. The percentage of students who had engaged in intercourse within thirty days of participating in the study broke down as follows: females, 60.4%; males, 49.8%; total, 55.4%. For more information, please see the Youth Behavior Risk Surveillance Summaries, http://www.cdc.gov/mmwr/preview/mmwrhtml/00049859.htm, accessed 8/28/2007.

See also W. D. Mosher, A. Chandra, and J. Jones, "Sexual Behavior and Selected Health Measures: Men and Women 15–44 Years of Age, United States, 2002," in *Advance Data from Vital and Health Statistics*, no. 362 (Hyattsville, MD: National Center for Health Statistics, 2005), which claims that 85% of men and 81% of women have had first intercourse by ages 20–21.

10. With regard to the topic of sex as a possible factor affecting the religious and spiritual identities of youth, though Regnerus's more recent *Forbidden Fruit*

extracts relevant data from the National Study of Youth and Religion about sex and religion, neither Christian Smith's published findings nor those of the Higher Education Research Institute study made it a primary goal to inquire, in depth, how romantic relationships and sexual activity coincide (or collide) with religious identity, nor did they investigate whether sex might be a uniquely significant catalyst within the college experience that sparks shifts in religious identity during adolescence.

Interestingly, only a single question on the UCLA survey even mentions romance. Here, "romantic relationship" is one choice among a list of possible change agents in a person's spiritual life. This same list includes parental divorce, personal trauma or injury, death of a close friend or family member, post-9/11, and natural disaster. Question 53 of the questionnaire asks: "In what ways have the following changed your religious/spiritual beliefs?" "Romantic relationship" is on the list of items, and the four possible answers are "strengthened," "no change," "weakened," and "not applicable."

Since I proposed my study, the results of several interesting, smaller studies about sexuality in relation to spirituality among college students were published. See, for example, Nichole A. Murray-Swank et al., "At the Crossroads of Sexuality and Spirituality: The Sanctification of Sex by College Students," *International Journal for the Psychology of Religion*, vol. 15, no. 3 (2005): 199–219; and Henry D. Beckwith and Jennifer Ann Morrow, "Sexual Attitudes of College Students: The Impact of Religiosity and Spirituality," *College Student Journal*, vol. 39, no. 2 (June 2005): 357–66.

11. Dr. Patrick G. Love, a professor of higher education and student affairs and associate provost at Pace University, has long been engaged in research about meeting college students' interest in spirituality and spiritual quests in practice—focusing on college students' "spiritual development" from within the realm of student affairs and residential education/life on campus. See, for example, Love, "Spirituality and Student Development: Theoretical Connections," *New Directions for Student Services*, no. 95 (Fall 2001): 7–17; Patrick Love et al., "Identity Interaction: Exploring the Spiritual Experiences of Lesbian and Gay College Students," *Journal of College Student Development*, vol. 46, no. 2 (March–April 2005): 193–209; Patrick Love and Judy L. Rogers, "Exploring the Role of Spirituality in the Preparation of Student Affairs Professionals: Faculty Constructions," *Journal of College Student Development*, vol. 48, no. 1 (January–February 2007): 90–104. Judy Rogers, an associate professor in the Department of Educational Leadership at Miami University in Ohio, has also taken the lead in the area of higher education by addressing questions about "authenticity" in relation to spirituality among college students. See, for example, Rogers, "Preparing Spiritual Leaders: One Teacher Takes on the Challenge," *About Campus*, vol. 8, no. 5 (November 2003): 19–26; "Role-Modeling Authenticity in Higher Education," *Spirituality in Higher Education Newsletter*, vol. 3, no. 1 (September 2006), http://209.85.165.104/search?q=cache:psXemzGHoNAJ: www.spirituality.ucla.edu/newsletter/past/vol.%25203/2.html+%22judy+l.+

rogers%22&hl=en&ct=clnk&cd=6&gl=us, accessed 5/19/2007. Much of the research within theory in higher education about college students' spiritual development is influenced by Parker Palmer's many books, most notably *The Courage to Teach* (San Francisco, CA: Jossey-Bass, 1998), as well as Sharon Daloz Parks's *Big Questions, Worthy Dreams: Mentoring Young Adults in Their Search for Meaning, Purpose, and Faith* (San Francisco, CA: Jossey-Bass, 2000). See also A. W. Chickering et al., *Encouraging Authenticity and Spirituality in Higher Education* (San Francisco, CA: Jossey-Bass, 2006).

12. This study was generously funded by the Louisville Institute in Louisville, Kentucky. The Louisville Institute is part of the Lilly Endowment. I am the primary researcher for this study and conducted all interviews with students and all campus interactions with staff and faculty. This study could not have happened, however, without the survey expertise of my colleagues Jeffrey Adams and Molly Millwood, both psychologists, who worked for many hours designing the extensive online survey based on the topics I hoped to investigate and interpreting the data after the online survey was distributed at all seven schools. Regarding the qualitative work that is the backbone of this project, I am indebted to the advice and direction of my colleague Sharon Lamb, who has done a great many qualitative studies. She also put me onto two books that proved indispensable in my preparation for this project: Deborah L. Tolman and Mary Brydon-Miller (eds.), *From Subjects to Subjectivities: A Handbook of Interpretive and Participatory Methods* (New York: New York University Press, 2001); and Deborah L. Tolman, *Dilemmas of Desire: Teenage Girls Talk about Sexuality* (Cambridge, MA: Harvard University Press, 2002).

Please also note: This book does not by any means exhaust either the qualitative or quantitative data and will not be the only product that will result from this national study. Most of the findings among the quantitative data will be published in other forms, in particular in journal articles written in conjunction with the online survey developers, Dr. Jeffrey Adams and Dr. Molly Millwood.

13. The evangelical colleges I visited for the study are middle-of-the-road when it comes to how they view Christianity—and are unlike what I would regard as extremist evangelical colleges, such as Bob Jones University in Greenville, South Carolina, or Pensacola Christian College, about which the *Chronicle of Higher Education* reports:

The rules ... govern every aspect of students' lives, including the books they read, the shoes they wear, the churches they attend, and the people they date. ... Demerits are common and discipline swift. It's all in the name of preserving Pensacola's "distinctives"—the word the college uses for what sets it apart, and these "distinctives" apparently required faculty chaperones if a female and male student go to dinner off campus, and where students are disciplined for what is known on the campus as "optical intercourse"—staring too intently into the eyes of a member of the opposite sex. This is also referred to as "making eye babies." While the rule does not appear in written form, most students interviewed for this article were familiar with the concept.

See Thomas Bartlett, "A College That's Strictly Different," *Chronicle of Higher Education*, vol. 52, no. 29 (May 24, 2006): A40. Most evangelical colleges do not fit this extreme picture.

14. Finding secular schools to participate was easy, and several religious institutions were eager to be part of the study. The decision to promise anonymity was, in part, to protect the privacy wishes of the religious colleges in particular. In my search for participant schools, the most difficult task was finding willing religious colleges. Though I found many contacts who pushed the study through the highest levels of approval, from the formal Internal Review Board (for studies using human subjects) to the provost and president, there were two colleges where faculty, students, and the IRB boards approved the schools' participation in the study, but whose provosts and/or presidents stepped over faculty wishes and academic interest to forbid involvement in the end. One was a mid-Atlantic Catholic university and the other a Christian college. At the Catholic college, the faculty sponsor for the study, after getting approval from the college IRB, was told by the vice president for enrollment and academic affairs and the president—in rather angry terms—that there would be dire consequences if this faculty member took the university forward with this study, as the administration greatly feared students telling their parents that they were being polled about their sex lives. At the Christian school, again after a faculty member and student jointly received IRB approval, the provost yanked the college's participation because of concerns about asking students to talk explicitly about their sexual pasts. At both institutions, administrators' unwillingness to allow the college contacts to move forward with the study on their campuses caused great frustration and dismay—especially since, at both schools, there were faculty who believed that conversations about the relationship between sex and religion among students were not only important but needed.

15. Please note: More than 2,500 students across the seven schools took at least some part or all of the online survey. Students were free to skip questions they did not want to answer or to simply answer part of the survey and not the entire thing. As a result, the number of student answers for each topic fluctuates, depending on how many students chose to answer the relevant question(s), as readers will see as the chapters continue. For students who answered questions at the end of the survey providing basic demographic data, here is some information about the sample as a whole: gender: 67% female, 33% male; religious preference: Roman Catholic 20%, evangelical Protestant 32%, mainline Protestant 19%, no religious affiliation 14%; number of states represented among participants: 45; white/Caucasian participants: 86%; lesbian, gay, bisexual participants: 5.1%; first-year students: 28.4%, sophomores: 22.5%, juniors: 23.4%, seniors: 25.8%.

16. First, regarding interviewee selection: the only factor affecting participant selection at each campus was the goal to achieve gender balance. Otherwise, students were selected at random, promised confidentiality, and paid $25 each for their participation in the interview process. Second, at each participating

college, I had a campus contact, in some cases a professor, in others a campus minister or related administrative staff member. Students were invited to take the online survey via an e-mail sent from the campus contact. At the three smaller colleges (with populations under 5,000)—both evangelical Protestant schools and one of the Catholic schools—the survey invitation was e-mailed to the entire student body via the campus listserv. At the remaining four schools, students were invited via e-mail listservs of large, general-education required courses, and at one school, via the listserv for a large residential hall of approximately 1,400 students. In addition to being given information about the study, the survey, and confidentiality, the invitation to participate was sweetened by offering a random drawing for three "prizes," one of $100 and two of $25 in cash at each participating school.

17. For an overview of recent trends in American Catholicism, see Dean R. Hoge, *Young Adult Catholics: Religion in the Culture of Choice* (Notre Dame, IN: University of Notre Dame Press, 2001), chap. 1. For a bleaker prognosis in terms of the "further erosion of Catholic identity, and a declining sense that the Church is worth supporting," see James D. Davidson et al., *The Search for Common Ground: What Unites and Divides Catholic Americans* (Huntington, ID: Our Sunday Visitor, 1997), 204.

18. Not helping matters are articles such as Alexandra Jacobs, "Campus Exposure," *New York Times Sunday Magazine* (March 4, 2007). Her subject was a "new crop of college sex magazines [that] shows students baring it all" (44). Several recently launched college sex and pornographic publications are highlighted, including the Boston University–affiliated *Boink*, which its editor, Alecia Oleyourryk, describes as "user-friendly porn" and Jacobs calls "an unblushing assortment of bared private parts, lewd prose and graphic caricatures" (44), and *H-Bomb*, Harvard's milder equivalent launched in 2004 by Katharine Cieplak-von Baldegg and Camilla Hardy as a "literary arts magazine about sex and sexual issues" (44). These magazines feature naked college students, mostly women but also men, mostly heterosexuals but also gays and lesbians, some explicit and others more discreet.

The stated purpose of these magazines is to champion sexual freedom on American college campuses. While a few students doubtless subscribe to the level of "sexual freedom" celebrated by such publications as *Boink* and *H-Bomb*, most college students are far from champions of the extremely sexed-up life these publications glorify.

See also Janet Reitman's article, "The Duke Lacrosse Scandal: Sex, Rape, and the Myth of the Post-Feminist Hookup," *Rolling Stone*, no. 1002 (June 15, 2006). Page 1 of the article has two photographs. The first shows an idyllic Duke quad on a beautiful day. Students soak up the sunshine as they cross campus, and a stunningly beautiful chapel is in the background. The other photo shows women in bikinis writhing in pools of baby oil with half-naked guys; giant pull quotes are superimposed that read: "Girls poured shots of chocolate syrup on each other and smeared their chests with whipped cream. Then they made the boys lick it off" (70–72). These two different images are juxtaposed to show readers two wildly distinct sides of Duke: its pristine popular image and its garish sexual underbelly. Unlike the rest of the media at this early time in the Duke lacrosse scandal, Reitman didn't visit Duke to talk to lacrosse players. She realized that the most interesting angle on the scandal was about the girls on campus and their attitudes about sex. "I've begun to see the story as not a 'he said/ she said' tale, nor a story about sexual violence, but rather a story about sex itself," Reitman writes. "Not sex in its nitty-gritty, anatomical sense, but more in the collective sense: sex as a sport, as a way of life, as a source of constant self-scrutiny and self-analysis" (72). Reitman was surprised by the lack of concern many Duke girls showed about the alleged rapes and their tendency to rally around the la-crosse players (or "laxers," as they are popularly known on campus). Girls were skeptical about the charges, Reitman reports, because these guys were the type "who could get any girl they wanted" and who "don't need to stoop to that level [of raping a stripper] in order to have sex with somebody" (72). The "laxers," in short are the gods among kings on campus, and highly accomplished, stunning, articulate, and wealthy young female students will happily service them; they do it for *prestige*. The girls Reitman interviewed counted themselves "lucky" to be associated with certain "big men on campus" in any way they could be—including through behavior that is "completely inconsistent with the type of person I am, and what I value," as one girl told Reitman. Women who by day dress as if they just walked off a fashion magazine shoot go out by night dressed like prostitutes, do pole dances in cages at the local watering hole while guys look on, or willingly act as the sexy entertainment for freshmen pledges at the most popular frat house, giving lap dances and performing dominatrix acts to turn the boys on—all while getting completely wasted themselves (74, 76, 109). Overall, sex is a sport like any other at Duke, Reitman argues. Girls both go to strip clubs and hire strippers themselves, occasionally. "Traditional intercourse is common," Reitman writes, "and oral sex nearly ubiquitous, regarded as a form of elaborate kissing that doesn't really mean very much." And within all this "hedonistic stew," dating is simply nonexistent (74). On top of it all, Reitman continues, feminism at Duke is more of a joke than anything else to the women students. These girls are from the Britney Spears generation, which sees taking off their clothes and making men drool as one of the most powerful things a girl can do. Having sex "like a man" is their feminist right. "[T]hese girls too, can have sex—with whomever they choose and whenever they might want it, in a number of ways, without even thinking about what it all means," writes Reitman. "That men and women play on an even sexual playing field is a given ... or should be. As [one young woman] sees it, 'It's *our* decision if we're going to allow ourselves to be subjected to negative treat-ment. It's all framed by the way the girls behave'" (72). Yet, as Reitman rightly explains, even the dominatrixes aren't dominating the men. What is worse is that the girls don't seem to realize that all this supposedly empowering sexy behavior is "done at the direction of the boys" (109). Moreover, in addition to playing their assigned roles and keeping the boys sexually satisfied, the girls *also* have to have perfect bodies, keep up amazing grades, and pursue high-powered careers, while somehow maintaining a positive self-image. This last goal is difficult, since this "partying" makes most of them feel insecure and ashamed (76).

19. For some examples of the media hype about girls finding empowerment and understanding feminism by performing oral sex on boys with no strings attached, see Benoit Denizet-Lewis's "Friends, Friends with Benefits, and the Benefits of the Local Mall," *New York Times* (May 30, 2004), accessed 8/12/2007, http://select.nytimes.com/search/restricted/article?res=F60713FA3C5A0C738FDDA C0894DC404482; and Caitlin Flanagan's "Are You There God? It's Me Monica," *Atlantic*, vol. 297, no. 1 (January–February 2006): 167–82.

20. Ariel Levy, *Female Chauvinist Pigs: Women and the Rise of Raunch Culture* (New York: Free Press, 2005), 29–30.

21. Again, this is especially the case with women. See also American Psychological Association, "Report of the APA Task Force on the Sexualization of Girls" (2007), http://www.apa.org/pi/wpo/sexualization.html.

22. Levy, *Female Chauvinist Pigs*, 31.

23. Based on a study conducted with 1,000 college women for the Institute for American Values, investigators Norval Glenn and Elizabeth Marquardt report: "The most common definition [we] heard was that a hook up is anything 'ranging from kissing to having sex,' and that it takes place outside the context of commitment." See *Hooking Up, Hanging Out, and Hoping for Mr. Right: College Women on Dating and Mating Today* (New York: Institute for American Values, 2001), 13. For a similar description, see Laura Sessions Stepp's discussion of the hookup as "un-relationship" in *Unhooked: How Young Women Pursue Sex, Delay Love, and Lose at Both* (New York: Riverhead, 2007), 24–31.

24. This is a similar reality to that which Laura Sessions Stepp chronicles poignantly in *Unhooked: How Young Women Pursue Sex, Delay Love, and Lose at Both*.

25. When I use the term "evangelical," I follow Randall Balmer's definition. He describes evangelicals as those who subscribe to two fundamental tenets: (1) the conversion or "born again" experience as the central "criterion for entering the kingdom of heaven": and (2) the Bible upheld as "God's revelation to humanity," often interpreted literally. Within those bounds, however, he allows for "various permutations." See Randall Balmer, *Encyclopedia of Evangelicalism*, rev. ed. (Waco, TX: Baylor University Press, 2004), *s.vv.* "evangelical," "evangelicalism."

26. The use of "sacred canopy" is derived from Peter Berger's classic, *The Sacred Canopy: Elements of a Sociological Study of Religion* (Garden City, NY: Doubleday, 1967).

27. Like researchers Conrad Cherry, Betty A. DeBerg, and Amanda Porterfield in *Religion on Campus: What Religion Really Means to Today's Undergraduates* (Chapel Hill: University of North Carolina Press, 2001), 2–6, I am suspicious of secularization theories in general.

28. As I've gathered the results of this study, noticing how so many students are left adrift and alone in their spiritual seeking, I think of Robert D. Putnam's

Bowling Alone: The Collapse and Revival of American Community (New York: Simon & Schuster, 2001), which contends that Americans have become increasingly isolated from one another, in part because of a drop in regular church attendance. I find it rather stunning and ironic that even within communities such as college campuses, students experience such isolation in their spiritual searches.

Chapter 1

1. For more information on liberation theology, please see Gustavo Gutierrez, *A Theology of Liberation* (Maryknoll, NY: Orbis Books, 1990).
2. I interviewed 75 students overall from Catholic, nonreligious private, and public schools. Out of the 36 evangelical Protestant students interviewed, only 7 (19%) identified as simply "spiritual" or "spiritual but not religious," a significantly lower percentage in comparison to the other school types.
3. Identifying as "more spiritual than religious" was popular among evangelical Protestant students, with 9 out of 36 (25%) claiming this label.
4. Again, when I use the phrase "searching alone," I am alluding to Robert D. Putnam's coining of the phrase "bowling alone" in his book of the same name, a phrase that has come to indicate the peculiarity of the American experience of isolation from community. In many ways, I believe that "searching alone" equally captures the religious experience of Generation Next, particular during their college years.
5. Please note: there were none of these "nones" at evangelical colleges.
6. Please note: The demographic information requested from each student at the beginning of each interview included name, age, school year, major, housing type, sexual orientation, ethnicity, and religious affiliation, if any. The 22 students mentioned here who answered "none" did so during this beginning information collection, when asked to state their "religious affiliation, if any." Further into the interviews, all students were asked a separate, open-ended question about "labels" such as "religious," "spiritual," and "spiritual but not religious," and were asked to define those terms, at which time it was not uncommon for the students who had labeled themselves as having "no affiliation" to apply the label "spiritual" to themselves.
7. One of these students was a 20-year-old junior at the public university named Lucy. "I feel like maybe because so many people believe in a higher being that maybe I'm missing out on something," Lucy said. Lucy, as one of the religious "nones," confessed to having no idea about how her parents feel about faith or God—it simply wasn't something talked about in her house while she was growing up. She'd been to a Baptist church three times, but only because a friend invited her. Otherwise she had no knowledge or experience of any religious tradition. But rather than making her feel free, this bothered her. It also bothered her when friends were "shocked" to learn that she had "no religious beliefs." Lucy was reluctant to label herself either spiritual or religious, but she

spoke of various experiences that might qualify as spiritual—like taking in the beauty of a sunset or getting lost playing the piano—and she showed signs of hunger to find a faith of her own. "I've taken religion classes. I find different religions extremely interesting," Lucy explained. "It's almost to the point where I think about maybe taking on a religion. But then there's a lot of stuff that I just can't make myself believe. I really have no belief in a higher being. I've tried. But it's just, it's a concept that I just can't buy into. I don't know why. I just can't." Lucy took hope, however, in her belief that a person can be spiritual without believing in God.

8. For those interested in the breakdown of religious diversity among interview participants at the private-secular and public schools, I will list the specifics here. At the nonreligious private university from Visit #4, they affiliated in the following ways: "none," 5; nondenominational Christian, 2; "exploring Eastern spirituality," 1; Hindu, 1; agnostic, 1; Jewish, 2; Catholic, 3; Sikh, 1; undecided, 1. At the nonreligious private university from Visit #2, participants affiliated in the following ways: "none," 5; nondenominational Christian, 1; atheist, 1; Jewish, 2; Quaker, 1; Presbyterian, 1; Greek Orthodox, 1; Latvian church, 1. At the public university from Visit #5, affiliations were: "none," 6; nondenominational Christian, 3; pagan, 1; agnostic, 1; Methodist, 1 (not practicing); Episcopalian, 2.

9. See Stephen Prothero's *Religious Literacy: What Every American Needs to Know— and Doesn't* (New York: HarperSanFrancisco, 2006) for the case for why religious education and religious literacy in particular is paramount in today's society, and why all educational institutions, regardless of whether they are public or nonreligious private, have a responsibility to find ways to open up productive conversation about religion.

10. While at religiously affiliated schools, both Catholic and evangelical Protestant, for those students I interviewed who did not, unprompted, mention the religious affiliation of the institution as part of their reason for attending, I then asked specifically if religious affiliation was a consideration; likewise, at all the non–religiously affiliated schools that participated in the study, I asked students whether they had considered religiously affiliated colleges or universities in their application process, or considered religious affiliation at all when choosing to what institutions to apply and eventually attend. Across the three schools, student answers broke down into three categories. At the nonreligious private university from Visit #4, 2 out of 17 considered attending a religiously affiliated institution, but then decided they didn't want to attend a religiously affiliated school; 8 said explicitly that they had wanted to attend a secular institution and actively avoided applying to religiously affiliated schools; 7 didn't consider religion as a relevant factor in their choice of college. At the nonreligious private university from Visit #2, 3 of 13 people interviewed considered attending a religiously affiliated institution, but then decided they didn't want to attend a religiously affiliated school; 3 others said explicitly that they had wanted to attend a secular institution and actively avoided applying to religiously affiliated schools; 7 didn't consider religion

as a relevant factor. At the public university from Visit #5: 3 of 14 considered attending a religiously affiliated institution, but then decided they didn't want to attend a religiously affiliated school; 6 said explicitly that they wanted to attend a secular institution and had actively avoided applying to religiously affiliated schools; 5 didn't consider religion as a relevant factor.

11. Spirituality falls mostly into the realm of the "experiential and emotional" if we use Ninian Smart's seven dimensions of religion to help categorize their answers—though the fact that student expression of the spiritual often includes private prayer and meditation also edges it into Smart's "ritual" dimension as well. Student understandings of the religious typically fit the "ritual" (in a communal sense this time), "social and institutional," and "ethical and legal" dimensions, according to Smart's categories. See Ninian Smart, *Dimensions of the Sacred: An Anatomy of the World's Beliefs* (Berkeley: University of California Press, 1996).

These self-descriptions also fit into Robert Wuthnow's proposition that "spirituality consists of all the beliefs and activities by which individuals attempt to relate their lives to God or to a divine being or some other conception of a transcendent reality" (*After Heaven: Spirituality in America since the 1950's* [Berkeley: University of California Press, 2000], viii). Wuthnow also argues that historically this form of relating to the divine has been moving away from the institutional constraints of organized religions since the middle of the twentieth century. Wade Clark Roof echoes that sentiment in claiming that when "Americans speak of spirituality today, the term may and most often does, include religion in the sense of a tradition, yet for many it is not bound by doctrinal, creedal, or ecclesiastical categories" (*Spiritual Marketplace: Baby Boomers and the Remaking of American Religion* [Princeton, NJ: Princeton University Press, 1999], 34).

12. Again, I do not intend to suggest that the spiritual colleges do not offer opportunities to practice a variety of faith traditions on campus, host related lectures, or offer a wide variety of courses to students. I am concerned here about the peer-to-peer campus culture in this regard, which indeed may have students taking classes and going to an occasional religiously affiliated program—yet these experiences do not make their way into friendships, relationships, or the overall peer culture on campus in any meaningful way.

13. The study chronicled in *Religion on Campus: What Religion Really Means to Today's Undergraduates* (Chapel Hill: University of North Carolina Press, 2001) by Conrad Cherry, Betty DeBerg, and Amanda Porterfield is a testament to the strong presence of interest in religion, spirituality, and even practice in certain circles at a variety of institution types, including a public school. My intention is *not* to dispute their finding that "if the definition of religion includes spirituality as well as the more traditional, denominationally based forms of religious expression...[then] opportunities [to] practice religions [are] widely available" nor that there was evidence of a "religious vitality" at the four distinct institutions that are the subjects of their study (*Religion on Campus*, 275–83). I agree that there is evidence that opportunities to explore and practice religion and spirituality on campus abound—and many students take advantage of these. How-

ever, I am interested here in whether that interest and even experimentation among nonevangelical college students "grip" them in ways that affect their decision making and behavior among their peers, and most especially, in how they interact with the social/party scene on campus, which is also tied to hookup culture and the dominant peer ethic about sex. As I will continue to show in this chapter and those that follow, at least when it comes to sex, religion and spirituality are rather ineffective within this realm in any meaningful way (short of some guilt), unless one attends an evangelical college.

Chapter 2

1. For a more complete picture of "evangelical Catholics," see William Portier, "Here Come the Evangelical Catholics," *Communio* 31 (Spring 2004): 35–66. Portier estimates that 10%–20% of contemporary Catholics under the age of 40 are evangelical in a style similar to that of evangelical Protestants.

2. Christian Smith, *Soul Searching: The Religious and Spiritual Lives of American Teenagers* (New York: Oxford University Press, 2005), 6–7.

3. See Carlin Flora, "The Decline and Fall of the Private Self," *Psychology Today*, vol. 40, no. 3 (May–June 2007): 82–87.

4. See Dean R. Hoge, *Young Adult Catholics: Religion in the Culture of Choice* (Notre Dame, IN: University of Notre Dame Press, 2001); Christian Smith, *Soul Searching*; and Colleen Carroll, *The New Faithful: Why Young Adults Are Embracing Christian Orthodoxy* (Chicago: Loyola Press, 2002). For a collective summary of two major recent studies of Catholic apathy/church attendance within Generations X and Next and the Millennials, see the article by sociologists Vincent Bolduc and William V. D'Antonio, "American Catholics: The 'Bookend' Generations," *National Catholic Reporter* [March 9, 2007] http://www.catholic.org/national/national_story.php?id=23289, accessed 11/10/2007.

5. Smith, *Soul Searching*, 207.

6. See *The New Faithful*, 33, 75, 102, for several of Carroll's many references to Notre Dame students; 38, 52, 74, for several of Carroll's many references to students at Franciscan University of Steubenville; and 1–3, 42, 51, for several of Carroll's many references to students at the Catholic University of America. See chapter 3 on Notre Dame University in Naomi Schaefer Riley's *God on the Quad: How Religious Colleges and the Missionary Generation Are Changing America* (New York: St. Martin's, 2005), 53–70, and chapter 4 on Thomas Aquinas College, 71–94.

7. Melanie M. Morey and John J. Piderit, S.J., *Catholic Higher Education: A Culture in Crisis* (New York: Oxford University Press, 2006). See also, for instance, a yearlong seminar at Georgetown University in 1996, which produced the notion of "centered pluralism" to explore the role of non-Catholic views in the university's identity. Centered pluralism led then-president Leo J. O'Donovan, S.J., in 1988 to create the Task Force on Georgetown's Catholic and Jesuit Identity, which produced a list of 20 recommendations. The following year, *The*

Application of Ex corde Ecclesiae for the United States (1999) was approved by the U.S. Conference of Catholic Bishops, 10 years after Pope John Paul II issued the original *Ex corde* in order to describe "the identity and mission of Catholic colleges and universities and [provide] General Norms to help fulfill its vision." Since the adoption of this document, Catholic universities across the nation have been forced to investigate how the *Ex corde* is to be implemented.

8. It should be noted that one Catholic school I visited was far more religious than the other, both in terms of the portion of students who self-identified as Catholic (13 out of 17 people I interviewed at one institution, 4 out of 14 at the other) when asked for religious affiliation at the beginning of the interview, and in terms of regular Sunday mass attendance (many of these Catholic students claimed to go about twice a month on average, whereas at the other Catholic school, claims of service attendance were negligible). Yet, with few exceptions, almost all students from both schools talked as if they could get through college without even realizing that they were at a Catholic institution.

Chapter 3

1. This figure of 45% comes from a 2000 Gallup poll reported in the *Princeton Religion Research Report*, 2002, "Describing Self as Born-Again or Evangelical," bar graph, http://www.wheaton.edu/isae/Gallup-Bar-graph.html, accessed 4/2/2007. Please note: I believe this figure is high—probably because of the manner in which people were polled. The religious affiliation studies break things down by denomination, which complicates the issue.

2. Aside from short stints at a public elementary school and then a middle school, my entire education took place at Catholic schools, from nursery school through my Ph.D. work at the Catholic University of America. Likewise, aside from four years teaching at a "multipartisan" nonprofit called the Close Up Foundation after graduating from college, and two years in the Department of Residential Education at New York University, I've spent most of my professional life teaching at Catholic universities and colleges, including the Catholic University of America, Marymount University in Virginia, St. John's University, and St. Michael's College in Vermont, and at a Catholic high school in Washington, D.C.

3. To give an idea of the breadth, diversity, and multimedia nature of evangelical Christian youth outreach available to teens and young adults (in addition to the mountains of books available from a wide variety of Christian publishers), which is designed to help youth navigate popular culture in relation to the Christian faith, please see the following. For Bible outreach, see Thomas Nelson's BibleZines, http://www.thomasnelson.com/consumer/dept.asp?dept_id=190900 &TopLevel_id=190000, which take the New Testament, the psalms, etc., and transform them into full-color, glossy magazines that resemble *Seventeen*, *Vogue*, and *GQ*. See, in particular, its first BibleZine, *Revolve: The Complete New Testament* (Nashville, TN: Thomas Nelson Bibles, 2003). For spiritual memoirs,

see, for example, Lauren Winner, *Girl Meets God* (New York: Random House, 2003); Donald Miller, *Blue Like Jazz: Nonreligious Thoughts on Christian Spirituality* (Nashville, TN: Thomas Nelson, 2003); and Rob Bell, *Velvet Elvis: Repainting the Christian Faith* (Grand Rapids, MI: Zondervan, 2005). Rob Bell is also one of a number of ultrahip, young, activist evangelical Christian pastors who have emerged over the last several years; in addition to writing memoirs and other popular books, they are producing multimedia sermons and other forms of access to their communities. If you don't live near Mars Hill, Bell's church in Grand Rapids, Michigan, you can check out his series of NOOMAs (http://nooma.com). NOOMAs—a play on the Greek *pneuma*, meaning "spirit"—are activist sermons/film shorts that have Bell preaching while, for example, planting a tree near an abandoned lot (see the NOOMA *Trees*). Then there are the media/publishing conglomerates: the more small scale like that of author/blogger Hayley DiMarco, called *Hungry Planet* (http://www.hungryplanet.net), and the giant scale like that of Cameron Strang's *Relevant Media* (http://www.relevantmediagroup.com), which has its own publishing imprint, and two magazines—one for young men (*Relevant*) and another for young women (*Radiant*)—does regular podcasts, and produces music, among other media outreach. The above list is a tiny slice of what is available for evangelical Christian youth to help negotiate popular culture, but it gives an idea of how far-reaching and creative the available resources are.

4. At the evangelical university from Visit #6, 12 out of 19 students who were interviewed offered, unprompted, that they had desired to be at a Christian college, among Christian peers, faculty, and community, and an additional 4 said the same when prompted. At the evangelical college from Visit #3, 11 of 17 offered, unprompted, that they had desired to be at a Christian college, among Christian peers, faculty, and community, and an additional 3 said the same when prompted.

5. The two Catholic schools I visited differed tremendously in terms of the religious affiliations of students. At the Catholic college from Visit #1, 13 of the 17 (76%) self-identified as Catholic; at the Catholic college from Visit #7, on the other hand, that figure was only 4 out of 14 (29%). Of the remaining students, 5 (36%) identified with mainline Protestantism, 2 (14%) with nondenominational Christianity, and 7 students (50%) said they had "no affiliation"; all of the "none" participants came from the seemingly less "Catholic" college—from Visit #7—of the two Catholic schools, making "none" a more widespread religious affiliation, at least on that campus, than Catholicism itself.

6. Sharon Daloz Parks, a former Harvard professor widely read in higher education circles, in *Big Questions, Worthy Dreams: Mentoring Young Adults in Their Search for Meaning, Purpose, and Faith* (San Francisco, CA: Jossey-Bass, 2000), rightly worries that "the practice and wisdom of mentoring [young adults] has been weakened in our society," especially during college, and argues that "restoring mentoring as a cultural force could significantly revitalize our institutions and provide the intergenerational glue to address some of our deepest and most pervasive concerns" (12). Faith is the place to begin this restoration, writes Daloz

Parks, not only because faith is crucial to meaning-making but also because it is of such keen interest to students entering college (as data from my study prove). Meanwhile, others have contended that institutions of higher education have gone wholly over to the secular side. See, for example, George M. Marsden, *The Soul of the American University: From Protestant Establishment to Established Nonbelief* (New York: Oxford University Press, 1996); and D. G. Hart, *The University Gets Religion: Religious Studies in American Higher Education* (Baltimore, MD: Johns Hopkins University Press, 2002). Daloz Parks sees colleges and universities as places where spiritual exploration is already happening and spiritual mentoring is already taking place:

> When we speak of the academy as a place for the formation of faith, this may appear to run counter to the commitments of the academy, as well as to speak of a domain beyond the academy's purpose and responsibility. Yet if we recognize faith as meaning-making in its most comprehensive dimensions, higher education inevitably functions, at least to some degree, as a mentoring community for those who are young adults in faith, even if only by default. It is primarily to this institution that young (and older) adults come to be initiated into critical thought and must make meaning in new ways on the other side of that discovery. Thus every institution of higher education serves in at least some measure as a community of imagination in which every professor is potentially a spiritual guide and every syllabus a confession of faith. (*Big Questions*, 159)

Yet, with the notable exception of evangelical schools, universities seem to be doing more "covering" than mentoring when it comes to faith. "Covering" is what Kenji Yoshino, a professor at Yale Law School and the author of *Covering: The Hidden Assault on Our Civil Rights* (New York: Random House, 2006), defines as "the new discrimination." According to Yoshino, "Courts will protect traits like skin color or chromosomes because such traits cannot be changed." But "the courts will not protect mutable traits, because individuals can alter them to fade into the mainstream, thereby escaping discrimination" (Kenji Yoshino, "The Pressure to Cover," *New York Times Sunday Magazine* [January 15, 2006], http://select.nytimes.com/search/restricted/article?res=F30F11F 834540C768DDDA80894DE404482, accessed 3/30/2007). Religious clothing—clothing such as the Jewish man's yarmulke or the Sikh's turban that explicitly marks a person as belonging to a particular tradition—is one such area. Here Americans are taught, even legislated, to cover—to erase from public view. "The demand to cover is anything but trivial," Yoshino writes. "It is the symbolic heartland of inequality—what reassures one group of its superiority to another. When dominant groups ask subordinated groups to cover, they are asking them to be small in the world, to forgo prerogatives that the dominant group has and therefore to forgo equality" (ibid.).

So whereas Daloz Parks idealizes colleges and universities as "communit[ies] of imagination in which every professor is potentially a spiritual guide and every syllabus a confession of faith," the reality of schools in the spiritual bubble is that students are masters at covering their spiritual lives—their spiritual questions, spiritual desires, and spiritual commitments—from peers, from faculty, from friends. Daloz Parks makes a profound case for meaningful mentorship and attention to college students' spiritual longing on campus at every level, most especially in relationships between faculty and students both within and outside of the classroom—but the evidence from the young women and men with whom I spoke at Catholic, nonreligious private, and public institutions shows that college students are overwhelmingly adrift when it comes to spiritual seeking. Most specifically, this covering hampers their ability to use religious resources to say no to unhealthy cultural norms about sex or, for that matter, to use religious resources to foster commitment to any moral norms whatsoever.

As a last note, there is no doubt that what Daloz Parks asks of faculty and professionals in student affairs is a tall order in terms of the time, training, and open-mindedness necessary to effectively mentor and support students during the college years. However, her overarching vision of a campus community is one that supports mentoring communities, where all parties, including the students themselves, become mentors engaged in the life and development of the community and its constituent individuals; therefore, this mentoring responsibility does not fall solely on the backs of already stretched professors. The hope is that campus culture can be transformed to support this type of mentoring community in which faculty have an important function and ideally will play a role in shaping campus communities in this direction. For more on this issue, see Daloz Parks, *Big Questions*, 158–205.

7. Daloz Parks, *Big Questions*, 159.

8. These admissions advertisements: "the sky's the limit," "anything is possible," and "the whole world at your fingertips," are paraphrased from actual admissions materials from a variety of school types (excepting evangelical colleges). I do not reveal the school names in the interest of maintaining the overall anonymity of schools within the context of this study.

9. As background for this study, I assigned two undergraduate research assistants to look into the admissions/marketing materials for a total of 20 colleges, inclusive of the 7 schools that participated in the study. This is how the "sky's the limit" admissions marketing was noted as a trend at Catholic, private-secular, and public institutions, and the "Christ-centered" admissions marketing was noted as a trend at evangelical Protestant schools.

10. Again, these admissions advertisements: "Burning with Jesus" and "Learning to Live for Christ" are paraphrased from actual admissions materials.

11. For articles that critique faculty's reluctance to involve themselves in in-depth ways with students, or to broaden their campus presence beyond the classroom, see Alexander W. Astin et al., "Meaning and Spirituality in the Lives of College Faculty," *UCLA Higher Education Research Institute* (November 1999); Philip L. Tite, "Reinforcing the Ivory Towers through Marginalization," *Council of Societies for the Study of Religion Bulletin*, vol. 31, no. 1 (February 2002): 14–17; John B. Bennett, "The Academy and Hospitality," *CrossCurrents*, vol. 50, nos. 1–2 (Spring–Summer 2000): 23–35; Mark R. Schwehn, "The Academic Vocation:

Specialists without Spirit, Sensualists without Heart," *CrossCurrents*, vol. 42, no. 2 (Summer 1992): 185–99; Myron B. Bloy, Jr., "Faith Communities in the Academic World," *CrossCurrents*, vol. 43, no. 4 (Winter 1993): 437–52; and John B. Bennett, *Collegial Professionalism: The Academy, Individualism, and the Common Good* (Phoenix, AZ: Oryx, 1998).

Chapter 4

1. Using data from the National Longitudinal Study of Adolescent Health, Peter Bearman and Hannah Brückner found that although abstinence pledgers waited longer to have intercourse, they did not have lower sexually transmitted disease (STD) infection rates, because they were less likely to use condoms during their first encounters. See "Promising the Future: Virginity Pledges and First Intercourse," *Journal of American Sociology*, vol. 106, no. 4 (January 2001): 859–912; and "After the Promise: The STD Consequences of Adolescent Virginity Pledges," *Journal of Adolescent Health*, vol. 36, no. 4 (April 2005): 271–78. Drawing from the same data set, Janet E. Rosenbaum found that more than half of abstinence pledgers deny ever having taken a pledge in the years following it, and these denials are highest among those who subsequently initiated sexual activity. See "Reborn a Virgin: Adolescents' Retracting of Virginity Pledges and Sexual Histories," *American Journal of Public Health*, vol. 96, no. 6 (June 2006): 1098–1103.
2. *Oxford English Dictionary*, 2nd ed., s.v. "Purity," www.oed.com, accessed 3/25/2007.
3. Mary Douglas, *Purity and Danger: An Analysis of Concepts of Pollution and Taboo* (New York: Routledge, 2002), 12.
4. Ibid., 17.
5. Ibid., 48.
6. One biblical verse commonly quoted (or rather, paraphrased) by evangelical Christian dating manuals is the following: "In the dense, immoral fog of this generation, shine your life as a beacon, guiding others to the goodness and grace of God. Though this world is polluted, live in spotless purity, uncontaminated by all the garbage around you" (Philippians 2:15). This version is taken from Eric Ludy and Leslie Ludy's *When God Writes Your Love Story* (Colorado Springs, CO: Multnomah, 2004), 104.
7. Stephen Arterburn, *Every Young Man's Battle: Strategies for Victory in the Real World of Sexual Temptation* (Colorado Springs, CO: WaterBrook, 2002), 73, 145.
8. Ibid., 140–41.
9. One of the only sex/dating books for the evangelical market that challenges stereotypes of men as primarily sexual (and sexually predatory) and women as emotional and *non*sexual is Lauren Winner's *Real Sex: The Naked Truth about Chastity* (Grand Rapids, MI: Brazos, 2005). See, in particular, chapter 5, "Straight Talk II: Lies the Church Tells about Sex," especially the section "Lie #2: Women Don't Really Want to Have Sex, Anyway."

10. Shannon Ethridge and Stephen Arterburn, *Every Young Woman's Battle* (Colorado Springs, CO: WaterBrook, 2004), 25.

11. Ibid., 119–21.

12. Ibid., 46.

13. Lisa Bevere, *Kissed the Girls and Made Them Cry: Why Women Lose When They Give In* (Nashville, TN: Thomas Nelson, 2002), 77. For more examples of evangelical dating and sex manuals for young adults, please see Jeramy Clark, *I Gave Dating a Chance: A Biblical Perspective to Balance the Extremes* (Colorado Springs, CO: WaterBrook, 2000); Justin Lookadoo and Hayley DiMarco, *Dateable: Are You? Are They?* (Grand Rapids, MI: Revell, 2003); Kay Arthur, *The Truth about Sex* (Colorado Springs, CO: WaterBrook, 2002); Jeff Taylor, *Friendlationships: From Like to Like, to Love in Your Twenties* (Orlando, FL: Relevant Books, 2005); Henry Cloud, *How to Get a Date Worth Keeping: Be Dating in Six Months or Your Money Back* (Grand Rapids, MI: Zondervan, 2005); and Alex Chediak, ed., *Defining Your Dating Style: 5 Paths to the Love of Your Life* (Colorado Springs, CO: Think, 2005).

14. Jessica's comments about "unwrapping" are almost uncanny in the way they resemble commentary in a popular online article about purity by Phil Ware called "Unwrapped Too Soon." Ware says:

> As I work with couples in pre-marital counseling, I am thankful to find that more and more are committed to not unwrapping their gift too soon. Even if they have opened packages early in their past, they have learned their lesson at a profound level. Unwrapping this gift before marriage robs it of the joy of discovery found only when it is received at the right time. Those who do wait find that special joy that comes from giving and receiving this precious gift in its proper place and time.

   See http://www.heartlight.org/two_minute/2m_981209_unwrap.html, accessed 3/25/2007.

15. Founded in 1995, the Silver Ring Thing received federal funding, which was subsequently challenged by the American Civil Liberties Union on constitutional grounds. See http://www.silverringthing.com; and Diana B. Henriques and Andrew W. Lehren, "Religious Groups Reaping Share of Federal Aid for Pet Projects," *New York Times* (May 13, 2007), http://select.nytimes.com/search/restricted/article?res=F40614FE39550C708DDDAC0894DF404482, accessed 5/13/2007.

16. In *I Kissed Dating Goodbye*, Joshua Harris alludes to this idea of a "depleted heart" through a supposed dream about which a friend named Anna writes to him. The person who possesses the damaged heart in this illustration, however, is a guy. "As the minister began to lead Anna and David through their vows, the unthinkable happened," Harris writes, describing Anna's wedding nightmare. "A girl stood up in the middle of the congregation, walked quietly to the altar, and took David's other hand. Another girl approached and stood next to the first, followed by another. Soon a chain of six girls stood by him as he repeated his

vows to Anna." Anna is horrified, and David tells her: "Anna, they don't mean anything to me now . . . but I've given part of my heart to each of them. . . . Everything that's left is yours," he adds, sheepishly. This makes Anna cry. See *I Kissed Dating Goodbye* (Sisters, OR: Multnomah, 1997), 17–18.

17. Started in 1993, True Love Waits is sponsored by LifeWay Christian Resources, a wing of the Southern Baptist Convention, and it stresses adherence to a "Christian" view of sexual purity. Its program includes several weeks of education culminating in a commitment ceremony in which a pledge of abstinence is made to God. See http://www.lifeway.com/tlw, accessed 5/7/2007.

18. "What Is a Purity Ball?" *Generations of Light,* http://www.generationsoflight.com/generationsoflight/html/PurityBall.html, accessed 4/21/2007.

19. See Stephen Arterburn et al., *Every Young Man's Battle,* for a thorough discussion of the Christian guy's tendency to get into pornography and how this damages a man's purity. There are so many references to pornography in this manual that they are too numerous to include here.

The topic of pornography never appears in books that identify women as their primary audience, however. Instead, manuals for women warn against watching romantic movies.

20. In the King James Version of the Bible, this verse says, "It is good for a man not to touch a woman," and the New International Version reads, "It is good for a man not to marry." So while Mark got the language right (at least, according to the King James), he got the book and chapter wrong—a mistake not uncommon among the many evangelical students who quoted Bible verses during our interviews.

21. Ludy and Ludy, *When God Writes Your Love Story,* 105–6.

22. Ibid., 106.

23. Mark is actually referring to 1 Corinthians 7:38 (New American Standard Bible): "So then both he who gives his own virgin daughter in marriage does well, and he who does not give her in marriage will do better."

Chapter 5

1. Please note: Laura M. Carpenter's *Virginity Lost: An Intimate Portrait of First Sexual Experiences* (New York: New York University Press, 2005) claims a serious dearth of information on youth and oral sex (234). Ariel Levy, *Female Chauvinist Pigs: Women and the Rise of Raunch Culture* (New York: Free Press, 2005), says that "there [are] no clinical data available comparing the percentage of girls vs. boys who perform oral sex" (144). Mark Regnerus, *Forbidden Fruit: Sex and Religion in the Lives of American Teenagers* (New York: Oxford University Press, 2007), has a table that shows virtually no difference between girls and boys ages 15–17 in the area of oral sex (166).

Whether the rumors are true or not—that girls perform oral sex more often than they receive it—seems difficult to ascertain. I asked every student I interviewed about oral sex on campus and whether or not they believed girls gave more than they received, boys gave more than they received, or performing and receiving were about equal. Perceptions were split down the middle. A large number of students said they believed it was "equal": there was almost no gender difference when it came to performing and receiving oral sex. Among the sizable number of students who perceived a gender difference, however, *all* perceived that girls give more than they receive.

Much ink has been spilled on articles about teenage girls talking about giving oral sex as a form of feminist empowerment and confirming or dispelling rumors about middle school and high school oral sex parties. In the *New York Times* article "Friends, Friends with Benefits, and the Benefits of the Local Mall" (May 30, 2004), accessed 8/12/2007, http://select.nytimes.com/search/restricted/article?res=F60713FA3C5A0C738FDDAC0894DC404482, Benoit Denizet-Lewis sat down with some teens from a "New England exurban world" to talk about what's happening with sex in high school these days—because clearly not much is happening with dating. One thing they told her was that "oral sex is common by eighth or ninth grade, and . . . hookups may skip kissing altogether." See also Caitlin Flanagan, "Are You There God? It's Me Monica: How Nice Girls Got So Casual about Oral Sex," *Atlantic* (January–February 2006), http://www.theatlantic.com/doc/200601/oral-sex, accessed 3/1/2007. Flanagan discusses her search for the truth (or falsity) behind all the rumors about oral sex parties where multiple teen girls service multiple teen boys in public settings—only to find out that what she hoped were "urban legends" about young girls proved to be true. In this vein, the release of Paul Ruditis's young adult novel *Rainbow Party* (New York: Simon Pulse, 2005)—also cited in Flanagan's article—caused huge controversy upon its release, with big bookstore chains like Barnes & Noble and Borders declining to carry it because of its portrayal of "rainbow parties," which are "group oral sex parties in which each girl wears a different shade of lipstick, and each guy tries to emerge sporting every one of the various colors," reports Tamar Lewin in "Are These Parties for Real?" *New York Times* (June 30, 2005), http://www.nytimes.com/2005/06/30/fashion/thursdaystyles/30rainbow.html?ex=1180324800&en=b77b89c87efeo30f&ei=5070, accessed 5/26/2007.

2. Though students in the spiritual bubble may not be reading books on dating and sex from a religious and/or spiritual perspective, a lot of young women admitted to having a copy of Greg Behrendt and Liz Tuccillo's *He's Just Not That into You: The No-Excuses Truth to Understanding Guys* (New York: Simon Spotlight Entertainment, 2004).

3. Coleman Barks, *Rumi: The Book of Love: Poems of Ecstasy and Longing* (San Francisco, CA: HarperSanFrancisco, 2003).

4. Dating from somewhere around the third century CE, the *Kama Sutra* is known as a Hindu textbook of erotic love. Yet the full translation, although emphasizing the erotic and sensual side of intimate human relations, is not simply a manual of sexual techniques, as is popularly believed. Only one of its seven sections focuses

primarily on sexual behavior, and others include advice and psychological insights on matters such as courtship and marriage. See Wendy Doniger and Sudhir Kakar, *Kamasutra: Mallanaga Vatsyayana* (New York: Oxford's World Classics, 2003).

5. Interestingly, in an article in the *New York Times*, "A Simple Show of Hands" (October 5, 2006), Stephanie Rosenbloom reports that *hand holding* on campus has become serious business. " If [college students] do [hold hands], it is likely only after they are deep into a relationship—not [like] in those early days of budding romance, when a touch of hands was the first act of intimacy between a couple," writes Rosenbloom.

> Among more than a half-dozen students at the University of Maine, there seemed to be two universal truths: that hand-holding is the least nauseating public display of affection and that holding hands has become more significant than other seemingly deeper expressions of love and romance. "It is a lot more intimate to hold hands nowadays than to kiss," said Joel Kershner, 23. Because of that, he said, reaching for someone's hand these days has more potential for rejection than leaning in for a smooch at a party where alcohol is flowing. Libby Tyler, 20, said it was "weird that hand-holding is more serious," but true. "It's something that you lead up to," she said. There is nothing casual about it any more, said Rachel Peters, 22. "Hand-holding is something that usually people do once they've confirmed they're a couple," she said. (http://select.nytimes.com/search/restricted/article?res=F70911FF3E540C768CDDA90994DE404482, accessed 10/19/2006)

6. Some of the grander romantic stories that students shared with me also underscored this point. One young man said that his girlfriend had wanted a picnic under the stars for weeks, but the weather just wasn't cooperating. "I put up glowy stars on the ceiling, cooked a good meal, and we had a candlelit dinner under the stars, on a table with a picnic cloth draped over it," he said. "She was so happy and that just made us both feel wonderful and very in love." Another boy spoke of wading into the ocean with a girl he was just getting to know and singing songs to her under the moonlight. "It was a beautiful experience," he said. And then there was a girl whose boyfriend, a lighting designer, asked her to come by the theater where he was working late.
"I went over at 7 PM," she writes,

> and found the whole stage glowing in pink and green, my two favorite colors, with red hearts projected on the floor. He had made me dinner and had his best friend serve us drinks and food. He took me back to his house and gave me the most beautiful heart shaped necklace. We spent the rest of the night cuddling and talking until we fell asleep together.

Then there was the occasional romantic outing where the student explicitly explained that there was no sex involved. "We walked to the . . . river and skipped stones before going back to her room at 3:30 AM. We didn't do anything physical at all and it was still incredibly romantic."

7. Almost all of these descriptions set the romantic encounter in a beautiful location, such as the beach at night, and many involved a surprise. Another commonality among these descriptions was time—long dinners, long conversations, and long walks. Some of those long walks involved holding hands, and some of the stories ended with a "long hug" or even "falling asleep in each other's arms." But that's about as far as the physical intimacy goes in the vast majority of these narratives. It is a widely held stereotype, of course, that women are interested in talking and men are interested in sex. But when it comes to the relationship between sex and romance, my male and female respondents were almost indistinguishable: when things turn to sex, the experience becomes something other than romance.

8. The other gay man who answered this question was more effusive, clearly overjoyed by the experience: "I was over at my friend's apartment," he writes:

> We watched some really funny shows, and then we exchanged shirtless massages. From there, we sensually began to kiss and touch. I had some kind of super-sensitivity with my body for some reason (an amazing connection, perhaps?), and whenever he touched my skin there was a sensually GLORIOUS feeling: a tickling mixed with warm beauty mixed with a sexual current. It was amazing. We rolled around the floor, laughing and joking, touching and kissing, telling each other what we loved about the other and their body. It was sensual. Personal. Connected. Beautiful (both him and the night).

Chapter 6

1. It's not that surprising that talk among evangelical Protestant students turns so quickly to marriage, since courtship—a special type of relationship formed with the express purpose of marriage as the outcome—is advocated over regular dating within evangelical youth culture, and especially in the popular dating manuals. See, for example, Joshua Harris, *Boy Meets Girl: Say Hello to Courtship* (Sisters, OR: Multnomah, 2000).

2. Apparently, this term circulates more in speech than on the page, because no one seemed to know just how to spell it. The first time I heard the word I responded, "Frugaling? Like Googling?" But the student told me, no, different spelling. One popular spelling is the one I'm using here, but no one seemed to know for sure.

3. Marie Griffith's scholarship suggests, however, that evangelical women find clever and subversive ways to be more active within the relationship and dating realm since they find it so frustrating to just wait around. See her book *God's Daughters: Evangelical Women and the Power of Submission* (Berkeley: University of California Press, 2000), which suggests that evangelical women find some of the so-called constraints of their faith empowering, even as they find ways to run around them. Perhaps Cara Walker, the born-again virgin whose story opens chapter 8, and Brook Lillith, the girl whose faith flourishes even while she

stretches her sense of when sex is acceptable within evangelical Christianity, also in chapter 8, are my best examples of what Griffith discusses here.

4. Virtually all popular evangelical dating/sex manuals, save *Real Sex: The Naked Truth about Chastity* (Grand Rapids, MI: Brazos, 2005) by Lauren Winner, portray the ideal Christian girl as sexually passive, emotional, and *patient*. In particular, please see Lisa Bevere's *Kissed the Girls and Made Them Cry: Why Women Lose When They Give In* (Nashville, TN: Thomas Nelson, 2002); and Joshua Harris's *Boy Meets Girl* for evidence of this.

5. Obviously, same-sex residence halls and visitation rules at evangelical campuses are biased toward the heterosexual population and simply ignore sexual minorities as a factor potentially affecting students' lives—as do most evangelical Protestant communities since they regard homosexuality as sinful, an issue I will discuss in further detail in the next chapter. But most student-life rules at colleges and universities, regardless of religious or secular affiliation, are still biased toward the heterosexual population.

6. This young woman is probably referring to the story of the woman taken in adultery in which Jesus says that those who are without sin among her accusers should throw the first stone.

Chapter 7

1. In *Female Chauvinist Pigs: Women and the Rise of Raunch Culture* (New York: Free Press, 2005), Ariel Levy writes about girls gaining acclaim socially by using "sexuality" as a "tool" (145–46). She also stresses the fact that sexuality for girls is not often about enjoyment, but instead, "it is something they embody to be cool" (163). See for Levy's discussion of how women became convinced that "raunch" culture is cool (17–45). To listen to Ariel Levy's NPR *Fresh Air* interview by Terry Gross, please see "Women in the 'Girls Gone Wild' Era," http://www.npr.org/templates/story/story.php?storyId=6549015&sc=emaf, accessed 11/29/2006. For a discussion of how the pornography industry is affecting women and girls' idea of sex, sexiness, and sexuality, as well as what men expect from women in the bedroom, see Pamela Paul's *Pornified: How Pornography Is Transforming Our Lives, Our Relationships, and Our Families* (New York: Times Books, 2005).

2. This form of stigma is so common that it often prompts young adults to disguise the exact timing of their virginity loss so as not to reveal their past virginity. See Laura M. Carpenter, *Virginity Lost: An Intimate Portrait of First Sexual Experiences* (New York: New York University Press, 2005), 107.

3. When it comes to defining hooking up, even Facebook—one of the most popular social-networking Web sites among American college students (and among teens and adults since May, 2007)—has gotten in on the act. Like the users at MySpace, Facebook users can and do put up extremely detailed virtual profiles of themselves, with all sorts of personal information from the most basic to the

most random, from their relationship status to explicit sexual information. When it comes to listing their relationship status, users can indicate, among other choices, "in an open relationship" or "it's complicated." The latter is usually taken to mean that the person engages in some sort of regular yet noncommittal hooking up. This connection can be made more explicit in category options. Under "Looking For," a user can list not only "friendship," "dating," and "a relationship" but also "random play" and "whatever I can get." "It's complicated" is also an appropriate way to characterize the many possible definitions that students give for how they understand hooking up.

A "Pew Internet Project Data Memo" (January 3, 2007), published by Pew Internet and American Life Project researcher Amanda Lenhart, estimates that 55% of American youth have already used social-networking sites like MySpace and Facebook by the age of 17. See http://www.pewinternet.org/pdfs/ PIP_SNS_Data_Memo_Jan_2007.pdf, accessed 5/7/2007. According to Internet intelligence service Hitwise.com, MySpace still dominates the overall market share with over 80%, although Facebook claims to be more popular with college students. See http://www.hitwise.com/press-center/hitwiseHS2004/social networkingmarch07.php, accessed 5/7/2007.

Based on a study conducted with 1,000 college women for the Institute for American Values, investigators Norval Glenn and Elizabeth Marquardt report: "The most common definition [we] heard was that a hook up is anything 'ranging from kissing to having sex,' and that it takes place outside the context of commitment." See *Hooking Up, Hanging Out, and Hoping for Mr. Right: College Women on Dating and Mating Today* (New York: Institute for American Values, 2001), 13. For a similar description, see Laura Sessions Stepp's discussion of the hookup as "un-relationship" in *Unhooked: How Young Women Pursue Sex, Delay Love, and Lose at Both* (New York: Riverhead, 2007), 24–31.

4. Please note that only 215 students at the evangelical colleges answered this question. The data with regard to how frequently students are sexually active while drinking or while under the influence are as follows: approximately 6.5% say they engage in this behavior "frequently" or "all the time"; 4.7% report that they "usually" do so; 12.5% answer that they are "equally as likely" to have been drinking or under the influence of drugs during sexual activity as not; and 76.3% answer they are "never" or "rarely" drunk during hooking up. Of course, overall, "hooking up" as understood at the spiritual colleges is virtually nonexistent at the evangelical ones, so I question the significance of these statistics with regard to the evangelical participant group.

For further data on the relationship between sexual activity and alcohol on college campuses, please see William F. Flack Jr. et al., "Risk Factors and Consequences of Unwanted Sex among University Students: Hooking Up, Alcohol, and Stress Response," *Journal of Interpersonal Violence*, vol. 22, no. 2 (February 2007): 139–57.

5. For discussions about teen girls and gossip, aggression, and "meanness," please see Sharon Lamb, *The Secret Lives of Girls: What Good Girls Really Do: Sex Play,*

Aggression, and Their Guilt (New York: Simon & Schuster, 2001); and Rachel Simmons, *Odd Girl Out: The Hidden Culture of Aggression in Girls* (New York: Harcourt, 2002).

6. For further discussion of how the pornography industry—in particular how "themes" once exclusively found in magazine and film pornography—is being proliferated and marketed through mass culture and, as a result, is affecting teen and young adult behavior, particular with regard to how male sexual fantasies and ideas about sexiness are becoming normative ideals for "sexiness" that young women are playing out through their attire and sexual activities as early as the tween years, please see again Ariel Levy's *Female Chauvinist Pigs: Women and the Rise of Raunch Culture* (New York: Free Press, 2005); Pamela Paul's *Pornified*; and Sharon Lamb and Lyn Mikel Brown, *Packaging Girlhood: Rescuing Our Daughters from Marketers' Schemes* (New York: St. Martin's, 2006).

7. For more on this, see Duncan Kennedy, "Sexual Abuse, Sexy Dressing and the Eroticization of Domination," *New England Law Review*, vol. 26 (1992): 1309–93. What Kennedy calls female "sexy dress" is inherently suggestive of a fantasy narrative. Duncan writes: "The dress alludes to that sexier setting, and then to the next after that, all in the direction of the settings in which men and women actually engage in sex. The sexy dresser invites the straight male audience to imagine being with her in the setting her dress alludes to" (1372).

8. Ibid.

9. See American Psychological Association, "Report of the APA Task Force on the Sexualization of Girls" (2007), http://www.apa.org/pi/wpo/sexualization.html, accessed 5/5/2007.

   "To say that a relationship is 'sexualized,' means that it is viewed as essentially sexual, and is not seen to be about commitment, communication, or love," writes Josephine Ross of the Howard University School of Law. For Ross, to "sexualize" something is to assume a "sexually charged" dimension to a relationship, comment, or situation which, within certain societal "norms" of heterosexuality (as one example), would not typically be assumed. Josephine Ross, "The Sexualization of Difference: A Comparison of Mixed-Race and Same-Gender Marriage," *Harvard Civil Rights–Civil Liberties Law Review*, vol. 37 (2002): 256.

   In "Sexed Up: Theorizing the Sexualization of Culture" (*Sexualities*, vol. 9, no. 1 ([February 2006]), Feona Attwood writes that "sexualization" involves "a highly individualized form of hedonism pursued through episodic and uncommitted encounters" (80)—making sexualization sound a lot like hookup culture.

10. See the executive summary in American Psychological Association, "Report of the APA Task Force on the Sexualization of Girls" (2007), http://www.apa.org/pi/wpo/sexualization.html, accessed 5/4/2007. Interesting to note: though there are many studies—both qualitative and quantitative—exclusively about girls and all manner of sex- and romance-related subjects, there is a striking *lack* of studies geared exclusively toward gathering qualitative and/or quantitative data about boys. As a result, sociologist Peggy Giordano made headlines when

she published a study about the romantic interests of adolescent boys. See Giordano et al., "Gender and the Meanings of Adolescent Romantic Relationships: A Focus on Boys," *American Sociological Review*, vol. 71, no. 2 (April 2006): 260–87. See also the *Time* magazine feature about Giordano's study: Lev Grossman's "The Secret Love Lives of Teenage Boys" (August 27, 2006), http://www.time.com/time/magazine/article/0,9171,1376235,00.html, accessed 9/4/2006.

11. Lamb and Brown, *Packaging Girlhood*, 13–56.

12. Tamar Lewin, "At Colleges, Women Are Leaving Men in the Dust," *New York Times* (July 9, 2006), http://www.nytimes.com/2006/07/09/education/09college.html?ex=1310097600&en=cd9efba2e9595dec&ei=5088&partner=rssnyt&emc=rss, accessed 5/3/2007. See also Robin Wilson, "The New Gender Divide," *Chronicle of Higher Education*, vol. 53, no. 21 (January 26, 2007): A36.

13. For more on how girls overachieve, especially with respect to college, see, for example, Alexandra Robbins, *The Overachievers: The Secret Lives of Driven Kids* (New York: Hyperion, 2006).

14. For more information about increased sexual promiscuity among women who have been sexually assaulted, please see B. L. Shapiro and J. C. Schwarz, "Date Rape: Its Relationship to Trauma Symptoms and Sexual Self-Esteem," *Journal of Interpersonal Violence*, vol. 12, no. 3 (June 1997): 407–19. See also W. van Berlo and B. Ensink, "Problems with Sexuality after Sexual Assault," *Annual Review of Sex Research*, vol. 11 (2000): 235–58.

15. A total of 668 students from all four institution types filled in a response to this question; however, 111 answers (94 from Catholic, nonreligious private, and public schools; 17 from evangelical schools) were thrown out because the responses either lacked enough information to categorize them or simply said "not applicable." Therefore, percentages within answer categories were based on the number of responses actually categorized. The breakdown of overall responses by school type is as follows: 79 out of 668 (12%) from evangelical schools; 195 of 668 (29%) from Catholic schools; 181 of 668 (27%) from nonreligious private schools; 127 of 668 (19%) from the public school (keep in mind that there was only one public school that participated in the survey); and 86 out of 668 (13%) students who answered the question did not indicate which school they attended, so their answers could not be categorized into school type.

16. In *Hooking Up*, Glenn and Marquardt report that college women often feel "awkward" and "hurt" after a hookup, and sometimes confused because they don't know if the hookup will "lead to anything else" (16). Other studies have gone further to suggest that there may even be a link between depression and casual sex in young women, and that women who have an "early transition to intercourse" are more likely to be depressed and to regret casual encounters. See Catherine M. Grello, Deborah P. Welsh, and Melinda S. Harper, "No Strings Attached: The Nature of Casual Sex in College Students," *Journal of Sex Research*, vol. 43, no. 3 (August 2006): 255–67.

17. Despite the frequency of negative or ambivalent descriptions of casual encounters, Glenn and Marquardt also note in *Hooking Up* that many of their
respondents used *both* negative and positive adjectives to describe the same event.
Grello, Welsh, and Harper's report ("No Strings Attached") also suggests that
college-age men are much less likely to "regret" a casual sexual encounter than
women are. For more data about teen and young adult perspectives about
hooking up, see Wendy Manning, Monica A. Longmore, and Peggy Giordano,
"Adolescents' Involvement in Non-Romantic Sexual Activity," *Social Science
Research*, vol. 34, no. 2 (June 2005): 384–407; and Wendy Manning, Monica
A. Longmore, and Peggy Giordano, "Hooking Up: The Relationship Contexts
of 'Nonrelationship' Sex," *Journal of Adolescent Research*, vol. 21, no. 5 (September 2006): 459–83.

18. Many of these respondents also said that this atmosphere was doubly hard to
navigate if you happened to be a woman. "I feel that sex [at my college] is
anticipated and expected overall," says one student. "I often feel that campus is
like a sex market [where] people are just walking around trying to impress each
other and trying to find people to sleep with."

19. Please note: While this data point showing such a large gap between the
freshmen surveyed and seniors who claim virginity is interesting, because this is
not a longitudinal study, this difference does not prove that *between* the first year
and senior year, it is likely that a large percentage of students who entered
college as virgins will no longer remain such. That would require following a
group of freshmen through to their senior year. However, within my study, these
percentages certainly show that senior-year respondents are more sexually active
than are first-year respondents.

20. In *Forbidden Fruit: Sex and Religion in the Lives of American Teenagers* (New York:
Oxford University Press, 2007), Mark Regnerus refers to members of this gap as
"technical virgins," because they believe that only vaginal sex "technically"
counts (167). See also Carpenter, *Virginity Lost*, 44–56. Although there is some
ambiguity in how her informants defined the concept of virginity loss, Carpenter
claims that most heterosexuals "assumed that virginity loss constituted vaginal
intercourse" (44). For earlier studies on the concept of technical virginity and the
many ways that teens and young adults rationalize engaging in explicit sexual
acts while still calling themselves virgins, as well as the high-stakes nature of
remaining a virgin for certain demographics, please see, for example, Jamie
Mullaney, "Like a Virgin: Temptation, Resistance, and the Construction of
Identities Based on 'Not Doings,'" *Qualitative Sociology*, vol. 24, no. 1 (March
2001): 3–24; and Stephanie Sanders and June Machover Reinisch, "Would You
Say You 'Had Sex' If...?" *Journal of the American Medical Association*, vol. 281,
no. 3 (January 20, 1999): 275–78.

21. What I am calling the virgin gap constitutes those who answered yes, they have
engaged in oral, anal, and/or vaginal sex, yet still consider themselves virgins.

22. Regnerus reports that whereas evangelical youth have the most conservative
sexual attitudes, they do *not* have the most conservative sexual behaviors. In

terms of behavior, they "are largely indistinguishable from the rest of American adolescents" (*Forbidden Fruit*, 153). My findings contradict his argument in this regard. I have discussed this point of difference at length in chapter 4.

Chapter 8

1. Please see, for example, the cover story by Lorraine Ali et al., "Choosing Virginity," *Newsweek*, vol. 140, no. 24 (December 9, 2002).
2. Again, in this study, 56% of participants describe themselves as both spiritual and religious, and 27% call themselves "spiritual but not religious." So roughly 83% self-identify as religious and/or spiritual in some measure. This percentage falls in line with both Christian Smith's findings about religiosity and spirituality among teens and the findings by the UCLA Higher Education Research Institute study of college students.
3. Mark Regnerus, *Forbidden Fruit: Sex and Religion in the Lives of American Teenagers* (New York: Oxford University Press, 2007), 154. For Regnerus's "several part" explanation as to why his findings turned out in this way, please see 154–61.
4. For more information about the NYSR sampling methods (Regnerus's research is drawn from Christian Smith's same research project), please see ibid., 239–47.
5. By "tightly knit campus culture," I mean the kind of culture that anthropologist of religion Mary Douglas would say is high on both the grid line and the group line. See Mary Douglas, *Natural Symbols* (New York: Routledge, 1996), 63–66. For Douglas, the idea of grid and group has to do with assessing the strength of a social system, such as a religious tradition. A system that is high on both grid and group is "likely to remain stable, unless counter-pressures develop from the outside or unless new knowledge weakens the credibility of the classifications" (62). Persons who are high on group are the converted, committed individuals who are "increasingly under the bond of other people" (63); and those who are high on grid subscribe to "a shared system of classifications" (64). See Douglas's helpful table, "Grid and Group" (64).
6. Jeramy Clark, *I Gave Dating a Chance* (Colorado Springs, CO: WaterBrook, 2000), 12–13.
7. Joshua Harris, *I Kissed Dating Goodbye* (Sisters, OR: Multnomah, 1997), 39.
8. Ibid.
9. Ibid., 141.
10. Of all the students I interviewed at all four types of institutions, the only students who spoke of pregnancy scares and having unprotected sex came from the evangelical colleges. Katrina Tan, who also had a pregnancy scare, confirms this tendency, which is supported by statistics about Christian students, who are more likely to delay sex, yes, but when they do engage in sex, they are more likely to have unprotected sex.

11. Of the 37 evangelical college students I interviewed, only 3 called themselves "spiritual but not religious." Aside from Katrina, there was one other woman, who identified as lesbian, and a young man, who identified as gay and about whom I speak in the next section.

Chapter 9

1. Paul VI, "On the Regulation of Birth," *Humanae Vitae* (July 25, 1968), http://www.vatican.va/holy_father/paul_vi/encyclicals/documents/hf_p-vi_enc_25071968_humanae-vitae_en.html, accessed 5/9/2007.

2. John Paul II, "The Church Family in the Modern World," *Familiaris Consortio* (November 22, 1981), http://www.vatican.va/holy_father/john_paul_ii/apost_exhortations/documents/hf_jp-ii_exh_19811122_familiaris-consortio_en.html, accessed 5/9/2007.

3. Please see Thomas Aquinas, *Summa Theologica* II.II, 151–154 (Question 151 on chastity, Question 152 on virginity, and Questions 153 and 154 on lust); *Summa Theologica* III, 64, 1–10 (on paying the marital debt); and finally, Thomas Aquinas, *Summa Contra Gentiles*, III, 122 & 126 (question 122 on fornication and the natural institution of marriage, & question 126 on not all sex being a sin.)

4. See Christopher West, *The Good News about Sex and Marriage: Answers to Your Honest Questions about Catholic Teaching* (Ann Arbor, MI: Servant Publications, 2004). For more information on Christopher West, his lectures, and many publications, please see http://www.christopherwest.com.

5. David Hajduk, *God's Plan for You: Life, Love, Marriage, and Sex (The Theology of the Body for Young People)* (Boston, MA: Pauline Books & Media, 2006). Hajduk's book is his interpretation of relevant material about love, marriage, and sex from John Paul II's *Theology of the Body: Human Love in the Divine Plan*, a collection of lectures that John Paul II gave between 1979 and 1984.

6. Hajduk, *God's Plan for You*, 166.

7. Ibid., 169–71.

8. Luke Timothy Johnson, "Sex and American Catholics," Annual Currie Lecture in Law and Religion, Emory University, Atlanta (October 9, 2002), http://www.law.emory.edu/cslr/documents/lukespeech.pdf, accessed 5/9/2007.

9. See Lisa Sowle Cahill's *Sex, Gender, and Christian Ethics* (Cambridge: Cambridge University Press, 1996).

10. See James F. Keenan, "Can We Talk? Theological Ethics and Sexuality," *Theological Studies*, vol. 68, no. 1 (March 2007): 113–31; and "Virtue Ethics and Sexual Ethics," *Louvain Studies*, vol. 30, no. 3 (Fall 2005): 180–97. See Margaret Farley, *Just Love: A Framework for Christian Sexual Ethics* (New York: Continuum, 2006).

11. Ibid., 232–35.

12. Colleen Carroll, *The New Faithful: Why Young Adults Are Embracing Christian Orthodoxy* (Chicago: Loyola Press, 2002), 121–41.

13. Christian Smith, *Soul Searching: The Religious and Spiritual Lives of American Teenagers* (New York: Oxford University Press, 2005), 194.

14. For more information on InterVarsity Christian Fellowship/USA, please see http://www.intervarsity.org

Chapter 10

1. "[H]igher education has been increasingly dominated by a particular interpretation of academic objectivity that over time has appeared to preclude a self-conscious search for value and meaning," writes Sharon Daloz Parks of this dilemma. "As a result, commitment to the true has been divorced from the good. Responsible teaching has seemed to require dispassionate presentation of value-neutral fact, or the mere presentation of multiple points of view." Sharon Daloz Parks, *Big Questions, Worthy Dreams: Mentoring Young Adults in Their Search for Meaning, Purpose, and Faith* (San Francisco, CA: Jossey-Bass, 2000), vii.

2. Ibid., 159.

3. Evangelical colleges bring to mind the era in the 1960s when academic administrators first became aware that 1950s campus culture was under siege. This prompted what may be the first book about campus sex, *Sex and the College Student* (1966) with a foreword by Anna Freud. This path-breaking book was a response to a spate of "sex scandals" at prestigious American universities; see Committee on the College Student/Group for the Advancement of Psychiatry, *Sex and the College Student: A Developmental Perspective on Sexual Issues on the Campus: Some Guidelines for Administrative Policy and Understanding of Sexual Issues* (New York: Atheneum, 1966). In November 1963, the dean of Harvard College had written a letter to the *Harvard Crimson* lamenting the declining standards of decency on campus. The authors write: "What disturbed him most, he said, was the students' belief that a student's behavior in his room was of no concern to the college, that a student's room was his castle and his sexual behavior his private affair" (*Sex and the College Student*, 3). At Oxford University, two separate "scandals" involved "the presence of a girl in a boy's room—an offence for which students have traditionally been expelled" (4). And shortly before the book's publication, the dean of Columbia University had issued a public statement about how "institutions . . . have been remiss in their responsibility to show the 15-, 16-, 17-, and 18-year-olds entrusted to them how to make responsible judgments—on an individual basis—about sex" (4). At the time this book appeared, many colleges were struggling with the fact that students were "both testing authority" and "searching for guidelines" with respect to sex (4). In her foreword, Anna Freud comments, quite ominously, that "the position of the residential colleges who take over parental authority" is "unenviable" at best, and nearly impossible for outsiders to appreciate in all its complexity.

Appendix

1. See Mary Brydon-Miller, "Education, Research, and Action: Theory and Methods of Participatory Action Research," in *From Subjects to Subjectivities: A Handbook of Interpretive and Participatory Methods*, ed. Deborah L. Tolman and Mary Brydon-Miller (New York: New York University Press, 2001), 76–89.
2. Ibid., 77–81.
3. Again, for the traditional PAR guidelines, see ibid., 80–81.
4. Ibid., 45–56.
5. In this vein, my academic background is heavily influenced by the postmodern, psychoanalytic, and feminist work of scholars such as Grace Jantzen, Luce Irigaray, Amy Hollywood, and Toril Moi.

Index

Page numbers in **bold** indicate charts, *italics* indicate tables.

premarital sex, 195–96
sexual ethics, 198–99
teachings about sex, 194
Catholic University of America, 56, 291n6, 292n2
CCCU (Coalition of Christian Colleges and Universities), 261–63
CCD (Confraternity of Christian Doctrine), 55
centered pluralism, 291n7
Centers for Disease Control (CDC), 281n9
CEOs and office ho's, 13, 148. *See also* theme parties
Chang, Chris, 203–4
chastity. *See also* purity culture
evangelical colleges, 14, 219
peer attitudes about sex, 123, **124,** 125, 159–60
purity standards, xix
Real Sex: The Naked Truth about Chastity, 211–12, 301n4
sex talk, 239
Cherry, Conrad, 287n27, 290n13
Christianity. *See also individual denominations*
Christian walk, 65–66
church hopping, 190
evangelical sex manuals, 79–80, 114, 297n13, 301n4
evangelical youth and faith, 45
GEMS: Girls Everywhere Meeting the Savior, 58
and homosexuality, 188–89
InterVarsity Christian Fellowship/USA, 35
liberalism, 185
liberation theology, 27
The New Faithful: Why Young Adults Are Embracing Christian Orthodoxy, 199
purity culture, 75–78, 92
and science, 58, 188
True Love Waits, 298n17
witnessing, 51
women and marriage, 116, 118
youth outreach, 292–93n3
Christian walk, 65–66
church hopping, 180–81, 190
Cieplak-von Baldegg, Katharine, 285n18
Clark, Jeramy, 178, 297n13
clergy
Catholic colleges, 56
Catholic sexual ethics, 198
evangelical colleges, 219–20, 226
religion and spirituality talk, 228, 240–41

Close Up Foundation, 292n2
Coalition of Christian Colleges and Universities (CCCU), 261–63
college marriage, 233
Columbia University, 309n3
Committee on the College Student/Group for the Advancement of Psychiatry, 309n3
communication
Catholic teachings and youth, 197–99
in hookup culture, 260
religion and spirituality talk, 241
sex and romance, 106–9, 300n5
void at evangelical colleges, 125
Confraternity of Christian Doctrine (CCD), 55
contraception
Catholic teachings, 196
courses about, 233–34
hookup culture remorse, **154**
Julia Tanner, 150
pregnancy scares, 180, 183–84
safe sex, 157
The Courage to Teach, 283n11
courtship, 301n1, 301n4
covenant ring, 76–77
"covering," 293–95n6
creation science, 58

Dalai Lama, 26
Daloz Parks, Sharon
Big Questions, Worthy Dreams: Mentoring Young Adults in Their Search for Meaning, Purpose, and Faith, 236, 283n11, 309n1
mentorship, 67, 71, 293–95n6
dancing ban, 64
Danni, 83–84
Dasari, Padma, 32–33
data sampling. *See also* Sexuality and Spirituality in American College Life
anonymity, 273–74, 278, 279n1
Catholic colleges, 10–11
evangelical colleges, 11–12, 283–84n13
online survey, 11, 284n15
public colleges, 11
secular colleges, 284n14
Dateline SMC, xvi–xx, 271
date rape, 305n14. *See also* sexual assault
dating
admissions tour questions, 232–33
bisexuality and, 189
Cal Saunders, 176

student spirituality, 308n11
virgin gap, 162, 164
virginity and marriage, 92
evangelical religion, definition, 39. *See also* Christianity
Ex corde Ecclesiae for the United States, 291–92n7

Facebook, 54, 138, 234, 251, 302–3n3
faculty. *See also* mentorship
 admissions tour questions, 237
 campus contacts for survey, 273
 Catholic colleges, 49–50, 56, 69
 evangelical colleges, 64–66, 76, 123, 226
 "Meaning and Spirituality in the Lives of College Faculty," 295n11
 religion and spirituality talk, 240
 sex talk, 238, 250–51, 295n11
 and sexual minorities, 104, 189
 statement of faith, 11–12
 strategies for responding to hookup culture, 265–67
 study participation, 284n14
faith
 Big Questions, Worthy Dreams: Mentoring Young Adults in Their Search for Meaning, Purpose, and Faith, 236, 283n11, 309n1
 and campus culture, 228
 evangelical youth and, 45
 The New Faithful: Why Young Adults Are Embracing Christian Orthodoxy, 199
 statement of faith, 11–12
Familiaris Consortio, 197
Farley, Margaret, 199
fellatio. *See* oral sex
Female Chauvinist Pigs: Women and the Rise of Raunch Culture, 13, 302n1, 303–4n6
females. *See also* feminism; sexual assault; slutty dressing
 alcohol consumption, 5
 alpha females, 129
 depression, 305n16
 frugaling, 116
 God's Daughters: Evangelical Women and the Power of Submission, 301n3
 gossiping, 138, 143–44, 234, 303–4n5
 hookup culture, 95–96, 127, 157, 271
 marginalization of, 213
 objectification of, 147
 online survey, 12
 and oral sex, 125, 128

peer attitudes about sex, 157–58, 306n18
promiscuity and, 102, 305n14
purity culture, 82–83, 85–86, 91–92
and reputations, 6, 98, 234
senior scramble, 113–14
sexual activity, 161, 161–62
feminism
 Catholic sexual ethics, 198
 Duke Lacrosse scandal, 285–87n18
 Female Chauvinist Pigs: Women and the Rise of Raunch Culture, 13, 302n1, 303–4n6
 and hookup culture, 246–47
 Molly Bainbridge, 59
 and oral sex, 13, 287n19, 298–99n1
 research approaches, 272–73
 and sexual assault, 148
 and theme parties, 146–47, 232
Firth, Gabriel, 105–6
Flack, William F., Jr., 303n4
Flanagan, Caitlin, 299n1
Forbidden Fruit: Sex and Religion in the Lives of American Teenagers, 174–75, 280n6, 306n20, 307n3. *See also* Regnerus, Mark D.
Franciscan University of Steubenville, 56
frat boy, 101
Freitas, Donna
 educational background, 292n2
 implications of findings, viii–ix
 postmodernism, 310n5
 Sexuality and Spirituality in American College Life, 269
 survey interviews, 271
 teaching philosophy, 270
freshman frenzy, 116
Freud, Anna, 309n3
friends with benefits, 14, 134, 299n1
From Subjects to Subjectivities: A Handbook of Interpretive and Participatory Methods, 272
frugaling, 115–17, 301n2

Gallup poll, 292n1
gays. *See* lesbian, gay, bisexual, transgender (LGBT) persons
GEMS (Girls Everywhere Meeting the Savior), 58
"Gender and the Meanings of Adolescent Romantic Relationships: A Focus on Boys" (Giordano), 305n10
Generation Next, 288n4, 291n4

interview topics, 277
as justice issue, 247–48, 250
lesbianism, 105
LGBT community, 141–42
male remorse, 155–56, 305–6n17
the morning after, **152**
the morning after, 153, 155–56, 305nn15–16
MySpace, 138, 302n3
NCMO (noncommitted making out), 119
oral sex, 95–96, 131
peer attitudes about sex, 157–58, 200, 231, 290–91n13
players, 101–2
raunch culture, 13–14
and religion, 16–17, 228, 254
remorse over, 119–20, **121, 154,** 205, 271
residential vs. commuter institutions, 244
resistance to, 235, 239
and romance, 109
sexualization of women, 304n9
sexually active seekers, 222
slutty dressing, 94
spiritual colleges, 15–16, 118, 179, 213–14, 217–18
steady hookup, 138
strategies for responding to, 265–67
stress of, 194
Tom Beecher, 130–31
and virginity, 131, 136–38, 202
walk of shame, 137
"Hookup in theory," 245
ho train, 143–44, 234
Humanae Vitae, 197
humanism, 39–41

I Gave Dating a Chance: A Biblical Perspective to Balance the Extremes, 178, 297n13
I Kissed Dating Goodbye, xiv, 178–79, 297–98n16
informed consent, 276
Institute for American Values, 287n23, 303n3
intelligent design, 58
intercourse
    Brook Lillith, 192
    contraception, 157
    and homosexuality, 197
    hookup culture, 128
    interview topics, 277
    one-night stands, 155
    and orgasm, 198

Promising the Future: Virginity Pledges and First Intercourse, 296n1
    by school type, 162, 163
    technical virgins, 306n20
    virgin gap, 306n21
Internal Review Board (IRB), 273–74, 284n14
InterVarsity Christian Fellowship/USA, 35, 204–7
interview topics, 276–77
IRB (Internal Review Board), 273–74, 284n14
Irigaray, Luce, 310n5

Jacobs, Alexandra, 285n18
James, Taneesha, 104–5
Jantzen, Grace, 310n5
jock pros and sport ho's, 145. *See also* theme parties
John Paul II, 197, 292n7, 308n1, 308n5
Johnson, Luke Timothy, 198, 308n8
Johnson, Mark, 88–92, 298n20
John Templeton Foundation, 280n6
journal entries. *See also* Sexuality and Spirituality in American College Life
    Amy Stone, 8, 20–21, 279n2
    Catholic colleges, 56
    Emily Holland, 76
    Jake Stein, 29–30
    Juanita Alvarez, 43
    Kylie David, 205
    Madanjit Singh, 45
    Mara, Mandy, 51
    methodology, 279n2
    payment to interviewees, 276
    romantic encounters, 107, 300n6, 301n7
    spiritual autobiography, 33–35
    study participants, 12
    and youth culture, 54
Judaism, 26, 29, 31
Just Love: A Framework for Christian Sexual Ethics, 199

Kama Sutra, 100, 299–300n4
Keenan, James F., 198–99
Kennedy, Duncan, 304n7
Kim, Jeremy, 140–42
Kissed the Girls and Made Them Cry: Why Women Lose when They Give In, 79–80, 82, 297n13, 301n4
kissing
    Catholic teachings about sex, 199
    covenant ring, 77

West, Christopher, 197, 308n4

When God Writes Your Love Story: The Ultimate Approach to Guy/Girl Relationships, 89–90, 296n6

whores, 5, 13, 143–45, 148. *See also* reputation; theme parties

Wilson, Robin, 305n12

Winner, Lauren, 211–12, 301n4

witnessing, 51

Woodhouse, Jamie, 99, 100–101, 127

Wuthnow, Robert, 290n11

yes girls, 142–44, 234

Yoshino, Kenji, 294n6

Young, May, 88

youth outreach, 292–93n3

Zen, 29